PHENOMENOLOGY AND EXISTENTIALISM

PHENOMENOLOGY AND EXISTENTIALISM

Edited by

EDWARD N. LEE AND MAURICE MANDELBAUM

THE JOHNS HOPKINS PRESS: BALTIMORE

Preface

The essays collected in this volume were (with one exception) first presented as a lecture series at The Johns Hopkins University in the spring of 1966. That lecture program—the first in a projected series of "Johns Hopkins Seminars in Philosophy" —was designed to provide a moderately advanced introduction to the contemporary movements of phenomenology and existentialism. This remains the intention of the present volume. No attempt has been made to give a full or comprehensive history of these movements here, but the basic approach of these essays is historical. They focus in sequence upon main figures and topics connected with each movement and so provide a selective overview of certain main themes and controversies that have characterized the relationships between the two movements. Each essay, then, provides an exposition of some special aspect in this complex story, though beyond this common purpose they differ widely in method and in point of view. For example, Professor Chisholm concludes his account of Franz Brentano's fundamental work on the concept of intentionality by formulating an original logical criterion to distinguish precisely intentional concepts from nonintentional ones. Professor Gurwitsch's analytical review of Husserl's position includes a criticism of the status he accorded to the ego, as well as a development of his theory of the object. Professor Olafson elucidates features of the conflict between Husserl and Merleau-Ponty by comparing it with the controversy (more familiar to most American students of philosophy) concerning phenomenalistic analyses of perception. And Professor Paul Ricoeur is also concerned with that gap which tends to separate recent Anglo-American philosophy from Continental thought. At home in France, he has supported the study and translation of Wittgenstein, Austin, Quine, and others; his

v

present essay on the theory of language in Husserl and in Wittgenstein may further serve to augment the dialogue between those who have been absorbed in one of the two traditions to the exclusion of the other. We believe that each of the following studies may similarily make more accessible to Anglo-American readers some important aspect of Continental philosophical thought. In addition to the papers presented during the lecture series, we were most fortunate in obtaining J. Glenn Gray's essay on Martin Heidegger for inclusion in this volume.

During the actual course of lectures at Johns Hopkins, each week's speaker also conducted an exploratory seminar on his subject. These lively and enlightening sessions were extremely rewarding for those who attended—most of them students in philosophy for whom this series was an introduction to the movements of phenomenology and existentialism. As editors, we warmly hope the essays gathered here may serve to inform and stimulate their readers, just as they did their original hearers.

M. M.
E. N. L.

Spring, 1967

Contents

PHENOMENOLOGY AND EXISTENTIALISM

Essay One

Brentano on Descriptive Psychology and the Intentional

RODERICK M. CHISHOLM*

1. According to Edmund Husserl, Brentano's "conversion of the scholastic concept of intentionality into a descriptive root-concept of psychology constitutes a great discovery, apart from which phenomenology could not have come into being at all."[1] It is fitting, therefore, to begin a course of lectures on phenomenology and existentialism with a discussion of what Brentano had to say about descriptive psychology and the intentional. We should remind ourselves, however, that the primary significance of Brentano's philosophy does not lie in the philosophical movements to which it happens to have given rise. This may be said with all due respect to the work of Husserl, Meinong, Twardowski, Marty, and the countless other philosophers who have been influenced by his work. Franz Brentano, as Husserl suggested to Kraus, was a philosopher of the ages and his greatness should not be measured by reference merely to the philosophical movements of our own time.[2]

* Dept. of Philosophy, Brown University, Providence, Rhode Island.

1. See the "Author's Preface to the English Edition" of *Ideas: General Introduction to Pure Phenomenology* (London: 1931), p. 23.
2. "Brentano ist eine historische Grösse—was keinesfalls heisst ein fur allemal erledigt—eine gewisse Überzeitlichkeit sollte in der Edition walten." Husserl was speaking of the edition of Brentano's writings which was being prepared by Oskar Kraus and Alfred Kastil. The quotation appears in the Introduction to Brentano's *Vom sinnlichen und noetischen Bewusstsein*, also referred to as *Psychologie, Band Drei*, ed. Oskar Kraus (Leipzig: 1928), p. xlviii.

1

2. Brentano's doctrine of the intentional, as well as much of the rest of what we would now call his philosophy, was a part of what he called "descriptive psychology." Brentano's "descriptive psychology" and Husserl's "phenomenology" are closely related. Husserl had studied with Brentano in Vienna from 1884 to 1886.[3] Brentano had used "beschreibende Phänomenologie" as an alternative name for descriptive psychology but evidently did not use "Phänomenologie" in this way after 1889.

The relation that descriptive psychology bears to genetic or explanatory psychology, Brentano said, is analogous to the relation that anatomy bears to physiology and to the relation that "geognosy" bears to geology (hence "psychognosy" was still another term that Brentano used for descriptive psychology).[4] Genetic or explanatory psychology is concerned with the causal status of psychological phenomena and hence with the relations that such phenomena bear to physical and chemical processes. It is not an exact science but, like meteorology, must qualify its generalizations with such terms as "on the average" and "for the most part." But descriptive psychology, Brentano thought, was an exact science.

The descriptive psychologist is concerned with "the totality of ultimate psychological elements":

> All other psychological phenomena are derived from the combinations of these ultimate psychological elements, as the totality of words may be derived from the totality of letters. Completion of this task would provide the basis for a *Characteristica universalis* of the sort that had been conceived by Leibniz, and before him, by Descartes. Genetic psychology, on the other hand, is concerned with the laws in accordance with which psychological phenomena come into being and pass away. Since these phenomena are undoubtedly dependent upon processes in the nervous system, the conditions of their coming and going are largely physiological; hence the investigation of genetic psychology must be entwined with that of physiology.[5]

3. See Husserl's *"Erinnerungen. an Franz Brentano,"* in Oskar Kraus, *Franz Brentano: Zur Kenntnis seines Lebens und seine Lehre* (Munich: 1919).

4. See Franz Brentano, *Grundzüge der Ästhetik,* ed. F. Mayer-Hillebrand, pp. 36ff., and *Meine letzten Wünsche für Oesterreich* (Stuttgart: 1895).

5. *Meine letzen Wünsche für Oesterreich,* pp. 34–5.

The task of descriptive psychology to which this passage refers has been described as being, in part, a matter of taking a "psychological inventory."[6] But it is also possible for descriptive psychology to formulate laws or theorems, and these laws or theorems, like those of mathematics and logic and unlike those of genetic psychology, are exact and apodictic. They hold universally and not merely "for the most part." Examples of such laws are the following, from the theory of evidence (which Brentano regarded as a part of descriptive psychology) : Every judgment is either correct or incorrect; if one person makes a correct judgment about a certain object, then no other person can make a similar judgment about the same object without also judging correctly.[7]

But we cannot properly understand Brentano's descriptive psychology unless we have a more detailed example. I shall attempt to summarize, therefore, what Brentano says about the nature of an act of will (*das Wollen*). I choose this particular example partly because of its intrinsic merit, partly because it provides an introduction to Brentano's doctrine of the intentional, and partly because it may be useful as a means of contrasting Brentano's psychological descriptions with those of subsequent phenomenology.

I refer to the account of willing that is set forth in Brentano's posthumous *Grundlegung und Aufbau der Ethik* (Bern, 1952), constructed by F. Mayer-Hillebrand from the notebooks that Brentano had used in lecturing on ethics at the University of Vienna from 1876 to 1894. Brentano here describes the way in which an act of will is constituted out of elementary psychological phenomena.

6. Oskar Kraus, *Franz Brentano*, p. 21.

7. Brentano is frequently charged with "psychologism." But if by psychologism we mean the doctrine according to which the laws of logic, evidence, and morality are merely contingent generalizations about the way in which people happen to think or feel, then the charge is not just. Brentano had criticized psychologistic theories of the evident in the first edition (1889) of the *Ursprung sittlicher Erkenntnis* (3rd ed.; Leipzig: 1934). Part of this critique is reprinted in *The True and the Evident*, ed. Oskar Kraus (English edition, ed. Roderick M. Chisholm [London: 1966], pp. 52–9; see also pp. 110–1, and Kraus's Introduction, pp. xx–xxii).

Within the sphere of the intellect, according to Brentano, the elementary phenomena are accepting and rejecting; within the sphere of the emotions they are loving, hating, and preferring. The terms "love" and "hate" should here be construed broadly: We love an object or state of affairs if we take a pro attitude toward that object or state of affairs; and we hate an object or state of affairs if we take an anti attitude toward that object or state of affairs. These phenomena—accepting, rejecting, loving, hating, and preferring—all presuppose and involve still another elementary phenomenon—that of having an idea of a thing (*das Vorstellen*). But although they do thus involve this further phenomenon, they may still be called elementary, for they are not themselves constituted by combining this further phenomenon with still *other* elementary phenomena. Being "red," similarly, involves or presupposes being "colored"; but red is not a combination of color and something else. How, then, is an act of will to be constituted out of such phenomena as these?

An act of will is, in part, a wish or want that involves a decision. And a wish or want that involves a decision is, in part, an act of love that involves a preference. What, then, is the difference between an act of love *simpliciter* and an act of love that involves a preference?

Of two situations, each of which is an object of my love or favorable inclination, I may yet *prefer* one to the other. For example, my friend's receiving a sudden stroke of good fortune might be something that I prefer as such, taken in itself and as if alone, to a similar stroke of good fortune on the part of a certain man who happens to be a total stranger. Here, then, we have love that involves a preference: I think of an object; I take a pro attitude toward it; and I prefer it to another object.

The good fortune of my friend is something that I prefer as such, taken in itself and as if alone, to the good fortune of the stranger. I may yet decide, however, that the latter rather than the former is the one I want to see realized. I thus arrive at a wish or want that involves a decision when (a) I have considered these two situations in the contexts of what I take to be their

total consequences and then (b) arrive at a preference with respect to these two sets of total consequences. Hence Brentano
says that a wish that involves a decision is related to a love or
preference that does not involve a decision in the way in which,
according to the traditional theological doctrine, the "consequent
will" of God is related to his "antecedent will."[8]

We have, then, the concept of a wish that involves a decision,
but we have not yet arrived at the concept of an act of will.
Although, as our example may suggest, "coming to a decision
does not always involve an act of will, an act of will always
involves coming to a decision."[9] What further differentiates an
act of will is the fact that its object is "always something that we
ourselves have to bring about. We can will only those things that
fall within our power, or, at any rate, those things which are
such that we earnestly believe that they fall within our power."[10]

And now Brentano is prepared to give us his definition of an
act of will. "Thus we can define an act of will as a wish or want
having these characteristics: it is such that it involves a decision
and it has as its object something that we are to bring about
ourselves and that we confidently expect will result from the
desires that we have. Hence one might say that an act of will
is a want or a wish such that we have arrived at it by coming
to a decision and such that we believe it can be realized by our
own endeavors."[11]

This complex concept of an act of will, then, contains a multiplicity of elements: love, conviction, preference, and causation.

8. Compare Franz Brentano, *Vom Ursprung sittlicher Erkenntnis* (3rd ed.
Leipzig: 1934), pp. 112–15, 156–58. The first edition of this work was
translated into English by Cecil Hague as *The Origin of our Knowledge
of Right and Wrong* (London: 1902). The third edition contains much
more important material, including the passages cited, which did not appear
in the first edition. The third edition is now being translated into English
by Roderick M. Chisholm and Elizabeth Schneewind.
9. *Grundlegung und Aufbau der Ethik*, p. 219.
10. *Ibid.*
11. "Wir können das Wollen also definieren als ein entscheidendes
Wunschen, das etwas von uns selbst zu Verwirklichendes zum Gegenstand
hat und von uns als Wirkung unseres Begehrens überzeugt erwartet wird.
Es ist m. a. W. ein Wunsch, für den wir uns entschieden haben und an
dessen Realisierbarkeit durch unser Eingreifen wir glauben." *Ibid.*

The first three of these are psychological and the fourth—that of causation—occurs only as part of the intentional object of the second.

Here, then, we have what seems to me to be a paradigm case of descriptive psychology, as Brentano conceived it.

3. Now we may turn to Brentano's conception of the intentional, beginning with the doctrine of intentional inexistence which he propounded in 1874 and was subsequently to abandon.

In his *Psychologie vom empirischen Standpunkt,* first published in 1874, Brentano proposed the doctrine of intentional inexistence as a means of distinguishing the mental or psychical from the physical. The familiar passage follows:

> Every mental phenomenon is characterized by what the scholastics of the middle ages called the intentional (and also mental) inexistence of an object, and what we would call, although not in entirely unambiguous terms, the reference to a content, a direction upon an object (by which we are not to understand a reality), or an immanent objectivity. Each one includes something as an object within itself, although not always in the same way. In presentation something is presented, in judgment something is affirmed or denied, in love something is loved, in hate something is hated, in desire something is desired, etc. This intentional inexistence is exclusively characteristic of mental phenomena. No physical phenomenon manifests anything similar. Consequently, we can define mental phenomena by saying that they are such phenomena as include an object intentionally within themselves.[12]

We have here an ontological thesis concerning "intentional inexistence," which Brentano was later to abandon, and a psychological thesis, implying that reference to an object is what distinguishes the mental from the physical. Each of these theses seems to me to be important. The ontological thesis seems to me to be problematic and not, as Brentano subsequently thought, to be obviously false. And the psychological thesis seems to me to be true. Let us consider them in order.

12. The passage may be found on pp. 124–5 of Volume I of the Second Edition of the *Psychologie vom empirischen Standpunkt* (Leipzig: 1924). The present version is from D. B. Terrell's translation of the chapter in which it appeared ("The Distinction between Mental and Physical Phenomena"), in *Realism and the Background of Phenomenology,* ed. Roderick M. Chisholm (Glencoe, Illinois: 1960); the passage appears on pp. 50–51.

We are readily led to the ontological doctrine of intentional inexistence, though not, of course, to the particular terminology that Brentano used, if we ask ourselves what is involved in having thoughts, beliefs, desires, purposes, and other intentional attitudes that are directed upon objects that do not exist. There is a distinction between a man who is thinking about a horse and a man who is thinking about a unicorn. The distinction lies in the *objects* of their respective thoughts. It does *not* lie in the fact that where the first man has an object the second man does not, for this is not a fact. There is a distinction between a man who is thinking about a unicorn and a man who is thinking about nothing at all; *this* distinction lies in the fact that where one man has an object of thought the other man does not.[13] What, then, is the ontological status of the object that the man is intentionally related to when he is thinking about a unicorn?

One is tempted to say that although the man's thought quite obviously has an object, this object—also quite obviously—cannot be a unicorn. For one might reason as follows: If the man's thought is directed upon *something* and if there are no unicorns, then his thought must be directed upon something other than a unicorn. But what could this something possibly be? Moreover, if the man is thinking about something that is *not* a unicorn, how, then, can we say that he is thinking about a unicorn?

The doctrine of intentional inexistence may seem, at first consideration, to provide us with answers to our questions. It seems to tell us three different things. It tells us, first, that the object of the man's thought *is* a unicorn. It tells us, secondly,

---

13. Compare Plato's *Theaetetus* 189a–b:

Soc. And does not he who thinks, think some one thing?

Theaet. Certainly.

Soc. And does not he who thinks some one thing, think something which is?

Theaet. I agree.

Soc. Then he who thinks of that which is not, thinks of nothing?

Theaet. Clearly.

Soc. And he who thinks of nothing, does not think at all?

Theaet. Obviously.

Soc. Then no one can think that which is not, either as a self-existent substance or as a predicate of something else?

Theaet. Clearly not.

that this unicorn is not an actual unicorn (for there are no actual unicorns). And it tells us, thirdly, that this unicorn has a certain mode of being other than actuality. Whatever has this mode of being—called "intentional inexistence" or "immanent objectivity"—is an entity that is mind-dependent and therefore appropriately called an *ens rationis,* in the traditional sense of this term. The intentionally inexistent unicorn is an entity that is *produced* by the mind or intellect; it comes into being as soon as the man starts to think about a unicorn and it ceases to be as soon as he stops.[14]

Are there, then, certain objects such as intentionally inexistent unicorns which are produced by the mind? In *The True and the Evident,* we find this interesting passage, which was written sometime prior to 1903. Brentano asks us to consider a person whose thought is directed upon a certain object A and, in this case, an A that happens also to be actual:

> The concept of this object A, like that of the person who is thinking, is the concept of a thing. We may also say of this thing A that it is an object which is thought about. It is just as true that this A is a contemplated A [ein gedachtes A] as it is that this A is an actual A, existing in reality. A can cease to be actual and yet continue to be thought about—so long as the thinking person does in fact think about it. And conversely it can cease to be thought about—if the person stops thinking about it—and yet continue to be actual.

14. This doctrine is at the basis of St. Anselm's ontological arugument; for St. Anselm takes it to be self-evident that if God is thought about then God does "exist in the understanding." William of Ockham contrasted the "intentional existence" (he did not use "inexistence") of the object of thought with the "subjective existence" of the thinking itself. "Objective existence" (meaning existence as an object of thought) came to be a synonym for "intentional (in)existence." Thus Descartes contrasted the *formale esse* of actual objects with the *objective in intellectu esse* of objects that are merely thought about. In the present century, the late Professor A. O. Lovejoy of Johns Hopkins appealed to those entitities that are objects merely of thought (unicorns, as well as many of the objects of dreams and hallucinations) in order to defend what he called "psychophysical dualism"— the view that there is, in addition to the world of physical things, a world of nonphysical, mental things, "a second world to which could be allocated all experienced objects which do not appear to satisfy the rules of membership in the physical system." See A. O. Lovejoy, *The Revolt against Dualism* (New York: 1930), pp. 28–29.

In contrasting the A which is contemplated or thought about with the A which is actual, are we saying that *the contemplated A is itself nothing actual or true?* By no means! *The contemplated A* can be something actual and true without being an actual A. It is an actual contemplated A and therefore—since this comes to the same thing—it is an actual contemplated A [ein wirkliches gedachtes A] which may be contrasted with what is a mere *contemplated* contemplated A [ein gedachtes gedachtes A]. (One may *think* that someone is thinking about an A.)

There cannot be anyone who contemplates an A unless there is a contemplated A; and conversely. But we must not infer from this fact that the one who is thinking about the A is identical with the A which he is thinking about. The two concepts are not identical but they are correlative. Neither can correspond to anything in reality unless the other does as well. But only one of these is the concept of a thing—the concept of something which can act and be acted upon. The second is the concept of a being which is only a sort of accompaniment to the first; when the first thing comes into being, and when it ceases to be, then so does the second.[15]

Brentano took these considerations to show that there *are* certain entities that are not concrete individual things. For, he says, the situation that he has described involves an actual thinker and an *actual contemplated A* (just as the situation he refers to parenthetically involves an actual, contemplated contemplated A). The contemplated A and the contemplated contemplated A are *entia rationis* that are *produced* by the mind.

According to Brentano's earlier doctrine, then, as soon as a man starts to think about a unicorn there comes into being an actual contemplated unicorn. This actual contemplated unicorn is an *ens rationis* that depends upon the thinker for its existence and that ceases to be as soon as the man ceases to think about a unicorn.

In the fourteenth century, Walter Burleigh had appealed to a slightly different aspect of the phenomenon of intentionality in order to make out a case for still another type of entity—an en-

15. *The True and the Evident*, p. 27; the passage appears on page 31 of *Wahrheit und Evidenz.* Compare also *The True and the Evident*, p. 64: "There is nothing universal in the things; the so-called universal, as such, is only in the one who is thinking." (*Wahrheit und Evidenz*, p. 74.)

tity that, like the merely contemplated A, is not a concrete individual thing, but that, unlike the merely contemplated A, exists "outside the mind." It will be useful at this point to recall Burleigh's argument, for, as we shall see, it will throw light upon Brentano's thought and upon the subsequent fate of the doctrine of intentionality. Burleigh argued in this way:

> Something about which real promises and contracts are made, such as buying and selling, donations, pledges, etc., exists outside the soul. But contracts are not always made about individual things. Therefore something exists outside the soul that is other than an individual nature. The major is obvious. The proof of the minor is that in the statement "I promise you an ox," something outside the soul is being promised to you, and yet no individual thing is being promised to you because you cannot lay claim to this or that particular ox on the strength of this promise.

Therefore something outside the soul that is other than an individual thing is being promised to you.[16] Since the entities with which Burleigh is here concerned are not produced by the mind and are not in any way dependent upon the mind, they are not properly called *"entia rationis."* Hence we need a more general term to cover non-things in general, non-things that may or may not be *entia rationis.* Brentano proposed the expressions *"entia non realia," "entia irrealia,"* or simply *"irrealia."*[17]

For the present, let us restrict ourselves to those *irrealia* that are also *entia rationis* and consider some of the difficulties involved in the concept of intentional inexistence.

4. The doctrine of intentional inexistence may seem at least to have this advantage: It provides us with a literal interpretation for the traditional dictum, "Veritas est adaequatio intellectus rei." One could say that an affirmative judgment is true pro-

16. Walter Burleigh, "On the Existence of Universals," in *Philosophy in the West: Readings in Ancient and Medieval Philosophy,* ed. Joseph Katz and R. H. Weingartner (New York: 1965), pp. 563–69. The passage appears on p. 564. For an account of Jean Buridan's treatment of the same problem, see Peter Geach, "A Medieval Discussion of Intentionality," *Proceedings of the 1964 International Congress for Logic, Methodology and Philosophy of Science,* Jerusalem, August 26–September 2, 1964 (Amsterdam: 1965), pp. 425–33.

17. Compare *The True and the Evident,* pp. 80f.

vided only that the properties of the intentional object are the same as those of the actual object.

But the very statement of this advantage betrays the fact that what the true affirmative judgment is directed upon is the actual object and not the intentional object.

To be sure, our intentional attitudes *may* be directed upon objects that do not exist. But they may also be directed upon objects that *do* exist: I may think of a golden mountain, but I may also think about Mt. Monadnock. Diogenes looked for an honest man and perhaps there was none; but there *are* many dishonest men who are also objects of quests, as the police files will indicate. And these objects are not things having mere intentional inexistence.

And even in those cases where the objects of our intentional attitudes do *not* exist, our attitudes are not normally directed upon an immanent, intentionally inexisting object. Whether or not there are honest men, Diogenes in his quest was looking for an *actual* 'honest man, not for an intentionally inexisting honest man. If the doctrine of intentional inexistence is true, the very fact that Diogenes was looking for an honest man implies that he already had the immanent object; hence *it* could not be the object of his quest. Thus Brentano was later to say that "what we think about is *the object* or *thing* and not the 'object of thought [*vorgestelltes Objekt*].' "18

18. *The True and the Evident,* p. 77. In this passage, Brentano also seems to deny ever having held the doctrine of intentional inexistence, as I have formulated it. Kraus believes, however, that by the time Brentano wrote the passage (March 17, 1905), the older doctrine (which, Kraus believes, Brentano had in fact held) "had become so foreign to him that he questioned whether he had ever enunciated it" (*op. cit.,* p. 154). One might try to reconcile this passage with what seems to have been Brentano's earlier doctrine by taking the earlier doctrine to be this: (1) an actual intentionally inexistent unicorn is *produced* when one thinks about a unicorn; (2) one's thought, however, is *not* directed upon this actual intentionally inexistent unicorn; and yet (3) it is *in virtue of* the existence of the intentionally inexistent unicorn that one's thought may be said to be directed upon a unicorn. But in this case, what point would there be in supposing that there *is* the inexistent unicorn? Compare Brentano's further remarks, *op. cit.,* pp. 77–79, and the notes by Oskar Kraus, *ibid.,* pp. 165–70. Compare also Jan Srzednicki, *Franz Brentano's Analysis of Truth* (The Hague: 1965), Chapter II.

The ontological use of the word "intentional," therefore, seems to undermine its psychological use. Intentionally inexistent objects were posited in the attempt to understand intentional reference, but the attempt did not succeed—precisely because the objects so posited *were* intentionally inexistent. Thus Husserl said, with the later Brentano, that the objects of our "intentional experiences" are never objects that exist merely in the understanding; they are always something "transcendent."[19]

There are still other difficulties in the ontological doctrine of intentionally inexisting objects, actual intentionally inexisting objects, as Brentano was later to emphasize. "If there are such objects, in the strict and proper sense of the term *are*, then, whenever anyone thinks of anything that is contradictory, there comes into being an object that *is* contradictory."[20]

Almost all intentionally inexisting objects, moreover, violate the law of excluded middle. Consider, for example, the promised ox that was the object of *our* thought a while back. It may have been brown and presumably it had four legs, a head, and a tail. Presumably also it was heavy. But was it such that it weighed 817 pounds, or was it such that it did not weigh 817 pounds? Evidently we must answer both of these questions in the negative. In this case, the actual intentionally inexisting ox was what Meinong called an "incomplete object."[21] Whatever the status of such objects in Meinong's realm of *Aussersein*, Brentano was certain, in his later thoughts, that there are *no* such objects, whether "in" or "outside" the mind. (This incompleteness of the immanent object would seem to insure disaster for the attempt to construe truth as a relation of correspondence or adequacy holding between the immanent object and the actual object. For, since all actual objects are complete and no immanent objects are complete, no immanent object can be adequate to any actual object.)

19. E. Husserl, *Logische Untersuchungen* (4th ed.; Halle: 1928), Vol. II, Part I, p. 425; compare 373–4.

20. Franz Brentano, *Kategorienlehre*, ed. Alfred Kastil (Leipzig: 1933).

21. See A. Meinong, *Über Möglichkeit und Wahrscheinlichkeit* (Leipzig: 1915), pp. 168–81.

And what, finally, of Walter Burleigh's *ens irreale*—the promised ox that is not identical with any individual ox? Brentano, in a letter to Kraus, had considered a slightly different example. You might promise to marry and yet not promise with respect to any particular person, to marry *that* particular person. But what happens if you keep the promise? "It would be paradoxical to the highest degree," Brentano said, "to suppose that you could promise to marry an *ens rationis* and then to keep the promise by marrying an actual, concrete particular."[22]

But it is much easier to ridicule the doctrine of *entia non realia* than it is to find a way of getting along without them. Let us consider, then, how Brentano himself made out in his subsequent attempts to get along without the ontology of intentionally inexistent objects.

5. Brentano's later thought was what Kotarbinski has called "reistic." The only things that can be said to *be,* in the strict and proper sense of the expression "to be," are particular, individual things. (But Brentano's reism, unlike that of Kotarbinski, is not also a "somatism." For Brentano held that there are concrete individual things that are not material things—for example, human souls and God.) Brentano thus repudiated all *entia rationis* and *entia irrealia.*

Our language contains a multiplicity of terms, purporting to refer to non-things, or *entia irrealia.* Brentano says that such terms are convenient fictions, comparable to such expressions as "negative quantities," "irrational numbers," "imaginary numbers," and the like.[23] When we find a true sentence, ostensibly referring to a non-thing, then, according to Brentano, we can "form an equivalent in which the subject and predicate are replaced by expressions referring only to things."[24]

For example, the sentence "There is a dearth of bread in the larder" may seem to affirm the existence of a *privativum*—that

22. Quoted by Oskar Kraus in his Introduction to *Psychologie vom empirischen Standpunkt* (2nd ed.; Leipzig: 1924), p. xlix. Presumably Brentano should have written *"ens irreale"* instead of *"ens rationis."*
23. *The True and the Evident,* p. 83.
24. *Psychologie vom empirischen Standpunkt,* 2nd ed., II, 163.

non-thing which is the absence of bread. But actually, according
to Brentano, it is concerned with the denial or rejection of a
thing: namely bread in the larder. Again, "There is redness"
and "Red is a color" may seem to pertain to *abstracta* and thus,
once again, to non-things. But "There is redness," Brentano
says, is just another way of saying "There are red things"; and
what "Red is a color" tells us is simply that red things, *as such,*
are colored.[25]

In a similar way, Brentano attempts to translate away all
ostensible reference to propositional objects. Thus, in the second
edition of the *Psychologie* and in *The True and the Evident,* he
defends a non-propositional theory of judgment. Language suggests that judgment involves a relation between a man and a
proposition (or content, state of affairs, or objective). We say,
"He believes that there are horses," thus seeming to describe a
relation between the believer and that non-thing named by the
propositional clause "that there are horses." But actually, Brentano says, what "He believes that there are horses" tells us is
simply that the believer accepts or affirms (*anerkennt*) horses.
And if we say, "He believes that there are no unicorns," we are
simply saying that he rejects or denies (*leugnet*) unicorns. "He
believes that some horses are red" tells us that he accepts red
horses, and "He believes that no horses are green" tells us that
he rejects green horses. Brentano's theory becomes complex, after
this point.[26] But what it is that he is attempting to do is clear
throughout: he wishes to translate those true sentences that
seem to refer to non-things into sentences that refer only to
things. In this way, he thinks, he will eliminate one of the most
fundamental sources of error and confusion in philosophy.
Philosophers go wrong and fall into confusion "when they take
some word to be a name when in fact the word is not a name at
all, and then look for the concept which this ostensible name

25. Brentano's reism is set forth in detail in *Kategorienlehre* and *The
True and the Evident.* Compare the exposition in Srzednicki, *op. cit.,* pp.
42–49.

26. See *Psychologie,* II, 158–72; part of this passage is translated by D. B.
Terrell in *Realism and the Background of Phenomenology,* ed. by Roderick
M. Chisholm, pp. 62–70.

designated."[27] Brentano's reism thus led him to revise his original doctrine of the intentional in two ways. First, he gave up the doctrine that our intentional attitudes are sometimes directed upon non-things or *entia irrealia*. Whatever language we may use for the description of our intentional attitudes—whether we use words ostensibly referring to *abstracta, privativa, negativa*, whether we use clauses ostensibly referring to propositions or what Meinong called *"Objektive"*—our attitudes are in fact always directed upon *things*. Second, Brentano gave up the doctrine that our intentional attitudes, whatever they may be directed upon, do somehow involve actual intentionally inexistent objects.

What, then, is the reistic replacement for the actual intentionally inexistent object?

6. The following passage, dictated in 1914, may be found in the *Kategorienlehre* (p. 8):

> Instead of saying that a person is thinking about a thing, one may also say that there is something which is the object of his thought. But this is not the strict or proper sense of *is*. For the thinker may in fact deny that there is any such object as the object he is thinking about. Moreover, one can think about what is contradictory, but nothing that is contradictory can possibly be said to be. We said above that roundness cannot be said to *be,* in the strict and proper sense of the term; that which is round, but not roundness, may be said to be. And so too, in the present case. What there is in the strict and proper sense is not the round thing that is thought about; what there *is* is the person who is thinking about it. The thing "as object of thought" is a fiction which, in many contexts, is perfectly harmless. But if we do not see that it is a fiction, then we will be led to the most blatant of absurdities. We are not dealing here with a type of being, in the strict sense of the term. What we say can be expressed in such a way that we do refer to a being in the strict sense of the term—namely, the thinker who has the thought. And what holds generally for that which is thought about also holds more particularly, for that which is accepted, that which is rejected, that which is loved, that which is hated, that which is hoped for, that which is feared, that which is willed, and so on.

27. Franz Brentano, *Die Lehre vom richtigen Urteil*, ed. F. Mayer-Hillebrand (Bern: 1956), pp. 45–46.

Saying that there *is* an immanent object, then, is just another way of saying that there *is* an actual person who is thinking about that object. *"Es gibt ein Gedachtes"* says no more nor less than *"Es gibt ein Denkendes."*[28] Hence if we continue to say, as Brentano had said earlier, that there is an *actual* intentionally inexistent unicorn when an actual man is thinking about a unicorn, we are using the first "actual" in its loose and improper sense and the second "actual" in its strict and proper sense. And where Brentano had said earlier that our thought *produces* an entity, he now denies that our thought thus produces any entity at all.

There are four possible views here that are easily confused with each other. There is what I have taken to be Brentano's original view; there is the later reistic view; and then there seem to be two different ways of combining the first two views. Let us consider these possibilities more explicitly.

i. According to what I have taken to be Brentano's view of 1874, when a man thinks about a unicorn there is *produced* an immanent or intentionally inexistent unicorn. This immanent or intentionally inexistent unicorn is an actual immanent or intentionally inexistent unicorn. And therefore it is an entity *in addition to* the man who is thinking.

ii. According to Brentano's later, reistic view, when a man thinks about a unicorn no intentionally inexistent unicorn is produced and therefore the situation involves no actual entity other than the man who is thinking.

iii. Suarez, in his *Metaphysicae Disputationes,* seems to combine these two views in the following way. He seems to suggest that when a man thinks about a unicorn, the act of thought *produces* an immanent or intentionally inexistent unicorn; hence we have an element of Brentano's first view. But Suarez adds that the unicorn that is thus *produced* is *not* an *actual* immanent or intentionally inexistent unicorn and therefore it is not an entity in addition to the thinker himself; hence we have an element of

28. *Wahrheit und Evidenz,* p. 79; compare *The True and the Evident,* p. 68.

Brentano's second view.[29] Now if this immanent or intentionally inexistent unicorn is produced, or (to use the terms that Suarez used) if this *ens rationis* that has only "objective being in the mind" had an efficient cause, then, one would think, the entity must be actual. If there *is* production or causation, then there must *be* that which is caused or produced.[30]

iv. There is, finally, still another way of combining the first and second views of Brentano; this final view is suggested by one passage in G. E. Moore. We could say (a) that when a man thinks about a unicorn, there is involved an *actual* intentionally inexistent unicorn; hence we have an element of Brentano's first view. And then we could add (b) that to say that there is such an actual intentionally inexistent unicorn is to say no more nor less than that the man is thinking about a unicorn.[31]

Do we have, then, a clear alternative to the original doctrine of intentional inexistence?

29. See disputation LIV ("*De Ente Rationis*"), Section 1. It is quite obvious that Brentano was influenced by this discussion in Suarez; compare the *Psychologie*, II, 272. I am indebted to the late Professor Ralph M. Blake for calling my attention to the importance of this and other discussions in the *Metaphysicae Disputationes*.

30. It should be noted that Suarez is fully aware of the difficulty (which he attributes to one Bernardinus Mirandulus) and that he attempts to resolve it. We *could* so interpret the view of Suarez that it becomes identical with Brentano's second view above. Where Brentano had distinguished a strict and proper sense and a loose and improper sense of "is," we might read into Suarez a distinction between a strict and proper sense and a loose and improper sense of "produce" or "cause." He could then be interpreted as saying that it is only in the latter sense of "cause" that an *ens rationis* may be said to have an efficient cause.

31. ". . . if it should happen that at the present moment two different people are having an hallucination of a different tame tiger, it will follow there are at the present moment two different imaginary tigers. . . . The sentence 'There are some tame tigers which do not exist' is, therefore, certainly significant, if it means only that there are some imaginary tigers. . . . But what it means is that either some real people have written stories about imaginary tigers, or are having or have recently had hallucinations of tame tigers, or, perhaps, are dreaming or have dreamed of particular tame tigers. If nothing of this sort has happened or is happening to anybody, then there are no imaginary tame tigers." G. E. Moore, *Philosophical Papers* (London: 1959), p. 120.

7. It seems to me that these alternatives to the doctrine of intentional inexistence involve a serious difficulty, and I am not at all sure that I know how it ought to be treated. The difficulty may be seen if we try to give a positive answer to the question "How are we using the word 'unicorn' when we say, 'John is thinking about a unicorn'?"

Brentano in his later view gives the question a negative answer. That is to say, he tells us how we are *not* using the word "unicorn" when we say, "John is thinking about a unicorn." But he formulates this negative answer affirmatively—in very much the way in which, according to him, "There is a dearth of bread in the larder" expresses a negative belief affirmatively. He tells us that in the sentence "John is thinking about a unicorn," the word "unicorn" is being used syncategorematically or synsemantically.[32] And this may be said to be a negative answer to our question, for to say that a word is being used syncategorematically or synsemantically is to say, negatively, that the word is *not* being used referentially—that the word is *not* being used to designate or to refer to an object. Thus our question now becomes, more positively: If the word is not being used to designate or refer to an object, how *is* it being used?

We may say, as Brentano suggests, that in "John is thinking about a unicorn" the word "unicorn" is being used to contribute to the description of John. But *how* does it contribute to the description of John? We are *not* saying, obviously, that John is a unicorn. We are saying that John is *thinking* about a unicorn, and so one might be tempted to say the word "unicorn" is being used to describe John's thought. But *how* does the word "unicorn" contribute to the description of John's thought? We are not saying, obviously, that John's *thought* is a unicorn. We are saying—again, obviously—that the *object* of John's thought is a unicorn. But, Brentano tells us, statements ostensibly about the object of John's thought are actually statements about John. And so we have completed a kind of circle. For now we can ask, once again: what does this use of "unicorn" tell us about John?

32. See *The True and the Evident*, p. 68.

One may be tempted to say that the use of "unicorn" in such sentences as "John is thinking about a unicorn" and "John believes that there are unicorns" has no connection at all with what would be its designative or referential use. What we have here, one is tempted to continue, are simply two different predicates of John—predicates that might be written as "thinking-about-a-unicorn" and "believing-that-there-are-unicorns." Better still, the hyphens could be removed, thereby making it clear that the predicates have no more to do with unicorns than they have to do with, say, ink, or with hats, or with corn, or with her, or with any of the other objects whose names happen to be imbedded in our intentional predicates.

That this suggestion will not do, however, is indicated by the fact that "John believes that there are unicorns" (or "John believesthatthereareunicorns") and "All of John's beliefs are true" together imply "There are unicorns"—a mode of inference that would not be valid if "unicorn" functioned here as an equivocal middle term.[33]

Alonzo Church has suggested that the English sentence "Schliemann sought the site of Troy" tells us that a certain relation obtains between Schliemann and the *concept* of the site of Troy, suggesting therefore that seeking is a relation between a person and an *abstractum*. But *what* relation is asserted to obtain between Schliemann and the concept of the site of Troy? He was not *seeking* the concept, since he already had it when he set out on his quest. Church says, negatively, that the relation that Schliemann bore to the concept of the site of Troy is "not quite

---

33. "One may have the feeling that in the sentence 'I expect he is coming' one is using the words 'he is coming' in a different sense from the one they have in the assertion 'He is coming.' But if it were so how could I say that my expectation had been fulfilled? If I wanted to explain the words 'he' and 'is coming,' say by means of ostensive definitions, the same definitions of these words would go for both sentences." Ludwig Wittgenstein, *Philosophical Investigations* (Oxford: 1953), p. 130e. The following passage occurs on this same page: " 'The report was not so loud as I had expected.'—'Then there was a louder bang in your expectation?' "

like that of having sought," but he does not tell us more positively what it is.[34]

Rudolf Carnap once suggested that *words* or other linguistic entities are the objects of our intentional attitudes. "Charles thinks (asserts, believes, wonders about) A," he said, might be translated as "Charles thinks 'A.' "[35] But when we say that Charles wonders whether there are unicorns, we do not mean to say that Charles wonders whether there is the word "unicorn." And when we make the semantic statement, "The word 'unicorn' in English designates unicorn," we cannot replace the last word in our statement with the expression "the word 'unicorn.' "[36]

One way out, if we are to avoid *entia irrealia* and at the same time do justice to the phenomenon of intentionality, is to follow Meinong's suggestion: There are certain truths which hold of objects that do not exist. There are no unicorns; yet there are certain truths that hold of unicorns; hence unicorns have certain properties, among them that of being the object, on occasion, of our intentional attitudes. But this suggestion was anathema to Brentano, as it is to most contemporary logicians.[37]

8. Brentano's doctrine of intentional inexistence was proposed as a way of distinguishing mental or psychical phenomena from physical phenomena: mental phenomena are distinguished by the fact that they contain objects immanently within themselves. If we give up the doctrine of intentional inexistence, how are we to make the distinction between the mental and the physical?

34. Alonzo Church, *Introduction to Mathematical Logic* (Princeton: 1955), p. 8n.

35. Rudolf Carnap, *The Logical Syntax of Language* (New York: 1937), p. 248.

36. Israel Scheffler's "inscriptionalism" might be interpreted as saying that linguistic entities constitute the objects of our intentional attitudes. But if we do interpret it in this way, it becomes very difficult to ascertain just what relation is being asserted to hold between a man and an inscription when we say of him that he is thinking, wondering, desiring, loving, and the like. See Israel Scheffler, *The Anatomy of Inquiry* (New York: 1963), pp. 57ff.

37. See A. Meinong, "The Theory of Objects," in *Realism and the Background of Phenomenology*, ed. Roderick M. Chisholm. I have attempted to defend Meinong in *"Jenseits vom Sein und Nichtsein,"* in *Dichtung und Deutung*, ed. Karl S. Guthke (Bern and Munich: 1961).

In the *Klassification der psychischen Phänomene,* published in 1911 and included in the second edition of the *Psychologie vom empirischen Standpunkt,* Brentano said that, since every psychical phenomenon involves a relation to something as object, psychical activity may be described as being essentially relational. But psychical relations, he said, are distinguished from other relations in the following way:

> In the case of other relations, the Fundament as well as the Terminus must be an actual thing. . . . If one house is larger than another house, then the second house as well as the first house must exist and have a certain size. . . . But this is not at all the case with psychical relations. If a person thinks about something, the thinker must exist but the objects of his thought need not exist at all. Indeed, if the thinker is denying or rejecting something, and if he is right in so doing, then the object of his thinking must not exist. Hence the thinker is the only thing that needs to exist if a psychical relation is to obtain. The Terminus of this so-called relation need not exist in reality. One may well ask, therefore, whether we are dealing with what is really a relation at all. One could say instead that we are dealing with something which is in a certain respect similar to a relation, and which, therefore, we might describe as being something that is "relation-like" [*etwas "relativliches"*].[38]

This passage suggests the possibility of a logical distinction between the mental and the physical. We might say that the language we use in characterizing the mental has certain logical properties that are not shared by the language we use in characterizing the physical. We could say, for example, that in characterizing the mental we must use "intentional terms" and that we do not need to use such terms when we characterize the physical; and we might then attempt to characterize intentional terms logically. The following definition of "intentional sentence," which is suggested by the passage from Brentano above, may be found in *Webster's Third New International Dictionary*: A simple categorical statement (for example, "Parsifal sought the Holy Grail") is intentional if it uses a substantival expression (in this instance "the Holy Grail") without implying either that

38. *Psychologie vom empirischen Standpunkt,* II, 133–34.

there is or that there isn't anything to which the expression truly applies.

But this characterization of "intentional sentence," as it stands, is too broad. The following sentences, none of them concerned with what is mental, satisfy the conditions of the criterion: "The site of Troy is not New Zealand"; "That lady has a profile like the profile of Satan"; "It is possible that the Loch Ness monster exists."

We will be more faithful to Brentano's intention if we look for a peculiar characteristic of the expressions we use to designate "intentional relations." And possibly we will find one if we remind ourselves of the type of situation involved in Walter Burleigh's promise: The man promised to deliver an ox, but there was no particular ox that he promised to deliver. Expressions for intentional relations may exhibit a unique type of behavior when they are found in contexts of quantification.[39] An example involving believing will illustrate the point; similar examples may be constructed which will hold of knowing, desiring, doubting, being pleased, being displeased, hoping, fearing, and still other intentional attitudes.

Consider the two formulae

$$(1) \quad (Ex) \quad (Ey) \quad (y = a \ \& \ xRa)$$
$$(2) \quad (Ex) \quad (Ey) \quad (y = a \ \& \ xRy).$$

Let us here restrict the values of variables to concrete entities. An expression which may occupy the place of "R" in such formulae could be said to be intentional if there is an individual term that may occupy the place of "a" with the results that (1) does not imply (2); (2) does not imply (1); and no well-formed sentence that is part of (1) is noncontingent.

We find an example of such an intentional expression if we replace "a" by "the next President" and "R" by "believes that the Mayor of New York is." Let us now suppose that Senator Robert Kennedy is the next President and that one of Mayor Lindsay's supporters believes that he, the Mayor of New York, is the next

39. In "Notes on the Logic of Believing," *Philosophy and Phenomenological Research*, XXIV (1963), 195–201, I described one such possibility, somewhat different from the one referred to here.

President. In this case (1) will be true. But (1) is consistent with the negation of (2). That is to say, affirming (1) is consistent with denying that there is anyone who mistakes Kennedy for the Mayor, i.e., with denying that there is anyone who supposes with respect to Kennedy that the Mayor of New York is he. But let us assume that there is, in fact, a man who mistakes Kennedy for the Mayor (expecting the Mayor on a certain occasion and then seeing the Senator in a conspicuous position, he takes it for granted that the man he sees, *viz.*, the Senator, is the Mayor). In this case (2) will be true. But (2) is consistent with the negation of (1). That is to say, affirming (2) is consistent with denying that there is anyone who believes that the Mayor of New York is the next President.

We might say, then, that a well-formed sentence is intentional if it contains an intentional expression (e.g., "believes that the Mayor of New York is") and in addition to that only individual terms or quantifiers and variables. We could also say that a well-formed sentence is intentional if it is consistent and implies a sentence that is intentional. The psychological thesis of intentionality could then be put by saying, "All intentional sentences pertain to what is psychological."

If I am not mistaken, no expressions designating nonpsychological phenomena have the logical properties that the expression "R" has just been described as having. And if this is so, then we may say with Brentano that what distinguishes the psychological from the physical is *"etwas 'relativliches.' "*[40]

40. Since the writing of this essay, the following work has appeared: Franz Brentano, *Die Abkehr vom Nichtrealen,* ed. Franziska Mayer-Hillebrand (Bern: 1966). This book is composed of selections, taken from Brentano's correspondence and hitherto unpublished manuscripts, concerning the repudiation of *entia irrealia.* It also contains a useful discussion of Brentano's reism by Professor Mayer-Hillebrand.

Essay Two

Husserl's Theory of the Intentionality of Consciousness in Historical Perspective

ARON GURWITSCH*

Though he was not a historian, either by temperament or by training, Husserl repeatedly and most emphatically insisted upon the continuity of his endeavors with the great tradition of Western philosophy, especially modern philosophy, which began in the seventeenth century. His insistence appears most explicitly in several of his writings of the twenties and thirties published in the course of the last decade.[1] Even as early as 1913, in the first volume of *Ideen zu einer reinen Phänomenologie und phäno-menologischen Philosophie,* the only volume published during his lifetime, Husserl speaks of his phenomenology as the "secret longing" of the whole of modern philosophy, referring especially to Descartes, Hume, and Kant.[2] Finally, it is significant that one of Husserl's presentations of phenomenological philosophy as a whole, a presentation in a highly concentrated, condensed, and, in comparison with *Ideen* I, abbreviated form (notwithstanding the discussion of the problem of intersubjectivity which is not

* Graduate Faculty of Political and Social Science, New School for Social Research, New York, New York.

1. Husserl, *Erste Philosophie,* Part I, *Husserliana* (The Hague: 1956), Vol. VII and *Die Krisis der Europäischen Wissenschaften und die transzenden-tale Phänomenologie* (henceforth referred to as *Krisis*), *Husserliana* (1954), vol. VI, secs. 15ff.

2. Husserl, *Ideen zu einer reinen Phänomenologie und phänomenologischen Philosophie* I (henceforth referred to as *Ideen* I), p. 118. The page numbers refer to the original edition; the edition in *Husserliana,* vol. III (1950), indicates on the margin the pagination of the original edition.

contained in *Ideen* I), bears the title *Cartesian Meditations,* which is to say meditations carried out in the manner of those of Descartes.

The phrase "secret longing" expresses the claim on Husserl's part to bring fulfillment to the intentions of his predecessors. This in turn implies that on the one hand their intentions were substantially the same as his, but that on the other hand they were unable to realize those very intentions and therefore did not reach the level or dimension of transcendental constitutive phenomenology. Thus, in his opening remarks in *Cartesian Meditations* Husserl characterizes his phenomenology as "a neo-Cartesianism," though he rejects nearly the whole doctrinal content of Cartesian philosophy—for the very sake of radicalizing Descartes' ultimate intentions.[3]

We therefore find ourselves confronted with a twofold task. In the first place, we must formulate what Husserl considers to be the fundamental intention which guides and dominates the whole of modern philosophy. In the second place, we must raise the question why, prior to Husserl, this intention could not find adequate fulfillment and satisfactory realization. We take our departure from Descartes, to whom Husserl repeatedly refers as having given to modern philosophy its distinctive character and physiognomy by orienting it towards transcendental subjectivism.

I

HISTORICAL ROOTS OF HUSSERL'S PROBLEMS

a. DESCARTES' SUBJECTIVE ORIENTATION AND ITS GENERALIZATION.

Descartes' discovery of consciousness, as his *sum cogitans* may be interpreted, amounts to and may even be said to consist in the disclosure of a double privilege pertaining to consciousness. There is, in the first place, its indubitability in the well-known sense. Whatever else may be, and is, open to the universal doubt—the existence of consciousness as such and as a whole, of actually experienced particular acts of consciousness of every de-

3. Husserl, *Cartesian Meditations,* trans. D. Cairns (The Hague: 1960), p. 1.

scription, the existence, finally, of the experiencing and conscious ego itself, to the extent to which it is conceived merely and exclusively as a conscious being (*res cogitans*) —is not engulfed by the doubt but, on the contrary, withstands such engulfment.

Of still greater importance in the present context is the second privilege of consciousness which Descartes indicates at the end of his second *Meditation* when he summarizes his famous analysis of the perception of a piece of wax.[4] According to this analysis we become assured of the existence of the piece of wax by the fact that we see it, touch it, hear the sound it emits when struck, etc., and bring further mental faculties into play, especially that faculty which Descartes calls inspection of the mind (*mentis inspectio*). At the end of the sixth *Meditation*,[5] Descartes points out that it is the convergence, concordance, and agreement between those mental operations and their yieldings which make us accept the objects thus encountered as really existing and which differentiate them from figments of the fancy and dream occurrences. It follows that in becoming convinced of the existence of any extramental objects, like the perceived piece of wax, we are a fortiori assured of the existence of the mental operations in question by means of which we come to accept those extramental objects as real and existing. To express it differently and in a more general manner, so as not to lay the main stress on the problem of existence and reality, Descartes' analysis of the perception of the piece of wax sets forth and makes explicit the essential reference of objects to consciousness, namely, to those acts of consciousness through which the objects present themselves. Descartes' analysis discloses consciousness as necessarily involved in whatever objects are encountered and dealt with. It may appear a truism to say that we cannot deal with objects in any manner except actually dealing with them and that such dealing denotes mental activities and operations

4. *Oeuvres de Descartes,* published by Ch. Adam & P. Tannery (henceforth referred to as *A-T*) (Paris: 1897–1910), VII, 33; IX, 25f. *The philosophical works of Descartes,* trans. E. S. Haldane and G. R. T. Ross (henceforth referred to as *H-R*) (Cambridge, England: 1931), I, 156f.

5. *A-T,* VII, 89f; IX, 71f. *H-R.,* I, 198f.

of various kinds. However, what appears as a truism expresses a profound and momentous discovery, namely, the insight into the nature of consciousness as the universal medium of access to whatever exists for us and is considered by us as valid.

As Husserl interprets Descartes' discovery of consciousness as to both the indubitability of its existence and its function as a universal medium of access, this discovery implies the principle of a subjectively oriented philosophy. It implies a goal pursued by Descartes himself as well as by the subsequent development of modern philosophy, a goal that is also the goal of Husserl's own endeavors. All that is required is a generalized expression of the mentioned reference of objects to acts of consciousness and conscious life as a whole and the formulation of that reference in sufficiently radical terms.

First of all, the term "object" must be understood in the widest possible sense. It is meant to apply to perceivable things encountered in everyday common experience; to things of cultural value and significance such as utensils, books, musical instruments, and the like; to all real beings both inanimate and animate, e.g., our fellow men with whom we deal in highly diversified social situations, where they play the roles of employers, employees, teachers, doctors, partners, collaborators, rivals, and so forth. Taken in this all-inclusive sense, the term "object" may also apply to the constructs of the several sciences, like matter, energy, force, atom, electron, and furthermore to ideal entities of every kind and description, like the general notions considered in traditional logic, propositions and systematic concatenations of propositions, relations of all sorts, numbers, geometrical systems. Finally, the term "object" may also denote specific social realities like the opinions and beliefs held in a certain society at a certain period of its historical development, political institutions, legal systems, and so on.

Every object—understood in this wide sense—presents itself to us through acts of consciousness as that which it is for us, as that which we take it to be, in the role which it plays and the function assigned to it in our conscious life, with regard to our several activities both practical, theoretical, and other, e.g., ar-

tistic. In and through specific acts of consciousness, the object
in question displays its qualities, properties, and attributes. It
exhibits the components that contribute towards determining
its sense; also the sense of its specific objectivity and existence,
which obviously is not the same in the case of numbers and
other ideal entities as it is in that of perceivable material things.
Because of their essential reference—in the sense which has just
been sketched—to acts of consciousness, objects may be said to
"depend upon" or—as we should prefer to express it—to be relative to consciousness. Hence a problem of a very general nature
and of universal significance arises. Given an object of any category whatever, the task is to set forth and to analyze descriptively
those acts of consciousness in their systematic interconnectedness
and interconcatenation through which the object in question
displays and presents itself, acts of consciousness in and through
which all its sense-determining components and constituents
accrue to the object. Hereby the task of constitutive phenomenology is defined, though in a somewhat sketchy way. It rests
on the principle that for an object of any class and sort to be
what it is and to have whatever existence, objectivity, or validity
pertains to it, acts of consciousness of a specific kind, as well as
typical organizational forms in which those acts are united and
concatenated with one another are required. Constitutive
phenomenology translates into concrete terms the essential reference of objects to conscious life (a reference that Descartes had
expressed in a more or less abstract and general way) insofar as
it makes every object arise, so to speak, out of the relevant acts
and operations of consciousness as accomplished (*geleistet*) by
them and, in that sense, as their product. Hence Husserl speaks
of an "equivalent of consciousness" related to every object,[6] and
he describes it as the task of constitutive phenomenology to lay
bare and to make explicit the correlation which a priori obtains
between objects of the different varieties on the one hand and
systematically organized groups of specific acts and operations of

6. Husserl, *Ideen* I, p. 319.

consciousness on the other.[7] For reasons that cannot be discussed in the present context, precedence in the order in which the constitutive problems are to be tackled belongs, according to Husserl, to the real perceptual world, the existents it comprises, and the events taking place in it.

Obviously, it is only by means of generalizations and radicalizations going far beyond not only Descartes' explicit statements but also his actual intentions that the program of constitutive phenomenology can be derived from his discovery of consciousness. As a matter of fact, what Husserl interprets as the central motif of Descartes' thinking was for Descartes himself rather a means to an end and stood in the service of a different purpose. Descartes' main intention was the validation of the incipient new science of physics, the justification of a tenet whose boldness we, the heirs to a scientific tradition, can appreciate only with considerable difficulty. This is the tenet that an external, extramental, and extraconscious world exists, but that this external world is in reality not as it appears in everyday perceptual experience but as it is conceived of and constructed in mathematical terms in the new science. This explains why neither Descartes himself nor any of the Cartesians proceeded to exploit the momentous discovery of consciousness, whose exploitation did not begin until prior to Locke's *Essay concerning the human understanding*. Having made the preceding remarks for the sake of the accuracy of the historical record, we must insist upon the legitimacy of isolating the discovery of consciousness and developing it in its own right. Understood along the general lines of Husserl's interpretation, though of course not in the sense of his extreme radicalization, the Cartesian philosophy takes on its fundamental significance within the course of the subsequent development of modern philosophy. It can be considered as the first expression historically of what was to become the ultimate intention of the whole of modern philosophy.

We already mentioned that in Husserl's judgment neither Descartes himself nor any of his successors, whom Husserl con-

7. Husserl, *Krisis*, secs. 46 and 48, and *Phänomenologische Psychologie, Husserliana*, Vol. IX (1962), sec. 3b and e.

siders as his own predecessors, has succeeded in adequately realizing the intention in question. Here Husserl points to what he calls "transcendental psychologism" as one of the main reasons for that failure. Succinctly stated, the task is to account for objects of every kind and description—in the first place, the real perceptual world and whatever it contains—by reference to subjective conscious life. Acts and operations of consciousness are as a matter of course interpreted as mundane events alongside other such events. They pertain to sentient living organisms, e.g., human beings, which obviously are mundane existents occupying determinate places within the spatio-temporal order of the real world. We thus seem to be caught in a circular reasoning insofar as the very terms in which the world is to be accounted for are themselves affected by the sense of mundaneity.[8] This situation leads to, motivates, and even necessitates transcendental reduction as a methodological device whose function is to strip conscious life of the sense of mundaneity.

Undoubtedly, transcendental reduction is of utmost importance for the foundation and consistent elaboration of constitutive phenomenology. Still, it is not along that line of thought that we shall pursue our discussion. We wish to point out a second and no less important reason for the failure referred to. To do so we raise the question of whether the theoretical means at the disposal of Descartes and his successors in the classical tradition of modern philosophy were sufficient for an adequate realization of what, following Husserl, we consider their ultimate intention to be. In other words, we turn to examining the general conception of consciousness as laid down by Descartes and taken over, almost as a matter of course, by his successors. Such an examination will enable us to see in its true proportions the radical and revolutionary innovation which is Husserl's theory of the intentionality of consciousness.

8. About the paradox involved in transcendental psychologism see Husserl, *Phänomenologische Psychologie,* pp. 287ff and 328ff; concerning Husserl's criticism of Descartes in the respect here relevant cf. *Cartesian Meditations,* sec. 10, and *Krisis,* secs. 17ff.

b. CARTESIAN DUALISM AND THE THEORY OF IDEAS IN THE "REPRE-
SENTATIVE VERSION."

Reality as whole is divided by Descartes into two domains.
The domain which withstands universal doubt is the domain of
consciousness (*cogitatio*), while the other domain, that of extension, is at first engulfed by universal doubt and subsequently
reconquered and so to speak reinstated in its right. Throughout
Descartes emphasizes the thoroughgoing heterogeneity of these
two domains. To be sure, with respect to both domains Descartes
uses the term "substance." However, the defining attributes of
these substances are so utterly different, the two substances have
so little in common, that the distinction between them amounts
to a profound dualism dividing reality.

As, in Descartes' view, a corporeal thing is nothing but a
delimited portion of space and, in this sense, a mode or modification of extendedness, so is a mental state, a *cogitatio,* nothing but
a modification of consciousness or, in more modern parlance, an
occurrence in conscious life. Because of the heterogeneity of the
two domains, either domain is completely self-contained and self-
sufficient, at least with respect to the other domain. Such self-
sufficiency justifies denoting both domains as substances within
the meaning of the specific Cartesian definition of that notion.

On account of its self-containedness and self-sufficiency, the
domain of consciousness forms a closed sphere, the sphere of
interiority or subjectivity. All mental states, which by definition
belong to the mental sphere, are on the same footing, for whatever differences may obtain between them in any other respect,
mental states are, all of them, modes of consciousness, subjective
occurrences, events taking place in conscious life. This holds
also for the particular class of mental states which Descartes
singles out under the heading of Ideas.[9] Hereby are meant such
mental states as have a presentifying function, that is to say,
make present a man, a chimera, the heavens, an angel, God, to

9. We are writing "Ideas" (with an "I") when that term is to be understood in the general sense as it is used by Descartes and "ideas" (with an
"i") when we refer to the specific sense that Hume gives to it.

abide by the examples Descartes gives in the *Meditations*.[10]
Ideas by the means of which or, more correctly, by the means of
some of which—as will presently be explained—contact is established with what pertains to the other domain, that of ex-
ternality, are, to begin with, subjective occurrences and events,
not different from other mental states, e.g., a feeling of pleasure
or pain, a desire, a hope, and the like.

At this point we may formulate two tenets that are connected
with and characteristic of both the theory of Ideas and the interpretation of consciousness as a closed sphere of interiority. On
the latter account, the mind is confined to its own states. Only its
own experiences, its modes and modifications, are directly and
immediately given to the conscious ego. Differently expressed:
*The only immediate and direct objects of knowledge are our
own mental states.* It is not Descartes himself who defined Idea
as that which is in our mind or thought,[11] but—as far as I see—
Antoine Arnauld[12] who was the first explicitly to lay down that
principle which has become a general and fundamental doctrine
accepted in the whole subsequent development of classical modern philosophy. Even thinkers who, like Hume and Kant, con-
siderably depart from Descartes maintain that, as Hume expresses
it, "Nothing is ever really present with the mind but its perceptions or impressions and ideas,"[13] or, as Kant has it, all our
representations, whatever their origin and nature, are nothing
but modifications of the mind (*Gemüt*) and therefore belong to
inner sense.[14]

The second doctrine is of a less general significance, because,
in contrast with the first one, it is not essential to the theory of
Ideas as such but only to a special version of that theory, the
version advocated by Descartes. As we noted, the goal of Des-

10. *A-T*, VII, 37; IX, 29. *H-R*, I, 159.
11. Letter to Mersenne, June 16, 1641: ". . . par le mot *Idea*, j'entends
tout ce qui peut être en notre pensée. . . ." (*A-T.*, III, 383.)
12. Compare C. E. Bréhier, *Histoire de la philosophie*, II, 219f.
13. D. Hume, *A treatise of human nature*, ed. L. A. Selby-Bigge (Oxford:
1888), p. 67; compare also pp. 197, 206, and 212.
14. Kant, *Critique of pure reason*, A, pp. 98f; compare also A, pp. 189ff =
B, pp. 234ff, and A, p. 197 = B, p. 242.

cartes is to prove the real existence of the external world, conceived to be of a mathematical, especially geometrical, nature, and to show that certain particularly privileged Ideas correspond to, and are in conformity with, corporeal things. Still, the Ideas in question are subjective occurrences in the sphere of interiority. Furthermore, on the strength of what has just been shown, the mind can never leave that sphere of subjective interiority but remains forever moving within it, so to speak—that is to say, among its own states. If, owing to the privileged Ideas, contact is to be established with extramental corporeal things, the contact can be only a mediated one. The Ideas in question must be considered as intramental representatives of extramental, i.e., extended objects. Deliberately we avoid the expression "representation," because the meaning of that term as usually understood in the psychological sense is too narrow. Being representative is meant to denote substituting for, standing in the place of, acting and functioning on behalf of, and therefore mediating. The conception of consciousness as the universal medium of access acquires an additional meaning, insofar as the term "medium" comes to be understood with respect to the mediating function that is attributed to certain mental states, i.e., those that are representative.

At this point the question must be raised as to how to account for the representative function by virtue of which certain Ideas play the role of mediators between the conscious ego and extramental corporeal things. The question concerns nothing less than the cognitive significance and objective validity of the Ideas under discussion. We are in possession of some knowledge concerning the extramental world of extension. Such knowledge is acquired by means of privileged Ideas and, more generally, through processes and operations of consciousness which—to repeat and stress it once more—are and remain subjective events occurring in the sphere of interiority. How under those conditions is it to be understood that subjective events within the sphere of interiority can have reference to, and significance for, what on principle lies outside that sphere? How do the role and function of mediators accrue to the Ideas in question?

Briefly we recall Descartes' well-known reasoning. Among the totality of Ideas he singles out a special class, namely, those which exhibit clearness and distinctness. Whatever formal definition Descartes gives of clearness and distinctness,[15] in view of the use he makes of these notions in actual practice, we may say that clear and distinct Ideas are in the first place mathematical, particularly geometrical, Ideas. At least, these alone are relevant within the present context. The special emphasis on geometrical Ideas is in conformity with his goal of vindicating the incipient new science. However, clearness and distinctness—whatever privilege they may bestow upon the Ideas concerned—are not the same as and do not even imply the objective reference of those Ideas. Descartes is fully aware of the necessity of establishing a connection between clearness and distinctness on the one hand and, on the other hand, objective reference—that is to say, reference to what is extramental. He must establish the principle that whatever is clearly and distinctly perceived is true, i.e., has objective reference and validity. For the establishment of that principle, Descartes, as is well known, resorts to the veracity of God. Divine veracity guarantees the existence of the external world.[16] In guaranteeing that principle, divine veracity also guarantees the validity of the mathematical conception of the external world—its interpretation in purely geometrical terms. Finally, although divine veracity does not guarantee the cognitive value of common perceptual experience, it does confirm its reliability for the practical conduct of our life. This reliability rests on the inner consistency and coherence exhibited by that experience.[17] By a veritable tour de force Descartes has cut the Gordian knot, which is to say that in the representative version of the theory of Ideas the problem of the objective reference and significance of subjective events and occurrences in the sphere of interiority proves insoluble.

Lack of space forbidding, we cannot enter into a detailed analysis of the work of Locke, who also advocates the theory of

15. R. Descartes, *Principia Philosophiae*, Part I, secs. 45f.
16. *A-T*, VII, 78ff; IX, 62f. *H-R*, I, 190f.
17. *A-T*, VII, 88ff; IX, 70ff. *H-R*, I, 198f.

Ideas in the representative version. A few remarks will have to suffice. Locke sets out to study what may be called the natural history of the human mind and of human knowledge in particular. He carries this study out on the basis of Newtonian physics, which he unquestionably accepts as a point of departure. This acceptance appears most clearly in his concept of the role of primary qualities. On the one hand they pertain to "ideas of sensation," which are psychological events, occurrences, within the mind. On the other hand they are assumed to correspond to and even to render faithfully the true state of affairs—that is to say, the state of affairs which in the physics of Newton passes for the true one. Whereas the objective reference of subjective events is seen by Descartes as a genuine problem—though he could find no solution to it except by a tour de force—that reference is for Locke no longer a problem at all but is taken for granted and underlies the elaboration of his whole theory. One may be tempted to say that divine veracity has been replaced in Locke by the authority of Newton, by the prestige and authority of Newtonian science. This is not merely a bon mot. The difference between Locke and Descartes seems to us to reflect the development of modern physics in the course of the seventeenth century from its incipient phase at the time of Descartes to the systematically developed form it had attained in Locke's time with the *Principia Mathematica Philosophiae Naturalis.* Needless to add, when the objective reference of certain mental states is taken for granted and assumed as a matter of course, the problem—as we have tried to set forth—which is involved in and besets that reference is eschewed rather than solved.

c. THE NONREPRESENTATIVE VERSION OF THE THEORY OF IDEAS.

In the version of the theory of Ideas to which we now turn, objects and Ideas are not opposed to, or even distinguished from, but on the contrary equated with one another. Hence there can be no question of Ideas functioning as representatives of extramental objects.

The nonrepresentative version of the theory of Ideas was first formulated by Berkeley and fully elaborated by Hume. We shall here concentrate on Hume's theory, the analysis of which will lead to the disclosure of a problem that is of utmost importance for the subsequent development of our argument.

According to Hume, "Almost all mankind, and even philosophers themselves," unless they are engaged in philosophical speculations, "take their perceptions to be their only objects, and suppose, that the very being, which is intimately present to the mind, is the real body or material existence."[18] The terms "object" and "perception" (Idea, in the sense defined above[19]) can be interchanged, since both of them denote "what any common man means by a hat, or shoe, or stone, or any other impression, conveyed to him by his senses."[20] The identification of objects and perceptions follows, according to Hume, from the fundamental principle of the general theory of Ideas. In fact, if the only data immediately given to consciousness are its own mental states—in Humean parlance, its impressions and ideas—the consequence is that it is "impossible for us so much as to conceive or form an idea of any thing specifically different from ideas and impressions."[21]

All mental states, whether "passions, affections, sensations, pains and pleasures, are originally on the same footing; . . . whatever other differences we may observe among them, they appear, all of them, in their true colours, as impressions or perceptions."[22] This also holds for their temporality or, as Hume puts it, for their being "perishing existences" and appearing as such.[23] No perception, once it has passed, can ever recur. A new perception may arise, highly similar to and even perfectly like the former one. Yet, as a new perception, that is to say, one occupying a different place in the order of time, it cannot be identified with the former perception and must not be mistaken for the recurrent former perception. On the other hand we are convinced that the object with which we are dealing now is identically the same as that which we encountered on a previous occasion. Considering that objects are nothing but perceptions

---

18. Hume, *A Treatise of human nature*, p. 206.   19. See n. 9.
20. Hume, *A Treatise of human nature*, p. 202.   21. *Ibid.*, p. 67.
22. *Ibid.*, p. 190.   23. *Ibid.*, p. 194.

and that the latter are "perishing existences," how can the consciousness of the identity of the object arise and how can that consciousness be accounted for?

Stating our problem in terms of consciousness, we follow the general direction of Hume, who does not ask whether bodies have in fact "an existence distinct from the mind and perception"—or even a continued existence, i.e., whether they continue to exist when they are not perceived—but rather how we come to believe in their continued and distinct existence.[24]

To account for the consciousness of the identity of an object, Hume refers to the high degree of resemblance between the perceptions arising on successive occasions—as when, for instance, in observing an object we alternately open and close our eyes or when, after an absence of shorter or longer duration, we return to the object in question, e.g., our room.[25] Because of that resemblance the mind passes readily, easily, and smoothly from perception to perception. Its disposition hardly differs from that in which it finds itself when it observes an invariable object for a certain length of time without any interruption. The smoothness of the transition makes us oblivious of, or at least inattentive to, the interruptions that are actually taking place. In this way there arises the illusion of the identity that the imagination ascribes to the multiple perceptions separated from one another by shorter or longer intervals of time. The consciousness of the identity of the object is due to the imagination mistaking a succession of perceptions for the continuous, uninterrupted presence of an unvarying perception. However, the obliviousness required for the consciousness or illusion of identity cannot endure indefinitely. As soon as we become aware of being confronted with multiple perceptions which, however similar and even alike, are different from, because they succeed upon, one another, the awareness of the true state of affairs conflicts with the propensity of the imagination to ascribe identity to the multiple perceptions. To reconcile this conflict, the imagination is led to contrive the fiction of the "continued existence" of perceptions. Finally, this

24. *Ibid.*, pp. 187f.   25. Compare *Ibid.*, pp. 202ff.

conflict and contradiction, according to Hume, give rise to what we have called the representative version of the theory of Ideas—namely, the distinction between objects and perceptions or, as he calls it, the hypothesis of "the double existence of perceptions and objects."[26] Under this hypothesis, identity or continuance is ascribed to the objects and interruptedness and multiplicity to the perceptions which, precisely as representatives of the objects, cannot coincide with them.

Our main concern is not with the details of Hume's theory but rather with the terms in which he formulates the problem of identity. As our sketchy exposition of his theory shows, Hume considers the "notion of the identity of resembling perceptions, and the interruption of their appearance" as "contrary principles," exclusive of one another.[27] Overcoming the conflict and the perplexity it gives rise to requires "sacrificing" one of the two principles to the other. By contriving the fiction of a "continued existence" of perceptions even when they are not actually given, we disguise, as much as possible, the interruption, or rather remove it entirely.[28] Hume's formulation of the problem, however, proves to be at variance with the phenomenal state of affairs. Having been absent from our room, we return to it and find the same furniture that we perceived before leaving. To make that identity explicit, far from having to become oblivious of or even inattentive to the difference between the occasions on which we perceived the object in question, we must on the contrary make that very difference explicit. Verbally expressing our explicit awareness of the identity of the object, we say that the object with which we are dealing now is the same as that which we encountered on previous occasions and to which as identically the same we may, under certain conditions, return as often as we wish. The consciousness of the identity of the object does not arise in spite of but on the contrary in explicit reference to the multiple perceptions of the object. Identity and multiplicity are indeed opposed to one another; however, they are not opposed as contradictory or in any sense incompatible

26. *Ibid.,* pp. 214ff.   27. *Ibid.,* p. 206.   28. *Ibid.,* p. 199.

terms, but rather as correlative ones, which mutually require and demand each other.

Hume's analysis of the notion of identity leads to the same result. According to Hume, the uninterrupted presence of an invariable perception conveys the idea of unity but not of identity. For the latter to arise, time or duration must be taken into account. "We cannot, in any propriety of speech, say, that an object is the same with itself, unless we mean, that the object existent at one time is the same with itself existent at another."[29] Hume's analysis is inadequate insofar as he ascribes to "a fiction of the imagination" the participation of the unchanging object or perception in the flux of time. When we are actually confronted with an uninterrupted and unvarying perception, e.g., when the same musical note resounds over a certain length of time, we are aware of its duration, which is to say that our auditory experience passes through different temporal phases.[30] Since what we experience is an identical note resounding for a certain length of time and not a sequence of notes that are all of equal pitch, intensity, and timbre, we are again confronted with the problem of the identity of the note in opposition and with reference to a multiplicity, in this case not of discrete occasions separated from one another by temporal intervals but of phases that pass continuously into one another, exhibiting various temporal characteristics.

The problem that appears in Hume's theory is of quite universal significance and goes far beyond perceptual experience. Consider one more example. Yesterday we were reading a fairy tale about a mythical person and today we resume our reading, taking the identity of the mythical person for granted without even making it explicit, though we are always free to do so. On the grounds of Hume's theory, we are presented with two ideas

29. *Ibid.*, pp. 200f.

30. See Husserl's detailed analysis of that phenomenon in *The Phenomenology of Internal Time-Consciousness*, trans. J. S. Churchill (Bloomington, Ind.: 1964), secs. 10ff, and *Erfahrung und Urteil* (Hamburg: 1954), sec. 23.

or, if one prefers, two sets of ideas; one being related to the present reading, the other being the memory of yesterday's reading. However similar those ideas may be to one another, it is hard to see how they can yield the consciousness of an identical mythical person.

As this example as well as the preceding analysis of Hume's theory show, the problem concerns the consciousness of the identity of any object whatever, understanding the term "object" in the broad sense in which we initially introduced it.[31] The problem is insoluble within the framework of the theory of Ideas—that is to say, on the basis of the principle that its own mental states alone are directly and immediately given to the mind. Its insolubility appears still more clearly if allowance is made for the further development that Hume has given to the theory of Ideas in emphasizing that the mental states (the "perceptions" in his terminology) form merely a one-dimensional temporal order, or, as he expresses it, "The successive perceptions only . . . constitute the mind."[32] How indeed can a mere succession of mental states ever yield the consciousness of the identity of anything?

It is possible to show that the problem in question does not find a solution within the context of Kant's *Critique of Pure Reason* either. Lack of space forbidding, we cannot enter into a detailed analysis to substantiate that assertion; we may be permitted to refer to the discussion we have presented elsewhere.[33] For our present purpose we abide by Hume's theory. By its critical analysis we have prepared the ground for the exposition of Husserl's theory of the intentionality of consciousness.

31. See p. 28 above.
32. Hume, *A Treatise of human nature,* pp. 252f.
33. A. Gurwitsch, "La conception de la conscience chez Kant et chez Husserl," *Bulletin de la Société Française de Philosophie,* Vol. LIV (1960), and "Der Begriff des Bewusstseins bei Kant und Husserl," *Kant-Studien,* Vol. LV (1964). [The first essay has now been translated into English. See Prof. Gurwitsch's *Studies in Phenomenology and Psychology* (Evanston: 1966), 148–60. Hereafter, we refer to this volume as "*Studies . . .*" eds.]

II

Outlines of the Theory of Intentionality

In the course of the preceding discussion two problems have emerged. The first, which arose from the analysis of some of Descartes' tenets concerns the objective and, we may say, objectively cognitive significance of mental states, their reference to extramental facts, events, and items of any kind. Perhaps of still greater importance is the second problem, with which the critical examination of Hume's theory presents us—namely, the problem of the consciousness of any object given as identically the same through a multiplicity of mental states, experiences, acts. Because of its fundamental importance we shall start by considering the problem of the consciousness of identity, which—we submit—has found a solution in Husserl's theory of intentionality. After that theory has been expounded, at least in its basic outlines, the problem mentioned in the first place will no longer present any considerable difficulties.

The notion of intentionality plays a major role in all Husserl's writings, with the exception of *Philosophie der Arithmetik*. Here we can obviously not enter into a study of the development which that notion has undergone along with that of Husserl's thought in general.[34] In view of Professor Chisholm's contribution we abstain also from presenting Brentano's conception of intentionality and setting forth its difference from that of Husserl.[35] Since we approach the theory of intentionality from a specific point of view, namely, the problem of the consciousness of identity, we shall have to overemphasize certain aspects of that theory or, more correctly, to emphasize them more than Husserl did himself. In doing so, however, we remain faithful to the spirit of Husserl's theory and its leading intentions. Finally,

34. Q. Lauer in his book *Phénoménologie de Husserl* (Paris: 1955) has followed up on the genesis of the theory of intentionality through four of Husserl's major works which appeared in his lifetime.

35. L. Landgrebe, "Husserl's Phänomenologie und die Motive zu ihrer Umbildung," I, *Revue Internationale de Philosophie*, Vol. I (1939), and H. Spiegelberg, *The phenomenological movement* (The Hague: 1960), I, 7, and III, C 2 c.

we shall exclude from our presentation a few doctrines, especially the notion of sense-data and the egological conception of consciousness, which play a certain role in Husserl's theory of intentionality. Not endorsing those doctrines,[36] we may abstain from dwelling upon them, because they do not seem to us to be of crucial importance for what we consider most essential to the concept of intentionality. The justification of our departure from Husserl would lead us too far afield to be attempted here.

a. THE NOTION OF THE OBJECT AS MEANT OR INTENDED (THE NOEMA).

From the critical examination of Hume's theory it has become clear that the consciousness of identity cannot be accounted for in terms of the theory of Ideas, that is to say, on the grounds of the traditional conception of consciousness. Hence a totally new and radically different conception is required in which the consciousness of identity no longer appears as an *explicandum* but, on the contrary, is made the defining property of the mind, that essential property without which the mind could not be what it is. For that reason it is insufficient, though true and valid as a first approximation, to define intentionality as directedness, saying that in experiencing an act of consciousness we find ourselves directed to something; e.g., in perceiving we are directed to the thing perceived, in remembering we are directed to the event recalled, or in loving or hating to the person loved or hated, and the like. Directedness merely denotes a phenomenal feature of the act, inherent and immanent, a feature that appears and disappears along with the act to which it pertains. If intentionality is thus defined, the question remains unanswered as to how we can become aware of the identity of the "something" to which the multiple acts are directed, considering that each one of those acts possesses directedness as a phenomenal

36. Compare A. Gurwitsch, "Phänomenologie der Thematik und des reinen Ich," chap. III, sec. 16, and chap. IV, sec. 4, *Psychologische Forschung*, Vol. XII (1929) [= *Studies* . . . 253–58 and 278–86]; "A non-egological conception of consciousness," *Philosophy and Phenomenological Research*, I (1941) [= *Studies* . . . 287–300]; and our book, *The Field of Consciousness* (Pittsburgh: 1964), Part IV, chap. II, 6.

feature of its own. Therefore the theory of intentionality must be based upon the notion of the "something" that we take as identical and whose identity we may disclose and make explicit by the appropriate considerations.

As a convenient point of departure we choose a special phenomenon, namely, the understanding of meaningful verbal expressions, a phenomenon whose analysis forms the subject matter of the first investigation of Husserl's *Logische Unter-suchungen.*[37] To lay bare what is involved in the understanding of meaningful expressions, let us contrast our experience in hearing a phrase like "the victor of Austerlitz" or "New York is the biggest city in the U.S.A." with the experience we have when we hear a noise in the street, a sound like "abracadabra" or an utterance in a foreign language with which we are not familiar. In the latter cases we have merely an auditory experience. In the former cases we also have an auditory experience, but one which supports a specific act of interpretation or apperception by means of which the auditory experience becomes a vehicle of meaning or a symbol. The same holds in the case of reading, except for the immaterial difference that the visual experience of marks on paper takes the place of the auditory experience. The specific acts that bestow the character of a symbol upon perceptual experiences may be called acts of meaning apprehension. Like all other acts, they, too, are psychological events occurring at certain moments in time. By means of the reasoning we used in the critical discussion of Hume's theory, we come to establish the distinction between the act of meaning apprehension and the meaning apprehended. We remember that on numerous occasions we uttered or heard the phrases mentioned. Recalling those occasions, we recall them as different from one another because of their different temporal locations. At the same time we become aware of the fact that what we meant and had in view on those occasions and what we mean now is the same: on all these occasions there presents itself to, and stands before, our mind "the one who

37. Husserl, *Logische Untersuchungen* (2nd ed.; Halle: 1913), Vol. II; see also the condensed but faithful rendering by M. Farber, *The Foundation of Phenomenology* (Cambridge, Mass.: 1941), chap. VIII.

won the battle of Austerlitz," or Napoleon as the victor of Austerlitz, or New York under the aspect of its number of inhabitants in comparison with the other American cities. Furthermore, we take it for granted that all who listen to our utterance, provided they are familiar with the symbolic system used—in this case the English language—apprehend the same meaning. Each person experiences his own act of meaning apprehension which he cannot share with anybody else. Yet through all these multiple acts, distributed among any number of persons, and for each person, varying from one occasion to the other in the course of his life, the same meaning is apprehended. If this were not so, no communication, either in the mode of assent or dissent, would be possible. For a proposition to be accepted or rejected it must first be understood.

The identical entity that we call "meaning" may be defined as a certain person, object, event, state of affairs which presents itself, taken exactly as it presents itself or as it is intended. Consider the two phrases: "the victor of Austerlitz" and "the initiator of the French legal code." Though both meanings refer to the same person, Napoleon, they differ from one another insofar as in the first case Napoleon is intended under the aspect of his victory at Austerlitz and in the second with regard to his role in the establishment of the French legal code. The difference in question has been expressed by Husserl as that between the "object which is intended" and the "object *as* it is intended."[38] It is the latter notion which we identify with that of meaning. For a further illustration we mention another of Husserl's examples.[39] In hearing the name "Greenland," each one of us has a certain thought or representation of that island; that is to say, the island presents itself and is intended in a certain fashion. The same holds for the arctic explorer. Both he and any one of us intend the same object. However, Greenland *as* intended and meant by some of us with our sketchy, highly vague, and indeterminate representation obviously differs from Greenland *as*

38. Husserl, *Logische Untersuchungen*, II, i, pp. 415f.
39. *Ibid.*, II, i, 418.

meant by the arctic explorer, who has been to the island and knows it thoroughly.

Two multiplicities, each related to an identical entity, must be distinguished from one another. On the one hand we have the multiplicity of acts through all of which the same meaning is apprehended; on the other hand there is the multiplicity of meanings, of "objects as intended," all referring to one and the same "object which is intended."

For the sake of simplicity we have confined ourselves to such meanings as refer to real objects, persons, or events. This simplification makes it easy to see that meanings cannot be identified with physical objects and occurrences any more than with psychological events. From the fact that a plurality of meanings can refer to the same object, it follows that none of the meanings coincides with the object. Real events like the battle of Austerlitz take place at a certain moment in time. But it is absurd to assign a temporal place to the meaning of the phrase "the battle of Austerlitz" and to ask whether it precedes, succeeds upon, or is simultaneous with another meaning, though any one of the acts through which the meaning is apprehended occupies a definite place in time. There are no spatial relations between meanings any more than there are causal effects exerted by meanings either upon one another or upon anything else. We are confronted with entities of a special kind—aspatial, atemporal, acausal, hence irreal or ideal—which have a specific nature of their own. Between these entities obtain relations of a particular sort, the like of which is nowhere else encountered. As a simple example we may mention the relations, studied in logic, that obtain between propositions as a special class of meanings.

Our results can easily be generalized. For the sake of brevity we limit ourselves to perceptual experience. When we perceive a thing, e.g., a house, we do so from the point of observation at which we happen to be placed, so that the house appears under a certain aspect: from one of its sides, the front or the back, as near or far, and the like. It appears, as Husserl expresses it, by way of a one-sided adumbrational presentation.[40] Maintaining

40. Husserl, *Ideen* I, sec. 41, and *Cartesian Meditations,* sec. 17.

our point of observation, we may alternately open and close our eyes. We then experience a sequence of acts of perception, all differing from each other by the very fact of their succeeding upon one another. Through all of these perceptions not only does the same house appear, but it also appears under the same aspect, in the same orientation—in a word, in the same manner of adumbrational presentation. Again we encounter an identical entity, namely, that which is perceived exactly as it is perceived, the "perceived as such" (*das Wahrgenommene als solches*). It stands in the same relation to the acts of perception as does the meaning apprehended to the acts of meaning apprehension. One may generalize the term "meaning" so as to use it beyond the domain of symbolic expressions and speak of perceptual meanings. Husserl also denotes the "perceived as such" as "perceptual sense" (*Wahrnehmungssinn*), because by virtue of it a given perception is not only a perception of a certain thing but also a determinate perception of that thing—that is to say, a perception through which the thing presents itself in this rather than another manner of adumbrational appearance.[41] Husserl's most general term here is that of *noema*,[42] a concept that comprises meanings in the conventional sense as a special class. Noema denotes the object as meant and intended in any mode whatsoever and hence includes the mode of perceptual experience.

Having distinguished the perceptual noema from the act of perception—the *noesis*—we have further to distinguish it from the thing perceived. The latter may be seen from different points of view—it may appear under a variety of aspects: from the front, the back, one of the lateral sides, and the like—while the perceptual noema denotes the thing perceived as presenting itself under *one* of those possible aspects. Again we have to apply the distinction between the "object which is intended"—the thing perceived—and the "object *as* it is intended"—the perceptual noema, or the thing perceived *as* it is perceived. A multiplicity of perceptual noemata are related to the same thing as, in the previous example, a multiplicity of meanings were seen to refer to the same object.

41. *Ideen* I, sec. 88.   42. *Ideen* I, Part III, chap. III.

Let us consider the difference between the perceptual noema and the thing perceived from a different point of view. The house may be torn down, but none of the pertinent noemata is affected hereby.[43] Even after its destruction the house may still be remembered, and it may be remembered as presenting itself under one or the other of the aspects under which it had previously appeared in perceptual experience. To be sure, the noema is no longer a perceptual one; it is rather a noema of memory. The point is that two or even more noemata, their difference notwithstanding, may have a certain stratum in common, a stratum that Husserl denotes as "noematic nucleus."[44] Within the structure of every noema, the distinction must be made between the noematic nucleus and "noematic characters," which, incidentally, belong to several dimensions.[45] By means of this distinction it is possible to account for the verification of a nonperceptual experience by a perceptual one. When in actual perceptual experience a thing proves to be such as it had been assumed, thought, believed, etc., to be, it is that the nucleus of the nonperceptual noema is seen to coincide and even to be identical with that of the perceptual noema, while the noematic characters indicating the mode of givenness or presentation remain different on either side.[46] Both the identity of the noematic nucleus and the difference concerning the characters are required for and essential to the phenomenon of verification.

b. CONSCIOUSNESS DEFINED AS NOETICO-NOEMATIC CORRELATION.

In the center of the new conception stands the notion of the noema, of the object meant and intended, taken exactly and only as it is meant and intended. Every act of consciousness is so essentially related to its noema that it is only with reference to the latter that the act is qualified and characterized as that which it is, e.g., that particular perception of the house as seen from the front, that determinate intending of Napoleon as the victor

43. *Ideen* I, p. 184.   44. *Ideen* I, sec. 91.
45. *Ideen* I, secs. 99 and 102ff.
46. Cf. Husserl, *Logische Untersuchungen*, Vol. II, i, chap. I, sec. 14, and vi, chap. I, secs. 8ff.

of Austerlitz and not as the defeated of Waterloo. Traditionally consciousness has been interpreted as a one-dimensional temporal order, a conception whose most consistent elaboration lies in Hume's theory. To be sure, acts of consciousness are psychological events that take place and endure in time and stand under the laws of temporality to which Husserl has devoted detailed analyses.[47] Though temporality undoubtedly denotes a fundamental aspect of consciousness, that aspect is not the only one. The temporal events called "acts of consciousness" have the peculiarity of being actualizations or apprehensions of meanings, the terms "apprehension" and "meaning" being understood in a very general sense beyond the special case of symbolic expressions. It pertains to the essential nature of acts of consciousness to be related and to correspond to noemata. Rather than being conceived of as a one-dimensional sequence of events, *consciousness must be defined as a noetico-noematic correlation,* that is to say, a correlation between items pertaining to two heterogeneous planes: on the one hand the plane of temporal psychological events, and on the other hand that of atemporal, irreal, that is to say, ideal entities that are the noemata, or meanings understood in the broader sense. Furthermore, it is a many-to-one correlation insofar as an indefinite multiplicty of acts can correspond to the same noema. Correlated terms demand and require each other. To establish the identity of the noema we had to contrast it with, and hence to refer it to, a multiplicity of acts. Conversely, it can be shown (though this is not the place to do it) that no account of the temporality and especially the duration of an act of consciousness is possible without reference to the noema involved.[48] Thus the conception of consciousness as noetico-noematic correlation brings to light the indissoluble connection between consciousness and meaning *(Sinn)*. It shows

47. See n. 30.

48. See our detailed analysis in "On the Intentionality of Consciousness," Part III, *Philosophical Essays in Memory of Edmund Husserl,* ed. M. Farber (Cambridge, Mass.: 1941) [= *Studies* . . . 134–38], and "William James' Theory of the 'Transitive Parts' of the Stream of Consciousness," Part II, *Philosophy and Phenomenological Research,* III (1943) [= *Studies* . . . 306–13].

consciousness to be essentially characterized by an *intrinsic duality*, which is to take the place of the Cartesian dualism.

To evaluate the historical significance of the innovation, let us consider in which respect it constitutes a break with the tradition. In the first place the theory of Ideas is relinquished, especially the principle that the mind is confined to its own mental states, which alone are directly and immediately given to it. Undoubtedly the mind lives exclusively in its mental states, its acts. Each act, however, is correlated to a noema which—as we have stressed—is itself not a mental state, an act of consciousness, a psychological event. Relatedness to essentially nonmental entities is the very nature of mental states. Furthermore, the noema is defined as the "object as it is intended," i.e., as the object in question appearing in a certain manner of presentation (under a certain aspect, from a certain point of view, etc.), an object capable, however—we must now add—of appearing in different manners of presentation. The definition of intentionality as directedness can now be given its legitimate meaning. Experiencing an act of consciousness, we are directed to an object insofar as in the structure of the noema corresponding to the act there are inscribed references to further noemata, to different manners of presentation of that object. Objective reference of mental states is no longer an insoluble problem as with Descartes; nor is it to be explained and accounted for subsequently. On the contrary, it proves essential to the acts of consciousness—not as an additional phenomenal feature of the acts, of course, but rather in the sense of the conception of consciousness as a noetico-noematic correlation.

As a consequence, consciousness can no longer be interpreted as a self-sufficient and self-contained domain of interiority. This interpretation follows from the Cartesian dualism, the severance of *res cogitans* from *res extensa* to which Descartes was led in endeavoring to lay the foundations of the incipient new science. It must be stressed that nature in the sense of modern physics is not the same as the world of common, everyday experience. In the latter world things not only present spatial forms, stand in spatial relations to one another, and change those relations in the course of time, but they also exhibit specific qualities, the so-called secondary qualities, and are endowed with characters which, like those of instrumentality, utility, and cultural value, refer to human purposes and activities.[49] Quite generally, in the world of common experience the corporeal in the spatiotemporal sense is intertwined and interwoven with the mental and the psychological in all its forms. Nature in the modern scientific sense is the result and product of an artful method applied to the world of common experience. That method consists, among other things,[50] in abstracting spatiotemporal extendedness to the disregard of whatever is mental or psychological, relegating the latter to the purely subjective domain. In this way one arrives at one single coherent and self-contained context encompassing all spatiotemporal things and events. The success of this abstractive procedure suggests its application in the opposite direction, namely, a counterabstraction of what is "subjective" to the disregard of what pertains to the spatiotemporal, hence "objective," domain. However, the attempt at such a counterabstraction fails to yield a self-sufficient and self-contained domain of interiority. Turning to and concentrating upon the life of consciousness, one does not discover occurrences that take place in a closed domain and merely succeed upon one another, as Hume's theory of the mind would have it. Rather one encounters apprehensions *of* meanings; perceptions *of* houses, trees, fellow human beings; memories *of* past and expectancies *of* future events; and the like. Generally speaking, one encounters dealings in several manners and modes with mundane things and events of the most diverse description as well as with nonmundane entities like numbers and geometrical systems, which are not mental states or psychological occurrences any more than they are mundane existents. The very failure of the counterabstraction discloses the essential reference of acts of consciousness to objective entities of

49. Cf. Husserl, *Krisis*, secs. 66ff, and *Phänomenologische Psychologie*, secs. 16ff.

50. For the sake of simplicity we omit mentioning the problems concerning mathematical idealization, which are extensively treated by Husserl in *Krisis*, secs. 8ff.

any kind, hence also to mundane, i.e., spatiotemporal objects. This failure marks the breakdown of the Cartesian dualisms.

Being based on the theory of intentionality, phenomenology must not be identified with or even too closely assimilated to intuitionistic philosophy or introspectionism as advocated by Bergson.[51] For consciousness to be grasped and studied in its authentic and aboriginal state, it must first, according to Bergson, undergo a purification from whatever contamination or admixture has accrued to it by way of contact with the objective external world, which is not only a spatial but also a social world. Obviously, such a methodological principle presupposes the Cartesian dualism. What Bergson considers a denaturalization of consciousness appears in the light of the theory of intentionality as an expression of its genuine nature. Insistence upon that difference, profound as it is, must not, however, preclude the recognition that many of Bergson's analyses have phenomenological significance or, to speak with greater prudence, may by a proper reinterpretation be given phenomenological significance.

Because of the intentionality of consciousness, we are in direct contact with the world. Living our conscious life, we are "at" the world, "at" the things encountered in that world. This should be seen as a consequence of the theory of intentionality rather than being credited as original with subsequent existentialist philosophies. A glance at the phenomenological theory of perception makes that clear. We recall the definition of the perceptual noema as the thing perceived appearing from a certain side, under a certain aspect, in a certain orientation—briefly, in a one-sided manner of adumbrational presentation. The decisive point is that notwithstanding the one-sidedness of its appearance, it is the thing itself that presents itself, stands before our mind, and with which we are in contact. Noetically speaking, perceptual consciousness is an originary, albeit incomplete because one-sided, experience of the thing perceived appearing in "bodily presence" (*in Leibhaftigkeit*). Perceptual consciousness must not be interpreted in terms of profoundly different modes

51. Bergson, *Essai sur les données immédiates de la conscience* (Paris: 1904).

of consciousness, as, e.g., by means of images, signs, symbols, and the like.[52] Accordingly, the perceptual noema must not be mistaken for an Idea in the Cartesian sense, that is to say, the substitute for or representative of a reality only mediately accessible. With the phenomenological theory of perception, we submit, the traditional theory of Ideas is definitively overcome.

c. ON THE NOTION OF OBJECTIVITY.

There remains the task of defining the relationship between the perceptual noema and the thing perceived. While actually appearing in a determinate manner of adumbrational presentation, the thing is capable of appearing in other manners. It actually so appears in the course of the perceptual process, when, e.g., we walk around the thing and, in general, perceive it under various conditions of different sorts. In the course of that process, the thing is perceived as identically the same, presenting itself from different sides, under varying aspects, in a variety of orientations. The thing cannot be perceived except in one or the other manner of adumbrational presentation. It is nothing besides, or in addition to, the multiplicity of those presentations through all of which it appears in its identity.[53] Consequently, the thing perceived proves to be the group, more precisely put, the systematically organized totality of adumbrational presentations. Both the difference and the relationship between the thing perceived and a particular perceptual noema can now be defined in terms of a noematic system as a whole and one member of that system. This is in agreement with the previous formulation that every particular perception, its incompleteness and one-sidedness notwithstanding, is an originary experience of the thing perceived appearing in bodily presence. In fact, it is the perceptual apprehension of a noematic system as a whole from the vantage point of one of its members.

Two questions arise. One concerns the organizational form of the noematic system, the other the manner in which its member-

---

52. Husserl, *Ideen* I, sec. 43.
53. Compare Husserl, *Phänomenologische Psychologie*, pp. 152f, 178f, 182f, and 430ff.

ship in the noematic system is inscribed in the structure of every particular noema. Both questions can here only be mentioned, but not discussed.[54] At present we must confine ourselves to stressing that the thing perceived also proves to have noematic status. As a noematic system it is a noema itself, but a noema of higher order, so to speak.

Just as the theory of intentionality involves a new conception of consciousness or subjectivity, so, too, it entails a reinterpretation of the notion of objectivity. Traditionally, the objective has been opposed to the subjective as entirely alien to it, so that for an object to be reached in its genuine and authentic condition, all mental, i.e., subjective activities and their contributions, must be disregarded if not eliminated altogether. In the light of the theory of intentionality, this conception of objectivity, which derives from the Cartesian dualism, can no longer be upheld. The objective reference that is essential to acts of consciousness corresponds to a no less essential relationship of objects to acts of consciousness, especially to their noemata. The disclosure of the thing perceived as a noematic system, that is to say, an intentional correlate,[55] is in perfect conformity with the here propounded general conception of consciousness as a correlation. Furthermore, several levels of objectivity must be distinguished from one another, in consequence of which the notions of subjectivity and objectivity prove affected by a certain relativity.

Every particular meaning or noema as an identical entity can be considered as objective in contrast to the multiple subjective acts that are correlated to it, especially if it is remembered that those acts may be distributed among a plurality of persons. A particular perceptual noema, defined as the thing appearing under a certain aspect, is in turn to be characterized as subjective with respect to the perceived thing itself, of which the former is a one-sided perceptual adumbration, with respect to the noematic system of which the particular noema is a member. The things perceived and perceivable form, in their totality, the

54. *The Field of Consciousness,* Part IV.
55. Compare Husserl, *Phänomenologische Psychologie,* p. 184.

perceptual world, the world of pure experience, or, as Husserl calls it, the life-world *(Lebenswelt)*. It is the world such as it is understood, conceived, and interpreted by a certain social group which unquestioningly accepts it as reality. The life-world is an essentially social phenomenon.[56] Accordingly, it differs from one social group to the other and also for a given social group in the course of its historical development. At every phase of this development and for every social group, the respective life-world counts as objective reality. Over against this multiplicity of life-worlds, the question arises of a world common to all social groups. This is an objective world in a second, more profound sense. More precisely, the question concerns a set or system of invariant structures, universal insofar as they are by necessity exhibited by every sociohistorical life-world.[57] Of this common world, which perhaps should not be called life-world but rather the world of pure perceptual experience, the diverse life-worlds in the proper sense appear as varieties to be relegated to the status of merely subjective worlds. Finally, there is objectivity in the specific sense of modern science: the objectivity of the scientific or scientifically true and valid universe as constructed on the basis of perceptual experience by means of mental operations and procedures into whose analysis we cannot enter here. From the point of view of the universe of science, the world of perceptual experience appears in turn as subjective.

Sketchy and incomplete though these remarks are, they might perhaps suffice to illustrate, if not substantiate, the thesis that what is to be meant by objective must not be conceived as severed from the life of consciousness. Moreover, the ascent to higher levels of objectivity, far from requiring the progressive elimination or, at least, disregard of mental activities and operations, on the contrary involves them in increasing complexity; it

56. The social aspect of the life-world is the persistent central theme in most of A. Schütz's writings; cf. his *Collected Papers*, Vol. I (The Hague: 1962). See also our article "The commonsense world as social reality," *Social Research*, Vol. XXIX (1962).

57. Compare Husserl, *Krisis*, secs. 36f, and *Phänomenologische Psychologie*, secs. 7ff.

involves syntheses of consciousness of ever-widening scope. As an intentional correlate, the object of every kind and level proves to be an accomplishment (*Geleistetes*) whose clarification, especially the clarification concerning its objectivity and existence, requires that it be referred to the accomplishing (*leistende*) mental operations. Accounting in this manner for an object of whatever sort is tantamount to disclosing its "equivalent of consciousness."

CONCLUSION

Our discussion has run full circle. By generalizing and radicalizing Descartes' discovery of consciousness, Husserl was led to conceive the program of constitutive phenomenology, which is to account for objects of all possible kinds in terms of subjective conscious life. A superficial survey of some levels of objectivity might give an idea of the extent of that tremendous task. For the sake of completeness we recall in passing the sense of objectivity which pertains to the ideal orders of being and existence in the Platonic sense or, in Husserl's parlance, to the eidetic realms. In the theory of intentionality we found the theoretical instrument both necessary and sufficient for the realization of that task. Herein appears the historical significance of that theory.

We could as well have started from the theory of intentionality, conceived as a theory of the mind in a merely psychological setting, regardless of philosophical interests. The radical innovation which that theory entails for the conception of the mind and thus for psychological thinking defines its historical significance in a further respect. Consistently developing the theory of intentionality conceived in a psychological orientation, and pursuing it in its ultimate consequences, would have led us to the idea of constitutive phenomenology in a way Husserl has followed himself in the Amsterdam lectures and the article in *Encyclopaedia Britannica*.[58] The theory of intentionality thus

58. *Phänomenologische Psychologie* contains the "Amsterdamer Vorträge" and the definitive German text as well as two preparatory drafts of the article in *Encyclopaedia Britannica*.

serves both as a motivating force, as far as the conception of the idea of constitutive phenomenology is concerned, and as the theoretical instrument for its realization. In other words, provided proper allowance is made for the transcendental reduction, which could here be mentioned in passing only, the full elaboration of the theory of intentionality proves coextensive and even identical with the philosophy of constitutive phenomenology.

Essay Three

Notes toward
an Understanding of
Heidegger's Aesthetics*

E. F. KAELIN**

PART I

On Being, Essence, and Truth

I

One of the prevailing mysteries in contemporary discussions of phenomenological aesthetics is the paucity of attention given the relevant work of Martin Heidegger. Although his three lectures on Der Ursprung des Kunstwerkes were delivered in the years 1935–36, first in Freiburg, then in Zurich and Frankfurt am Main,[1] they were not made available to the wider reading public until 1950, when they were published together as the first essay in *Holzwege*. And quite recently Heidegger's war-long reflection on the philosophy of Nietzsche was published with one section devoted to this philosopher's contribution to aesthetic theory. Even though the two volume work on Nietzsche did not make its

* The research reported on herein was supported by funds from two committees of the University of Wisconsin (Madison), which permitted the author to spend a year at Freiburg-im-Breisgau, 1964–65. To each of them, the Department of Philosophy's Committee on Comparative Philosophical Studies and the Graduate School's Research Committee, his thanks are due. Thanks are likewise due to Professor Sieghardt M. Riegel of the Department of German, University of Wisconsin, for suggesting corrections to the author's translations of Heidegger's sometimes difficult German.

** Department of Philosophy, Florida State University, Tallahassee, Florida.

1. See *Holzwege* (Frankfurt a. M.: Klostermann, 1950), p. 344.

appearance until 1961,[2] Heidegger's interpretation of the Will to Power considered as Art was composed in 1936–37. His reflections on art, then, have been known in restricted circles for about thirty years and should now become more widely, if not better, known than in the past.

In France, Mikel Dufrenne has made extensive use of Heidegger's first essay in his *Phénoménologie de l'expérience esthétique*,[3] but came a cropper on one of its central ideas, the expressiveness of a nonobjective work; and at his death Maurice Merleau-Ponty left unfinished a work that was to continue the inspiration he felt from Heidegger, the signs of which had already begun to show in his introduction to *Les philosophes célèbres*,[4] and became most apparent in *Signes*[5] as well as in the last of his articles he saw published, "L'oeil et l'esprit."[6]

In America, things have not been much better, even in phenomenological circles. In a curious paragraph on Merleau-Ponty's relationship to Heidegger, occurring in his introduction to the American edition of *The Primacy of Perception*,[7] Professor James M. Edie states: ". . . what radically separates Merleau-Ponty's existential analysis from Heidegger's is precisely his thesis of the primacy of perception, and his acceptance of the perceived world as the primary reality, as giving us the first and truest sense of 'real.' "[8] This was true of the earlier Merleau-Ponty (*The Structure of Behavior* and *The Phenomenology of Perception*); it was no longer true of the Merleau-Ponty of *Signs* and "Eye and Mind." For in these latter works Merleau-Ponty's central focus on the world had changed from an "acceptance of the perceived world as the primary reality" to an

2. *Nietzsche* (Pfullingen: Günther Neske, 1961), 2 vols.

3. Paris: Presses Universitaires de France, 1953, 2 vols.

4. Geneva: Mazenod, 1956.

5. Paris: Gallimard, 1960. Translated with introduction by R. C. McCleary as *Signs* (Evanston: Northwestern University Press, 1964).

6. In the inaugural issue of *Art de France*, I (1961). See Dallery translation in Edie, *The Primacy of Perception and Other Essays* (Evanston: Northwestern University Press, 1964).

7. *Ibid.*

8. *Ibid.*, p. xviii.

ontologico-eidetic description of the manner in which human beings come to the notion of a single perceived world whose structures are revealed to a community of perceiving subjects. In a word, his interest in the world of perception was temporarily being replaced by a notion of transcendence which was larger in scope, embracing the intentional arc established between "brute being" and "wild-flowering mind."[9]

What remained constant in the two periods of Merleau-Ponty's thought is the notion of mind as the integration of a corporeal schema. The *cogito* for him was always in the end a corporeal phenomenon; and the certitude for this *cogito* was guaranteed by the moment to moment perception of our own lived bodily schemata. The force of this *cogito* is so grounded in human experience that it would lead some unreflective philosophers of another persuasion to insist that the question of personal existence never arises. What Merleau-Ponty did not live long enough to explain, however, was the precise manner in which the human mind-body constitutes *its* world from a more fundamental relationship between itself and "brute being."

It is clear, from a first reading of "Eye and Mind," that Merleau-Ponty took the experience of painting as a direct revelation of "Being"; but it is also clear, from a sixth reading of the same essay, that he failed to provide the explanatory machinery necessary to show how the corporeal *cogito* is capable of developing the ontico-ontological distinction. What he does have to say on the matter reads like a careless repetition of Heidegger's *Sein und Zeit*. Thus, when Professor Edie continues—"For Heidegger, on the contrary, it is not this [the perceived] world but the Being of beings which is the primary reality, and any analysis of human experience, perceptual or otherwise, is only a means to pose the more fundamental question of this Being."[10]— the disinterested scholar no longer knows what to believe; for the being of an existent thing is not the same as Being. The one is a question of ontics and the other of fundamental ontology. Moreover, Heidegger had long ago explained that human exist-

9. See McCleary, *op. cit.*, p. xxxii.   10. *Op. cit.*

ence is nothing if not a manner of being in the world, and that
any analysis of this being must be made on the basis of "expli-
cata" proper only to it. This is a common phenomenological
idea, shared by Husserl, Sartre, and Merleau-Ponty.

Since the "categories" of the physical and biological sciences in
particular are not proper for an analysis of the human being,
Heidegger proposed a series of *existentialia* which he thought
could do the job. The successful use of these explicative notions
in the field of existential psychiatry would seem to constitute
some evidence that he was not entirely mistaken. In addition, his
analysis of a human subject's openness to the world (*Er-
schlossenheit*) clearly indicates the primacy of affectivity (*Befind-
lichkeit*) in our knowledge of both ourselves and the world. For
what is affectivity if not a perception of ourselves caught in a
certain pose before the objects of the world, if not one act of the
corporeal *cogito*?

Yet Professor Edie insists, "Heidegger's 'thought of Being'
escapes the methods of phenomenology altogether and certainly
has nothing to do with perceptual consciousness."[11] Like Merleau-Ponty in his later period, however, Heidegger insists that
our experience of the phenomena of art belie this contention.
One need only read the following—" 'Techne' does not in the
least mean a kind of practical accomplishment. Much more
appropriately, the word names a way of knowing. To know
means to have seen, in the broader sense of seeing, i.e., grasping
what is present as it is present."[12]—to understand that whatever
may constitute "the methods of phenomenology," art and technics have to do with knowing, knowing with seeing, and seeing
in its widest, most mysterious sense—the grasping of what is
present as it is present to us. The objects we see are merely the
closest at hand, not the most primary realities of human ex-

11. *Ibid.*

12. In Heidegger's German, *Holzwege,* p. 47: " 'Techne' meint überhaupt
niemals eine Art von praktischer Leistung. Das Wort nennt vielmehr eine
Weise des Wissens. Wissen heisst: gesehen haben, in dem weiten Sinne von
sehen, das besagt: vernehmen des Anwesenden als eines solchen." See also
Einführung in die Metaphysik (Tübingen: Niemeyer, 1957), p. 122, and
Vorträge und Aufsätze (Pfullingen: Neske, 1954), p. 160.

perience. But this, too, Heidegger had said quite long ago. And, apparently, in the latter days of his career Merleau-Ponty was led to agree with him.

As for Professor Dufrenne's aesthetics, whose "phenomenological" analysis of aesthetic objects includes three "worlds," the second of which is that of representation, even for works of nonobjective art such as a Grecian temple, there are even greater scholarly lacunae. Since his theory calls for the appearance of some kind of representation, he had to come up with something and, faced with the facts of a nonobjective universe, could find nothing better than an "idea of a temple" as object of a temple's representation. But the idea of a representational nonrepresentational work of art is a patent absurdity; and this is a logical, not a phenomenological, statement. Heidegger makes the same point somewhat differently in the very text Dufrenne cites: "But where and how then does this universal essence exist so that the work of art may correspond with it? With which essence of which thing, then, should a Grecian temple correspond? Who could assert the impossible, that in the edifice the idea in general of the temple is represented?"[13] Answer: Mikel Dufrenne.

Truth in art is not a matter of representation; for if we consult the things as they are we are forced to admit that works of art may be representational or they may be abstract, or they may be completely nonobjective and represent nothing at all. And "truth" need not be taken to mean "correspondence," so that the question of the truth of art works may be separated from the kinds of universe they present. If our phenomenological analysis of works of art is to be effective we must produce a description of works of the various kinds, whether or not there is a single description of the "essence" of art. What is more, the notions of "truth," "essence," and "art" must be considered in the light of an experience we have of the meanings of these terms if our

13. *Holzwege,* p. 26: "Aber wo und wie ist denn dieses allgemeine Wesen, so dass die Kunstwerke mit ihm übereinstimmen? Mit welchem Wesen welchen Dings soll denn ein griechischer Tempel übereinstimmen? Wer könnte das Unmögliche behaupten, in dem Bauwerk werde die Idee des Tempels überhaupt dargestellt?"

analysis of the truth of art is to be "phenomenological" in any workable sense of this term. It behooves us therefore to return once more to sources and to re-examine Heidegger's claim to having found truth revealed in art.

II

"Der Ursprung des Kunstwerkes" is an imposing title; we translate, "The Origin of the Work of Art" and immediately are faced with a host of linguistic problems. Why "the origin" and why "the" work of art? Is there only one source and only one work of art? Granted that many works of art could be traced to a common set of conditions—the creativeness of the artist, the *Zeitgeist* of his times, especially the socioeconomic conditions of his society, the level of sophistication and the aesthetic demands of the community of art consumers—what sense can be made of the attempt to reduce all works of art to a single description valid for them all?

What, for example, does a representational work have in common with a nonrepresentational piece, outside its sensuous surface? And can the notion of a sensuous surface exhaust, in its descriptive scope, all the felt expressiveness of works that represent objects realistically, abstractly, or do not represent objects at all? All these notions are important for a coherent theory of art, and Heidegger was not unaware of any of them. We can understand his answers to most of these questions by continuing to read beyond the title and to take the words Heidegger uses to mean what he says they mean. Most of the difficulty with understanding his philosophy seems to stem from his readers' refusal to take him at his word.

First, "der Ursprung." The origin of something need not be considered a cause in the sense of a prior set of conditions obtaining in the history of the natural world, or a reason by and through which the existence of something can be demonstrated to exist. The study of origins, in other words, need not be either "empirical" or "rational," as these terms are commonly used in contemporary theory of knowledge. The method to be used is "phenomenological" in the sense that a correct reading of the experience of the given object will reveal what it is and the source from which it springs. Nor is the phenomenological analysis of the language used to express the content of an experience foreign to Heidegger's approach.

To understand this method we must recall his prior descriptions of man's openness to the world as affectivity, understanding, and speech. Affectivity is the modification of a human being's existence in its relationship to *a world*; to its world, to one of those worlds that "world" owing to the context of meaning relations established by the purposeful activity of human subjects. Before the establishment of the single, natural world, primarily by means of speech and the adoption of univocally meaningful vocal gestures, this is the only kind of world there is. A child lives in such a world before "learning its language at its mother's knee"; and many, too distressingly many, adults are driven back to the same kind of world by their own inability to adjust to the prescribed structures of the one world described in scientific discourse. We call them "abnormal" and can do so only on the prejudice of the primacy of the "normal," or scientific, world. And, finally, the works of creative artists will always appear to be abnormal, odd, or queer, if not to say "obscene" or "sick," as long as we, as viewers, continue to look at their works as putative representations of some aspect of the world of nature.

We "understand" our own affectivity, in the second place, by having the experience of the feeling in question. Concern, boredom, anxiety, are merely the most widely known of Heidegger's affective terms, since these are given metaphysical, or ontological, interpretation. This is not to say, but expressly to deny, that we understand our feelings only when we can state their causes, their reasons, or otherwise classify them according to a programmed list of emotions found on a depth psychologist's chart. At this level of experience, which is yet an understanding, there is no "carte du tendre" such as the one drawn up by Mlle. de Scudéry in the period of preclassical French literature. We understand in this sense merely by keeping ourselves open to the influence of the world we ourselves are instrumental in creating.[14]

We speak, finally, not by repeating what is said by everyone in their idle talk (*Gerede*),[15] but by giving tongue to those sounds that express what is understood in the constant flux of our own affective conditions. In our speech, moreover, impression does not necessarily precede expression; or thought, the word. The sounds are simultaneous with the words, and these with meanings, or relationships to our experienced worlds. Thought is a creative act. Thus Heidegger can claim that man is the metaphysical animal, always living in the openness of Being, and this affectively, whether he "knows" it or not. Through man, Being is on the way to language (*Unterwegs zur Sprache*),[16] where it comes to revelation in poetic and philosophic thought.

These words are mysterious, but no more mysterious than the process by which "colors" take on essential determination by relatedness one to the other in a given visual context. Merleau-Ponty was fond of stating that in a living language there were no absolute counters, only sounds marking differences from other sounds. It is the context which allows us to perceive the word-sound entoned therein. For this reason I shall interpret the "openness of Being" as the permanent possibility of the appearance of new entities in the process of the world's becoming a world (*Die Welt weltet*),[17] in the context of which men become aware of things becoming things (*Das Ding dingt*).[18] These

14. Professor Werner Marx [*Heidegger und die Tradition* (Stuttgart: Kohlhammer, 1961)] finds Heidegger's interest in creativity one of the compelling reasons for taking him seriously. See p. 17.

15. *Sein und Zeit* (9th ed.; Tübingen: Niemeyer, 1960), pp. 167–70.

16. Pfullingen: Neske, 1959. Compare *Über den Humanismus* (Frankfurt a. M.: Klostermann, 1947), pp. 16, 45–7.

17. For the clearest presentation of this idea, see *Sein und Zeit*, pp. 63–88. The "World" is considered in relation to human transcendence in *Vom Wesen des Grundes* (Frankfurt a. M.: Klostermann, 1955). A later essay, "Das Ding," elaborates the relationship between our awareness of things and our living in a world. See *Vorträge und Aufsätze*, pp. 163–85. Compare Marx, *op. cit.*, pp. 183–202.

18. *Vorträge und Aufsätze*, p. 172.

things in their becoming constitute the objects of experience and the referents of the words we use to point them out. Thus the creative use of language presents a world to our experience and need not represent anything definite at all within the context of the real world, that world which forces our adaptation because we live in a society of common-language users. But from the foregoing it should be clear that life in a community of language users is not always an unmixed blessing. Sometimes our fellows can drive *us* mad.

The difficulty with Heidegger is that he insists upon using language creatively even when talking about the creative use of language. But this is determined by his method, which calls for the description of the "essence" of things—of what and how things are. This is not Husserlian "Wesensschau," true; there is no imaginative modification of the objects of perception through which there persists a single core of sedimented meaning. "The revelation" is claimed to be direct, there to be seen or heard by anyone who has eyes and ears *through which* to see and hear.[19] In making translations, therefore, one must be careful to hear the words as they grew out of the experience of the men who first used (read "spoke") them in such a way as to make a new meaning apparent.

Since, moreover, we see and hear *through* (*durch*) rather than with (*mit*) our organs of sense, we come into contact with the objects of our world by their means whether we see or hear *words* or the sensuous surface of actual things; all human expression mediated by seeing or hearing is so constituted as to produce this contact with the world, and engages the entire structure of the perceiving being. Like Merleau-Ponty, Heidegger considers perception a corporeal phenomenon and sensation an abstraction from the perceived thickness of things.[20] Painting presents us with a world directly through the medium of vision, and language presents a world in depth that may be sensuous, supersensuous, or however a world may be, indirectly through the

19. See *Der Satz vom Grund* (Pfullingen: Neske, 1957), pp. 85–90.
20. *Holzwege*, p. 15. See also *Nietzsche*, I, pp. 118–20, and *Die Frage nach dem Ding* (Tübingen: Niemeyer, 1962), pp. 163–4.

ear. As Merleau-Ponty pointed out,[21] it is for this reason that painting and literature can be reasonably compared: on the surface, each is a sensuous presentation of some kind of world: gestalt and symbol, neither of which is separable from the other without destroying the *working* of a work of art. In addition, according to Heidegger, both painting and literature are means of founding (*eine Stiftung*) [22] a novel meaning, which, when successful, adds a new direction to the course of our cultural history.

Such in very broad outline is the direction of Heidegger's musings on art. He has qualified his own work as an attempt to make clear the nature of "the riddle of art" and not as a solution to the riddle.[23] It is therefore apropos for someone to fill out the sketch in an effort to discern to what extent he has succeeded in indicating a way in which the riddle could ultimately be solved.

The first step in this process is to proceed with the analysis of Heidegger's terms. If the origin of a work of art is that from which (*woher*) and by means of which (*wodurch*) a thing is what and how it is,[24] we need to consider as the second term of our explication the peculiar twist he gives the word "Wesen."

Here again, we translate "essence" and chance to be misled by our knowledge of the history of philosophy, just as Sartre was misled.[25] For an essence is not only what a thing is, the quiddity of a thing—"This indifferent essence (the essentiality in the sense of *essentia*), however, is only the inessential essence."[26]—but what the thing is with all its particularities: "The true essence of a thing is determined by a relationship to its true being, to the truth of the momentarily existing things."[27]

21. In "Indirect Langauge and the Voices of Silence," *Signs,* p. 45.
22. *Holzwege,* pp. 62–64.   23. *Ibid.,* p. 66.   24. *Ibid.,* p. 7.
25. See Heidegger's criticism of Sartre's interpretation of his existential postulate in *Über den Humanismus,* pp. 16–21.
26. *Holzwege,* p. 39: "Dieses gleichgültige Wesen (die Wesenheit im Sinne der essentia) ist aber nur das unwesentliche Wesen."
27. *Ibid.*: "Das wahre Wesen einer Sache bestimmt sich aus ihrem wahren Sein, aus der Wahrheit des jeweiligen Seienden."

Although Heidegger owes this distinction to his earlier studies of Duns Scotus, the same distinction in meanings of the term "essence" is found in the ordinary English uses of the term. It may have a privative or a definitive sense.

We say, for example, "Don't tell me the whole story; give me the essence of it," meaning thereby the essentials, the gist, the story with all the inessentials removed. We are asking for quite another thing when we demand to know the essence (say) of justice, and expect a description of the concept. Any deletion of detail here is likely to lead to miscomprehension. In an older logic, the essence of a thing was called the "comprehension" of the term used to refer to it.

The peculiarity of Heidegger's interpretation of the non-privative essence is his addition of "the manner in which a thing is" to the notion of what a thing is; "essence" is not only a substantive but an adjectival or adverbial qualification as well. If we continue to use "essence" as the univocal translation of "Wesen," which is a noun in general use stemming from the infinitive of a verb no longer commonly used in German, Heidegger's thought will remain all but incomprehensible. He intends the word to be understood verbally.

Etymologically considered, "Wesen" is a verbal substantive, and the qualification suggested by the "how" (*wie*) is in consequence mainly adverbial. An essence in this sense is a coming to be, taking place in a determinate manner; the word denotes a well-defined process in which something appears and remains as it is.

It was Hegel perhaps who misled Sartre by his laconic "Wesen ist was gewesen ist," since this is the view which interprets the essence as a finished process in the same way Sartre interprets the essence of a human transcendence completed in death. His *Huis Clos* is a dramatization of a triangle of essences: the coward, the lesbian, and the nymphomaniac (in the order of their appearance), who can no longer be anything other than what they have been.

But it is a mistake, claims Heidegger, to derive "Wesen" from the perfect participle of *sein*; its true source is the archaic *wesen,* from the Old High German *wesan,* which means "to endure" (*währen*) or "to remain" (*bleiben*). It is for this reason that an essence names the manner in which a thing comes to be and remains what it is.[28] Of the essence, then, is how things are in play (*im Spiel*). And Heidegger does not hesitate to use this archaic word in its original sense, as when he says, "Technics comes to be and endures in that realm where disclosure and unconcealedness, where *aletheia* or truth happens.[29] Truth, too, is a "happening"; and it is more than a little ironic that some recent artistic events in America have been called by this name. For according to Heidegger it is the essence of art to "let truth happen."

The third and last term to be explicated is "truth" itself. Here, too, our love of substances or of nouns substantive may well lead us astray. Even if we assume, as we must, that truth is not a reified concept and that it is a shorthand expression used to name the condition of things that are true, our appeal to the adjectival sense may be misleading without further analysis. For what can be considered "true"? And what is the condition by which we know them as true? Ordinary usage is again of some help. We say, for example, that fool's gold is not "true" (or genuine) gold and that only something that corresponds to the essence of gold or has all the essential properties of gold can be truly so called. The question of truth in this concrete sense of the term, then, leads us back to the notion of essence, even if the essence is understood as a position in a chemist's periodic chart of elements.

But, speaking as logicians, we likewise say that only sentences are "true" in the technical sense of the term; and they are true only when what is said corresponds with matters of fact, i.e., when a representation gives, in some sense, a true picture of what is represented—the facts as they are. Such a view of the

28. See *Vorträge und Aufsätze,* p. 38, and *Was Heisst Denken?* (Tubingen: Niemeyer, 1961), p. 143.

29. *Vorträge und Aufsätze,* p. 21: "Die Technik *west* in dem Bereich, wo Entbergen und Unverborgenheit, wo aletheia, wo Wahrheit geschieht."

truth of sentences poses no problems if we can safely assume the oneness of the world and can have confidence in our manner of knowing what the facts are.

At one level of human experience, however, neither of these conditions obtains. They do not obtain each time it is asked what it means to say the world is one or, further, when it is said whether or not this statement is true. And these questions can be asked, as psychiatric evidence or the facts of scientific discovery and artistic creation attest. Any questioning of the facts in the case will once more repose the question of essence: "Every act of working and accomplishing, all acting and calculating, is maintained and stands in the openness of a context in the midst of which an existent thing, considered both as what it is and how it exists, can be expressly placed and referred to. This happens only when the existent thing comes to be represented in a declarative sentence, as the expression takes on itself the ordering which allows it to express what and how an existent thing exists."[30] The declarative sentence, in a word, must mediate the conception of an actual existent.

If the first notion of truth is genuineness (*Echtheit*), the second is correctness (*Richtigkeit*). And in our common sense view, a sentence is correct, or true, when what it says is correct, i.e., when it represents a true state of affairs. So far, common sense agrees with logic. But if this is so, it is false to assume that *only* statements are true; common sense here begins to diverge from logic, for statements can be true only if existents are revealed, and this in conformity to some concept so that the correspondence between reality and concept (or word) may in its turn be perceived. In his usual manner, Heidegger states the solution to this problem in an apothegm: ". . . das Wesen der Wahrheit ist die

30. *Vom Wesen der Wahrheit* (Frankfurt a. M.: Klostermann, 1954), p. 11: "Jedes Werken und Verrichten alles Handeln und Berechnen hält sich und steht im Offenen ins Bezirks, innerhalb dessen das Seiende als das, was es ist und wie es ist, sich eigens stellen und sagbar werden kann. Dazu kommt es nur, wenn das Seiende selbst vorstellig wird beim vorstellenden Aussagen, so dass dieses sich einer Weisung unterstellt, das Seiende so—wie es ist, zu sagen."

Wahrheit des Wesens"[31]—the essence of truth is the disclosure of being.

What at first reading appears to be a play on words, if not an explanatory circle, Heidegger states as an ultimate truth, for the upshot of his discussion is that truth is not *primarily* either of the senses heretofore denoted. Truth is not primarily a logical or scientific concept, but only secondarily so. There can be logical or scientific truths only because truth is metaphysical, implicit in all man's dealings with *his* world. And so, metaphysics points the way out of our circle.

Metaphysical truth is primary, and this truth is experienced as the disclosure (*Entbergen*) of an essence, of what and how a thing is. In this disclosure man first becomes aware of an existent thing qua existent (*ein Seiendes*). Moreover, each awareness of an individual thing takes place in situation—i.e., in an open field in which to reveal itself an object must conceal others (*Verborgenheit*)—as well as the totality of the field itself. This is the source of Heidegger's notion of *Seinsvergessenheit*, in which, according to him, contemporary philosophy has been stagnating in the past thirty years, as well as the basis of his interpretation of truth as the unconcealedness (*Unverborgenheit*) of existent things. The unveiling of the individual existent conceals the universe of existents considered as a whole (*das Seiende im Ganzen*).

The openness of the field of consciousness in which disclosure and concealment take place is the metaphysical precondition of having any truths at all. Heidegger refers to this openness as an illumination (*die Lichtung des Da*). In this light, in this relation of man to being, truth happens. And it happens in such a way as to conceal at the same time it discloses, for man cannot be aware of everything at once. When we are aware of anything, something lies unconcealed in the open field of human consciousness, while the rest of the field remains hidden; and when something appears *as* something it is not, man is led into error.

31. *Ibid.*, p. 26.

In sum, truth is neither an "objective" term qualifying the existence of a genuinely appearing object nor a "subjective" one qualifying man's knowledge as presented in correct sentences. It, too, is an existential explicative notion describing the conditions under which man lives in his world—in the truth as in untruth. Thus, Heidegger can say, " 'Truth' is no mark of the correct sentence, expressed of an 'object' by a human 'subject' and then somewhere—it is not known exactly where—holds as valid; it is rather the disclosure of a being by means of which an openness comes to be and endures. In this opening all human conduct and behaviour is exposed. It is in this way, therefore, that man is the ecstatic existent he is."[32] Truth in short is a phenomenon of human existence transcending itself toward a world and not strictly speaking the exclusive result of scientific or logical inquiry.

This last and most basic meaning of "truth" is what the Greeks, according to Heidegger, always called *aletheia*. It remains to be seen how this "truth" happens in art.

PART II

On Truth in Art

I

Phenomenological aesthetics, as it has developed in Europe, is a curious patchwork of diverse points of view. Ingarden describes a work of literary art as a multilayered yet "polyphonic harmony" of sound and sense,[33] the latter itself composed of three strata: propositions, represented objects, and concretizing imagery. His descriptions contain many insights into the struc-

32. *Ibid.*, p. 16: "Die 'Warhheit' ist kein Merkmal des richtigen Satzes, der durch ein menschliches 'Subjekt' von einem 'Objekt' ausgesagt wird und dann irgendwo, man weiss nicht in welchem Bereich, 'gilt,' sondern die Wahrheit ist die Entbergung des Seienden, durch die eine Offenheit west. In ihr Offenes ist alles menschliche Verhalten und seine Haltung augsgesetzt. Deshalb ist der Mensch in der Weise der Eksistenz."

33. *Das literarische Kunstwerk* (Halle: Niemeyer, 1931).

tures of the various strata but give little or no information on the manner in which the harmony of the whole is experienced. Sartre's phenomenological study of the imagination describes a work of art as the "absent" object to which the purely physical construct of the artist refers. In this procedure the sensuous surface of the work is reduced in importance to the function of a stimulus. Merleau-Ponty on the other hand begins with the analysis of the sensuous structures of the work as a perceptual object and is in his turn hard put to explain how the surface "thickens" into an experience of the depth content.[34] Sensation, perception, conception, representation, and imagination—each is a phenomenon of human consciousness and hence amenable to the techniques of phenomenological analysis, yet the description of the phenomenon in which all these "consciousnesses" flow into a single experience is singularly lacking. Heidegger's aesthetic writings may be viewed as an attempt to supply this want.

He will describe the essential structures of a work of art in metaphysical terms without, however, prejudging what must be found in a particular work of art. To avoid overemphasizing the surface qualities at the expense of the depth and vice versa, he will examine the expressiveness of an objective painting, a poem, and a Grecian temple; for the essence of art, if such there is, must be found in works of art and not in the lives of artists.[35] This primacy of the work is well attested in the critical practice even of those "biographical" critics who realize that whatever hypothesis they have gained from the knowledge of the author's nonartistic life must be checked against the facts of the art work's unique context of reference. The work is the thing, and if it can capture the conscience of a king the reason is that it is a work or a play only because it does engage the consciousness we call aesthetic: "Only this one thing in the work which reveals something else, this one which unites with the other, is the thing-

34. See my *An Existentialist Aesthetic* (Madison: The University of Wisconsin Press, 1962).
35. *Holzwege*, pp. 7–8.

like quality of an artwork."[36] Thus, works of art are like the other things we meet in our everyday lives, but what constitutes their essence is the way in which they work as allegory or symbol, i.e., as they function to reveal a second dimension of meaning.

How then does the perception of a *thing* become the experience of a *work* of art? Not, as some aestheticians have maintained, by a special attitude on the part of the perceiver, for "the aesthetic attitude" is not what makes a work of a thing; it is the work which controls the attitude. Our question is badly put. It should read, "How does the experience of a *work* of art come to be that of a thing?"

In Heidegger's metaphysical terms a work is not a thing that is transmuted by the magic of consciousness into something other than a thing grasped in an act of perception. A work of art exhibits its own way of being a thing, and this can be understood only by a "destructive" analysis of "the thingness of things" (*die Dingheit, das Dinghafte der Dinge*). And if this is true aesthetics cannot, any more than logic, be divorced from a sound metaphysical analytic. Aesthetics so pursued is the pursuit of philosophy in art.

From the foregoing analysis of Heidegger's discussion of essences (Part I, II), it is clear that a thing is a thing owing to the manner in which it "things," i.e., to the way in which it detaches itself from the context of meaning relations constituting the "world" of a human transcendence. But this is an idea that has come late upon the scene and not before philosophy had made a series of detours, having considered a thing as a substance bearing properties, some of which were essential and some accidental; as the unity of a manifold of sense impressions; and finally, as formed matter.

The difficulty of each of these conceptions is the assumption that a thing is a composite, understandable through the manner in which elements achieve summation. Our experience of the world indicates that things are given as they are and can only

36. *Ibid.*, p. 10: "Allein dieses Eine am Werk, was ein Anderes offenbart, dieses Eine, was mit einem Anderen zusammenbringt, ist das Dinghafte im Kunstwerk."

later be analyzed or decomposed into their elements. The same is true of our experience of works of art: all our aesthetic categories must be derived from our primary experiences of works. Even the notion of a sensuous surface is the result of aesthetic analysis and not a means for constructing an aesthetic experience in the first place.

Yet it is obvious that an artist constructs his work of art with the sensuous elements of his medium. The difficulty with this commonplace is that it leads no place; it merely serves to point out the thinglike understructure of works of art, which may, in a moment of theoretical aberration, be reduced to light and sound waves of a given frequency. Artists do not, however, work with waves of any kind or of any frequency. They create with pigments or stones or sound-producing machines, perceiving what they have already done and imagining what must be done on the basis of what has been perceived of the work in progress; in artistic creation, a thing comes to be within the artist's world out of a world that is as yet only a possibility. This is the view of artistic creation that comes to light in Heidegger's metaphysical analysis of things, tools, and works.

We may begin this analysis by considering his destruction of traditional metaphysics. Let us take first the thing as property-bearing substance. Expert opinion on this subject necessarily differs, for it is impossible to decide whether things appear as substance and attribute because our language is what it is or whether the subject-predicate sentence structure of declarative statements is what it is because things appear as substance and attribute.[37] Moreover, experience once again indicates that no substance ever appears, as the trenchant analyses of Berkeley and Hume succeeded in pointing out. But then this proposition had already been admitted by Descartes (*Principles* LI–LII).

If what appears is only the properties of things, it no longer makes sense to speak of "properties." A thing, then, is the unity of a manifold of sense impressions; and it matters not whether this manifold be interpreted as a "sum," a "totality," or a

37. *Ibid.*, pp. 13-14.

"Gestalt";[38] the sensations of which we speak are abstractions from the appearance of a thing: "Things themselves are closer to us than all sensations. In the house we hear the door slam, and never acoustical sensations or sheer noises. In order to hear a pure noise, we have to hear 'away from things,' to take our ear away from them; that is, to hear abstractly."[39] Concrete perception, it is claimed, must yield the thing itself.

The third and last interpretation of the thingness of things is not the most recent. It is merely the most persistent, and it has persisted because of the seeming success it has achieved in explaning how matter takes on form in aesthetic as well as in non-aesthetic contexts. So conceived, a thing is formed matter.

Form is the rational, matter the irrational, element of the thing, since form gives a determinate essence to the formlessness of matter. Thus, the artist's creation may be explained in terms of a rational process of introducing order into chaos. Unfortunately, however, the notions of matter and form are not unambiguous, especially in an aesthetic context. For what is matter, the sensuous stuff or the content of an experience? Is form the frame around sensuous materials or an ordering of content? Jugs, axes, and shoes have matter and form in the one sense but not in the other. Each has the form of a tool, which is determined by the purpose served in using the tool: the form of the jug, by its function to hold and pour water; of the ax, to cut wood; and of shoes, to protect feet.

Following this line of argument, Heidegger repeats the conclusions of his earlier philosophy. The being of a thing on hand (*ein Vorhandenes*) is not a primary object of awareness; things are primarily at hand (*ein Zuhandenes*) and are known essentially in their use. Is the work of art a tool?

38. *Ibid.*, p. 15.
39. *Ibid.*: "Veil näher als alle Empfindungen sind uns die Dinge selbst. Wir hören im Haus die Tür schlagen und hören niemals akustische Empfindungen oder auch nur blosse Geräusche. Um ein reines Geräusch zu hören, müssen wir von den Dingen weghören, unser Ohr davon abziehen, d. h. abstrakt hören."

In one sense, yes; in another, no. It is not a tool in the sense that its material stuff will be used up in serving an ulterior purpose.[40] Jugs, axes, and shoes wear out in use, while works of art preserve their materials in the achievement of form in the sense that form makes the materials visible as functioning in the context of the work. Moreover, when all the purposes or ends of an activity are internal to a single context, it hardly makes sense to speak of "means" and "ends" except within that context. The experience of art is a consummatory phenomenon, an enjoyment. If the work is its own end (autotelism) or contains its own end (endotelism), the work itself, considered as an experience, is never used for an external purpose.

Yet the working of a work does serve a purpose in the lives of both artists and appreciators. In "Der Ursprung des Kunstwerkes" this purpose is explained as the revelation of truth, and in *Nietzsche I* the revelation of truth is considered as a means of intensifying our sense of life. If art is *an* experience in the series of experiences we call a "life," art does serve a definite purpose; but at the same time the context of reference would have been modified from that of the work itself to the working of the work in the developing lives of art's connoisseurs. The context would have changed from the tool (open-ended means-ends complex), which cannot be taken for a work, to the work (closed means-ends complex) taken as a tool.

One context at a time. What is a tool? "Der Ursprung des Kunstwerkes" gives the answer in what can only be called an explanatory tour de force: Heidegger finds his answer by analyzing a painting by Van Gogh, *Les Souliers,* representing a pair of peasant's work shoes (see Fig. 1). If he is right, the toolness of these tools is there to be seen; and when it is seen, he will have made his point that paintings work as the revelation of a truth.

What we see in the painting is a pair of shoes worn in service, without wearer, placed in an indefinite space. The entire painting is done in monochromatic browns—somber, heavy, and oppressive as only work in the field can be. In the field alone

40. *Ibid.,* p. 36.

Figure 1. Vincent van Gogh, Les Souliers.
Stedelijk Museum, Amsterdam.

are those shoes the tool they were designed to be. They stand out, and their dignity is precisely in having been worn into the state they are in. In standing out they hide part of the earth, and at the same time reveal the relationship between the shoes and their wearer to the earth, which yields its harvest only to those not allergic to hard work. The crushing weight of the human body against the hard surface of the earth has produced these shoes. And all this can be seen in the painting if we look closely and allow it to engage our imaginations. Serviceability, dependability, contact with the earth—such is the toolness of a tool.

In the context of the working of Van Gogh's work, we perceive how and what the represented tool is: "The truth of the being has been set in the work of art. And 'to set' here means to bring to a stand. A being, a pair of peasant's shoes, comes to stand in the work in the light of its being. The being of the being is brought to the permanency of its appearance."[41] This is the sense in which art "lets truth happen." An essence appears as uncovered, as standing out from the rest of the world. And this can happen only because the work of art creates a world of its own—here, a world of human instrumentality.

Can this description be generalized? The first impulse is to answer no, for the painting represents an object and can be judged as true in the same sense that declarative sentences are judged true. Consider in comparison the imagistic poem, Meyer's "Der römische Brunnen" (The Roman Fountain):

> Up jets the stream and falling flows
> To fill the marble plate so round,
> Which, disappearing, overflows
> Into a second shallow ground;
> Too full it wells, and so pours forth
> Into a third its streaming jets;
> Each takes and gives—there is no fourth—
> And flows and rests.[42]

41. *Ibid.*, p. 25: "Im Werk der Kunst hat sich die Wahrheit des Seienden ins Werk gesetzt. 'Setzen' sagt heir: zum Stehen bringen. Ein Seiendes, ein Paar Bauernschuhe, kommt im Werk in das Licht seines Seins zu stehen. Das Sein des Seienden kommt in das Ständige seines Scheinens." See also, *Einführung in die Metaphysik*, p. 27; and compare, Albert Hofstadter, "Truth of Being," *Journal of Philosophy*, LXII (1965), 167–83; and his *Truth and Art* (New York and London: Columbia University Press, 1965).

42. By C. F. Meyer, entitled *Der römische Brunnen*. Heidegger, *Holzwege*, p. 26:

> Aufsteigt der Strahl und fallend giesst
> Er voll der Marmorschale Rund,
> Die, sich verschleiernd, überfliesst
> In einer zweiten Schale Grund;
> Die zweite gibt, sie wird zu reich,
> Der dritten wallend ihre Flut,
> Und jede nimmt und gibt zugleich
> Und strömt und ruht.

Does the poem picture an actual fountain or the essence of a Roman cascade? To answer yes is to forget the relation of the picture to the manner in which the words themselves "flow" and yet "remain at rest." To answer yes is to forget the experience of the poem in favor of the memory of an object seen.

The point may become clearer when we consider the manner in which an architectural masterpiece is said to let truth appear (see Fig. 2). Stone, mass, and empty space can hardly be taken as a picture of reality. Rightly ordered, however, they can become a work of art.

The temple performs a double function: it opens up a world at the same time it produces "an earth." The world is that of the godly. Experience the tranquillity of the Greek, the rising darkness of the Romanesque, the soaring pinnacle and flying buttresses of the Gothic, the somber austerity of the early Protestant,

Figure 2. The Temple of Hera at Paestum.

and you are in the presence of so many different gods, so many different forms of worship. Words such as "the altar," "the sanctuary," "the holy of holies," or simply "God's house" indicate the seriousness of this world, which, if it can be desecrated, is so only because it has previously been consecrated by a people's faith and an artist's work. Without the religious faith and artistic activities of the builders this world is nothing but a heap of stone, a museum, or a ruin and dead relic of a past way of life: "The god is present in the temple by means of the temple."[43] And He can flee from it, as He does when the religious way of life is lost.

Through the temple God comes down to earth, but not to the planet on which we live. The earth, our planet, is itself only a symbol for what takes place, a fixed point of reference for the "worlding" of the godly world. The stones and columns shimmer in the light as they rise; the horizon is cut into a significant form; day and night are measurable by lengthening shadows; and darkness follows dusk as death follows life. Around the holy ground, the human and nonhuman life finds its place—a nature, a living-ground, and a final resting place: "The earth is that to which the rise of everything rising falls back as such; its essence is to endure within the rising openness as the enclosing ground."[44] The openness of the religious world comes to closure, at least on one end, at the earth, where man builds, lives, and thinks.[45]

In such passages as these Heidegger's language exhibits a lyricism and degree of metaphorical statement rarely found in the writings of professional philosophers. He is in fact approaching the limits of meaningful expression. But, again, he is proceeding according to plan. He has excluded the physical notion of a thing as irrelevant to his subject, the working of a work of

43. *Ibid.*, p. 31: "Durch den Tempel west der Gott im Tempel an." Compare *Erläuterung zu Hölderlins Dichtung* (Frankfurt a. M.: Klostermann, 1951), p. 113.

44. *Ibid.*: "Die Erde ist das, wohin das Aufgehen alles Aufgehende und zwar als ein solches zurückbirgt. Im Aufgehenden west die Erde als das Bergende."

45. Compare *Vorträge und Aufsätze,* pp. 145–62.

art. Contemporary aestheticians know and speak of this experience as "expressiveness," which is precisely what cannot be expressed in symbols other than those of the medium being discussed. Heidegger can, therefore, only suggest and hope that his metaphors can turn the trick.

And they may, if we keep two further considerations in mind: he moves to the expressiveness of a temple by way of the temple's customary use, to house religious activity and to relate to other ordinary human activities, like living and dying. So far he is consistent in his moves from thing to tool to work. What he must yet do to complete his analysis is to cash in the metaphors he uses to explain the total expressiveness of religious architecture and then apply the concepts he has gained to the experience of a representational piece. Since the temple is nonobjective, he can rely on no representational imagery. "World" and "earth" must be given their metaphysical interpretation; and he proceeds to do just this, undaunted by our hesitations to follow: "The setting up of a world and the placement of the earth within are two essential characteristics in the being of the work."[46]

The explanation of these terms follows, first in the metaphysical and then in an aesthetic context. It is in this way we shall have tested the relevance of his thought for working aesthetic inquiry.

II

If a world and an earth are made to appear in a successful work of art, it should be possible to give a reasonable description of each of these, even if their relationship would at first blush seem to fall within the ineffable, within the area of our direct, consummatory experience. Aesthetics has traditionally attempted to treat of such experiences, and Heidegger's *Sein und Zeit* elaborated a technique for their analysis. He called it "Daseinsanalytik." "Der Ursprung des Kunstwerkes" merely repeats the conclusions of the earlier treatise, placing them in a specific aesthetic context.

46. *Holzwege*, p. 36: "Das Aufstellen einer Welt und das Herestellen der Erde sind zwei Wesenszüge im Werksein des Werkes."

The analysis of human existence (*Dasein*) begins with the relationship of transcendence to a world, which already obtains when the question of the being of this entity is posed. The question arises, then, on the basis of an original, implicit, yet unclear understanding of what it means to be in a world. The purpose of ontological analysis is to make the understanding consequent, explicit, and clear.

Heidegger describes our everyday experiences of objects in a passage that might have been written by Merleau-Ponty: "One existent heaves up before another, the one veils the other as the first overshadows the second; a little closes off much, and the isolated element disavows the whole. The concealment here is not this simple denial; the existent truly appears, but reveals itself as other than what it is."[47] What appears hides what does not and draws attention away from the entire context in which it does appear. Thus uncovering implies a double covering over. A figure appears on a ground but prevents the ground from appearing as a figure. Figure and ground each deny (*Versagen*) the other, yet neither can exist without the other. They exist in tension of strife (*Streit*), and as they come together in tension before our awareness ("perception" is too limited a notion to cover what is intended), the context of meaning relations which is a subject's world must itself recede into a background.

Nothing mysterious is being claimed here; this has always been true in aesthetic perception, in which the balance of our lives is "bracketed" out of relevance as we attend to the qualities of a specific work. How do we move from this common-sense notion of everyday experience to an understanding of the "ontological" structures implicit therein?

The first step in answer is to notice that figure and ground form a *Gestalt* in the flow of our conscious lives. A new entity appears where before consciousness there was none; within the density of the world there appears a light, an opening; and "This opening

47. *Holzwege,* p. 42: "Seiendes schiebt sich vor Seiendes, das Eine verschleiert das Andere, Jenes verdunkelt Dieses, Weniges verbaut Vieles, Vereinzeltes verleugnet Alles. Hier ist das Verbergen nicht jenes einfache Versagen, sondern das Seiende erscheint wohl, aber es gibt sich anders, als es ist."

occurs within the [phenomenally] existent thing."[48] Something is there, and the rest of our world recedes into unawareness. It would be too easy, however, to associate the light with the open-ness of the world and the darkness of unconsciousness with the closedness of the earth. For the light, too, can be covered over, as it is when appearances are deceiving.[49] Since the essence of the truth is to cover over what it does not uncover, truth is like-wise untruth (*Verborgenheit*). Truth and untruth happen simul-taneously; because something is true, something else must be false.

The earth is, however, what closes in upon itself (*das Sich-verschliessende*), what comes to closure within the context of the opening world: "The earth rises up only through the world; and a world is grounded only on the earth in so far as truth, as the primordial tension between light and concealment, comes about."[50] And for this reason it is said that truth is at work (*am Werk*) in the work (of art).[51] Consider our three examples, the painting of Van Gogh, the poem of Meyer, and the Grecian temple: they "reveal—strictly speaking they state nothing at all—not only what the essence of this isolated existent is, but they also permit the disclosure, the unconcealed truth, of the whole of Being."[52] So interpreted, the appearance of truth in the work of art is beauty; and beauty is one of the essential ways in which truth comes to be.

Yet we know that a work of art comes to be in the activity of the artist. What is the relationship between the creativity of the artist and the happening of truth? The Greek word "techne" is both a clue and a snare for further inquiry. It is a snare if we interpret the failure of the Greeks to distinguish between

48. *Ibid.*, p. 43: "Dieses Offene geschieht inmitten des Seienden."
49. *Ibid.*, p. 42.
50. *Ibid.*, p. 44: "Erde durchragt nur die Welt, Welt gründet sich nur auf die Erde, sofern die Wahrheit als der Urstreit von Lichtung und Verbergung geschieht."
51. *Ibid.*, pp. 44–54.
52. *Ibid.*, p. 44: "[Works of art] . . . bekunden nicht nur, sie bekunden streng genommen überhaupt nicht], was dieses vereinzelte Seiende als dieses sei, sondern sie lassen Unverborgenheit als solche im Bezug auf Seiende im Ganzen geschehen."

artisanry and artistry as a failure in thought or even as a dis-
inclination to distinguish between making an object according to
a predesigned plan and the discovery of a plan in the making of
an object.

It will be remembered that Kant referred to this distinction as
that between "industry" and "art," and contemporaneously we
distinguish between technique—whether it is found in science,
art, or everyday life—and creative vision. To call an artist a tech-
nician is to slander him and his works; only in the realm of
current pseudo-science and in some contemporary philosophies is
scientific knowledge confused with technology. But to say of a
successful business man—or even of a university administrator—
that he possesses vision is to praise his estimation of a future
state of affairs.

The clue provided by a translation of the Greek word for both
"art" and "technics" is precisely its reference to knoweldge as
"seeing" in its widest sense, which, it may be repeated, Heidegger
interprets as "the grasping of something present *qua* present,"[53]
even if what is present is so, in a paradoxical word of Sartre, only
in "absence"; for to imagine is to see something that is not
there to be perceived. Both the artisan and the artist must perceive *and* imagine what is to be done on the basis of what is
perceived as both work their materials. Such is the essence of
creativity, and one would be hard put to explain a premium to
be placed upon the one or the other activity (perception or
imagination) in the description of either art or technics.

Moreover, art and technics are not the only areas of human
experience in which truth may be seen happening. Heidegger
names others: the act of founding a state, living in the presence
of being itself, an act of sacrifice, and philosophical questioning.[54]
If this last is a correct example, one can witness truth happening
even when questioning the essence of art in the exercise of which
the artist has, in the first instance, set truth in his work.

53. *Ibid.*, p. 47: compare "Die Frage nach der Technik," *Vorträge und
Aufsätze,* pp. 13–44.
54. *Holzwege,* p. 50.

This does not mean of course that an artist must imagine what he will have done when his work is finished even before making a first stroke: "The arrangement of truth in a work is the bringing forth of such a being as that which before did not yet exist and which afterwards will nevermore come to be."[55] The artist creates his work by forming a *Gestalt* of the tension between world and earth, between that complex of sedimented meaning structures he has inherited from his culture and the new object he sets therein. His creative problem is to know when to stop manipulating materials, and this he knows in the same way that an appreciator knows, not by his signature but by an experience of the tension between expressing surface (sensuous *Gestalt*) and expressed depth (pregnancy, significance of the *Gestalt*).

As the French philosopher and critic Alain put the matter, the artist is the first one surprised by his work. Heidegger puts it in a slightly different manner when he says, "But what is more usual than this, that a being exists? In the work of art, however, that it should come to be is precisely the unusual."[56] To witness the unusual in the usual is to see, under one's hands as it were, truth having happened.

For the artist, this means that he must allow the work to be, once he has perceived the *factum est*.[57] No more changes or additions are allowable; the work is there to be perceived and preserved. Thus if the manipulation of materials into the significance of a *Gestalt* is the first phase, preservation (*Bewahren*) is the second phase of the artist's activity; and here the artist is joined by his fellow man: "The preservation of the work does not isolate men within the sphere of their own lived experiences, but moves them all into a togetherness with the truth as it comes to be in the work, and thus establishes a foundation of an existence with and for others as the historical endurance of

55. *Ibid.*: "Die Einrichtung der Wahrheit ins Werk ist das Hervorbringen eines solchen Seienden, das vordem noch nicht war und nachmals nie mehr werden wird."
56. *Ibid.*, p. 53: "Was aber ist gewöhnlicher als dieses, dass Seiendes ist? Im Werk dagegen ist dieses, dass es als solches *ist*, gerade das Ungewöhnliche."
57. *Ibid.*

human existence out of the relationship to truth."[58] The architects and masons had collaborated in making a temple, and they are joined by their fellow man in making the god descend.

The making of a work of art is thus the establishment of a tradition: a gift, a foundation, and a profound modification of the world as it had existed before—in a word, a new beginning. The origin of a work of art is to be found in the essence of art as "the creative preservation of truth in the work."[59]

III

Heidegger's study of the origin of art works presents a clear alternative to the phenomenological treatment of aesthetic objects elsewhere on the Continent, particularly in France. If Sartre could find little or no place for perception, and Merleau-Ponty little or none for the imagination, in their descriptions of an aesthetic object, the reason was that each began his investigation by considering aesthetic experience from the wrong starting point, i.e., from an encounter between a subject, and an object considered as a thing. The thing became for Sartre the occasion for the contemplation of an imaginary object and for Merleau-Ponty, the expressive organization of the sensible into a meaningful *Gestalt* grasped in the first instance by the readaptive modification of the subject's inner bodily schema. In terms of contemporary aesthetics, Sartre's theory is "depth"-centered while Merleau-Ponty's is centered on the "surface" of aesthetic expressions.

Yet at the time of his death, Merleau-Ponty was following a clue that might have led him beyond his "thin" doctrine of expressiveness. His "Eye and Mind"[60] is replete with references to "Being" which have a peculiarly Heideggerian ring. Having

58. *Ibid.*, p. 56: "Die Bewahrung des Werkes vereinzelt die Menschen nicht auf ihre Erlebnisse, sondern rückt sie ein in die Zugehörigkeit zu der im Werk geschehenden Wahrheit und gründet so das Für- und Miteinandersein als das geschichtliche Ausstehen des Daseins aus dem Bezug zur Unverborgenheit."

59. *Ibid.*, p. 59: ". . . die schaffende Bewahrung der Wahrheit im Werk."

60. See *The Primacy of Perception*, Edie, ed., pp. 159–90.

imprisoned himself earlier within his doctrine of the "primacy of perception,"[61] however, he was unable to provide a meaningful description of the ontological structures implicit in an act of artistic creation and appreciation. In every case his explanations return to the ground of the corporeal *cogito*: a result determined, if Heidegger is right, by the faulty point of departure. Any analysis of paintings which begins with the isolation of sensuous elements will have the same result: "In the experience produced by means of the sense organs of sight, hearing or touch; in the sensations of colored, of sounding, or rough and hard things, we are, literally so meant, attacked in the body."[62] It may come as somewhat of a surprise to reflect that these words are Heidegger's not Merleau-Ponty's. If we began our analysis of works of art as things, Heidegger claims, we shall be incapable of showing the particular manner in which works of art considered as works are things. And this is to say Merleau-Ponty of necessity failed to discover the "essence" of an artwork as it functions in the lives of artists and their audiences.

Heidegger accomplishes his explanation by seeking the essence of works of art as they function. He avoids Merleau-Ponty's problem of moving from the ontics of things to the ontological description of the being of things by reversing the order of procedure. The creation and the appreciation of works of art are "ontological" phenomena in that each of these activities affects a human subject's manner of being in the world. The world itself is the open context of sedimented meaning structures created in the first place by the purposeful activities of human transcendences. The ontological problem is to show how a single, newly created, meaningful structure comes to existence within this "world" because the artist and his society behave as they do.

That creative essences do come to being is hardly controvertible. Every successful work of art, as every other truly crea-

61. See the essay by this title, pp. 12–42.
62. *Holzwege*, p. 15: "In dem, was der Gesicht-, Gehör- und Tastsinn beibringen, in den Empfindungen des Farbigen, Tönenden, Rauhen, Harten rücken uns die Dinge, ganz wörtlich genommen, auf den Leib."

tive act, is as brute in its factuality as the givenness of any other conscious (or corporeal) event. This is what Emerson meant when he said every institution is but the shadow of a single (creative) individual. Institutions and works of art are created, but they are not amenable to the same sort of description used scientifically or philosophically to explain the existence of the things of nature. Works of art, in sum, are "daseinsmässig," i.e., existential phenomena.

Now, according to Heidegger, *Dasein* or human existence is such that it lives, moves, and has its being in the presence of Being, i.e., in the openness of the "worlding" world. The explanatory trick, therefore, is to show how "the earth" comes to the fore in this swirling meaning complex which is the world of the artistic personality.

The earth, it will be recalled, is that self-contained, newly fixed meaning structure which comes to be in the closure of a sensuous *Gestalt*. Thus the "sensuous surface" of a work of art is a description gained from an aesthetic-ontological analysis of aesthetic phenomena and not an element by means of which art works are constructed by a mysterious kind of conscious summation. The thingness of a work of art is the last, and not the first, content of our aesthetic awareness: "When we consider the work of art as an object, however, what appears as a thing in the current acceptation of the term is the earth-dimension of the work as it is experienced before analysis."[63] And this is only to say that our aesthetic categories must be derived from our experiences of authentic works of art; from those, in other words, in which the artist has succeeded in setting a truth and from which the truth shines, as much to the artist's surprise as to ours, as a beautiful "thing." Our aesthetic admiration is only an outward sign that we have witnessed this truth.

We must remember, however, not to confuse truth with the correspondence of statement to fact. Such a formulation of "truth" has vitiated most of the discussions of the appearance of

---

63. *Ibid.*, p. 57: "Was jedoch an dem als Gegenstand genommenen Werk so aussieht wie das Dinghafte im Sinne der geläufigen Dingbegriffe, das ist, vom Werk her erfahren, das Erdhafte des Werkes."

truth in art; for if this idea of the truth continues to hold sway, truth could be found only in representational art. It is for this reason that Merleau-Ponty could say in truth that the controversy over the relative merits of figurative and nonfigurative painting, for example, misplaces the emphasis on one or the other of our conscious activities: on the seeing of the eye or on the understanding of the mind.

Merleau-Ponty remains one of the greatest of the phenomenological aestheticians; not, as Professor Edie has suggested,[64] because he has accepted the perceived world as the primary reality—that is his weakness—but because he came as close as anybody to giving a description of "the working of a work." Heidegger has at least placed the inquiry in the context where fruitful investigation may take place. He has succeeded in showing what the problem is. For this reason, if for no other, he is worthy of being read.

But there are other reasons as well. If he is right, the ontological analysis of the working of works of art will yield still further results—call them "pragmatic" if you will. He has shown, for example, why it is fruitful to use paintings of healthy or of psychologically unbalanced persons to achieve an insight into the personality structures of the subjects involved. Margaret Naumberg has done this with great success.[65] And she has done nothing but work out the implications of the existence of a work of art as a tension between the world and the earth, between the open and the fixed, which tension is the work of art as experienced.

And there is more: Heidegger's view of creativity gives the same sort of foundation for the interpretation of art as an institution in the general society. For if it is true that the artist introduces a new meaning into his world, he is profoundly capable of modifying the world of others as this new meaning becomes a sedimented structure of a common world, the one referred to by every occurrence of the linguistic expressions

64. *Op. cit.*, p. xviii.
65. See her *Psychoneurotic Art: Its Function in Psychotherapy* (New York: Grune and Stratton, 1963).

going to make up "the common language." And this is to say only that art is a historical process uniting many human transcendences into a single "people."

Finally, if this view is correct the function of art criticism becomes the task of extending the scope of the society so created. Humanity is still in the making, and to be human in the fullest sense of this term we need only join in its further creation.

Poets and Thinkers
Their Kindred Roles in the Philosophy of Martin Heidegger

J. GLENN GRAY*

Some day the major significance of the existentialist movement may be seen to lie in the recovery of poetry (in the generic
sense of imaginative literature and art) as a subject matter for
philosophy. For many generations philosophers have looked to
natural science for a model of philosophic method as well as
for standards by which to judge the worth of philosophic effort. Anglo-Saxon philosophers have also used the findings of
the sciences, social and natural, increasingly as the proper material for reflection—indeed as the very core of their discipline.
In conceiving philosophy to be a criticism of culture, they have
been impelled to pay more and more attention to science as the
enterprise that has revolutionized the modern world.

Literature has inevitably suffered by philosophers' devotion
to the sciences. In America at least, and hardly less in Britain,
it has become a mark of derogation to refer to a philosopher
as essentially a poet. "I am an ignorant man, almost a poet,"
Santayana once remarked, and the remark is frequently understood in a sense which that ironic spirit did not intend. For
the impression is inescapable that many, if not most, English-
speaking philosophers not only consider poets ignorant of
knowledge worth having, i.e., scientific knowledge, but also find

* Department of Philosophy, The Colorado College, Colorado Springs, Colorado.

their utterances subjective and arbitrary. Poets do not tell us anything about the way things are in the world: they only reveal private moods. At most they celebrate values, whereas scientists and philosophers are charged with preserving and extending knowledge of nature and man.

This climate of opinion may be changing. With dismay many scientifically oriented philosophers have witnessed the rise to prominence of existentialism on the European continent since World War II. Even the British have turned away from preoccupation with science to the study of language, though not to the language of poetry. In an era when the effects of the scientific revolution are at their peak and in dire need of interpretation and mediation to the lay mind, is it not irresponsible of so many European philosophers to be looking to literature and language for the primary source of their eccentric analyses and doctrines? So it seems to many American academicians of philosophy. Yet history reveals, if we care to reflect, parallel instances of dramatic shifts of allegiance at unexpected times and places in the career of Western philosophy.

In the German tradition such a shift of allegiance hardly amounts to a revolution. Poets and philosophers have always been closely associated in Germany. It was Kant who insisted in his third *Critique* that for an adequate account of the world philosophers should investigate the ideas and visions of art and artists. As John Herman Randall has emphasized recently, it was Kant's *Critique of Judgment* that became a major source of inspiration for idealism and romanticism, which dominated the nineteenth century in Germany.[1] This close alliance of poetry and thought reached a peak but did not end in Schelling's conception of "productive imagination" as the way to philosophic wisdom. Later Germans such as Schopenhauer, Nietzsche, and most of the *Lebensphilosophen* preserved this alliance down to the present. "Poets and thinkers" is anything but a chance conjunction of terms in German intellectual

1. John H. Randall, Jr., *The Career of Philosophy* (New York: 1965), II, Book V, 175, 176 *et passim*.

history. When studying Nietzsche, Herder, Lessing, or many another German writer, it is difficult to discover where philosophy ends and poetry begins.

From this perspective Martin Heidegger's increasing preoccupation with the role of poetry in his philosophy is easily understandable. Though he is not a typical existentialist (if indeed he is one at all), his work has already been influential for the whole movement and likewise has had profound impact on the interpretation of literature and the other arts in Europe. In this respect at least Heidegger is far from revolutionary. On the contrary, he is a continuator of that long line of artist-philosophers which began in ancient Greece and which has long been so congenial to the German philosophic temperament. If we ever succeed in assimilating Heidegger's peculiar language, he may even become in the eyes of posterity a representative philosopher of the German tradition, if not of our whole era.

In what follows I want to sketch Heidegger's views, as they have developed over the years, on the interconnections of poetry and philosophy and the close affinities of poets and philosophers for one another. I shall try to clarify why he considers the utterances of poets like Hölderlin, Trakl, and Sophocles of such importance for philosophy. If I am successful, the attempt should throw some light on the general shift of allegiance from science to art, particularly the art of literature, which I believe to be characteristic of existentialist thought.

It is best to begin with Heidegger's conception of the essential task of philosophy, though "mission" perhaps would be the more appropriate word. This task he has stated very explicitly in a lecture series at Freiburg in the middle thirties, published in 1953 under the title *Einführung in die Metaphysik*.[2]

---

2. *An Introduction to Metaphysics,* trans. Ralph Manheim (New Haven: 1959; New York: 1961). In the quotations used I have generally followed Manheim's translation, taken from the Doubleday Anchor edition, except for his rendering of *das Seiende* and *das Sein.*

In the opening lecture Heidegger defines his conception of philosophy by first rejecting two current misconceptions of its function. The first of these is the demand that philosophy provide a foundation upon which a nation can build its historical life and culture. This asks too much of a philosophy, Heidegger insists, for "philosophy can never *directly* supply the energies and create the opportunities and methods that bring about a historical change."[3] The second misconception somewhat more modestly conceives philosophy as a cultural force because it provides an over-all view of the premises, basic concepts, and principles of the sciences. "Philosophy thus is expected to promote and even accelerate—to make easier as it were—the practical and technical business of culture."[4] According to Heidegger this second misinterpretation distorts the real function of philosophy.

In opposition to these views Heidegger believes that "philosophy is one of the few autonomous creative possibilities and at times necessities of man's historical existence."[5] It is not dependent on other disciplines nor is its mission to provide a systematic cultural perspective. No, philosophy must break new paths, open new perspectives, bring into radical question the very foundation of the values and norms by which a people live. By thinking more deeply and simply, philosophy must challenge conventional ways of viewing the world and thereby provide a more authentic knowledge of things than any social or natural science can achieve. The advance of any civilization tends to cover up and obscure man's fundamental relations to his environment and to his fellows. Hence philosophy's mission is to break new paths into strange and unfamiliar terrain—terrain that has become unfamiliar because a people forgets continually the points of reference of its historical existence and needs to be recalled to them.

In this connection Heidegger quotes Nietzsche, to whom he is clearly indebted for this conception of philosophy, with approval. "A philosopher is a man who never ceases to experience, see, hear, suspect, hope, and dream extraordinary things . . . ."

3. Manheim, p. 8.   4. Manheim, p. 9.   5. Manheim, p. 8.

"Philosophy . . . is a voluntary living amid ice and mountain heights."[6] The concern with philosophy, Heidegger continues, is of necessity restricted to the few, because only those of great spirit have eyes for the extraordinary and sufficient courage to bring the foundations into question. Though in later decades he has come to reject, I believe, Nietzsche's emphasis on the extraordinary nature of philosophy's subject matter in favor of meditating on the simple and commonplace objects of experience, he has certainly retained this basic conception of the essence of philosophic thinking as creative and pathbreaking.

It was in these lectures on metaphysics—rather than in his earlier *Sein und Zeit*—that Heidegger began to concern himself with the pre-Socratics, Parmenides and Heracleitus in particular, and to combine them with a long discussion of Sophocles' famous chorus from the *Antigone*. Here poets and thinkers were pathbreakers par excellence; they taught us what it means really to think, not simply in terms of ethics, metaphysics, or any of the later divisions of philosophy which first came into existence in fifth century Athens. Heidegger is convinced that crucial and originative thinking tends to cease when thinkers turn into philosophers, that is, into those who are professionally taught to think. Scholarship in philosophy is a necessary and useful occupation, he tells us in *Was Heisst Denken?*, but there is no guarantee that the philosophically learned know what thinking is. The pre-Socratics, on the other hand, were not learned men, but they knew how to think, Heidegger believes, as do few of us today. Indeed, the sentence that becomes a recurring refrain in *Was Heisst Denken?* is: "The most thought-provoking thing in our thought-provoking age is that we are still not thinking."[7]

Why does he believe that these earliest philosophers of the West, who lived before the very name "philosophy" was coined, are the models of what thinking ought to be? To provide a full answer to this question would exceed by far the limits of this essay. But to get at the essential relations of poetry and think-

6. Manheim, pp. 10, 11.
7. *Was Heisst Denken?* (Tübingen: 1954), p. 3 *et passim*.

ing, as he conceives them, it is necessary to suggest the outlines of an answer.

These first thinkers were concerned with *physis*, that fundamental reality which the Romans translated as *Natura*—thus perverting, so Heidegger thinks, the basic subject matter of philosophy, a perversion that endured throughout the Middle Ages and into modern times. Men like Anaximander, Parmenides, and Heracleitus conceived *physis* as "self-blossoming emergence . . . that which manifests itself in such unfolding and perseveres and endures in it . . . *Physis*, the realm of that which arises, is not synonymous with these phenomena, which today we regard as part of 'nature' . . . *Physis* is Being itself, by virtue of which existing things become and remain observable."[8]

Unencumbered with learning and pseudosophistication, the pre-Socratics were clear-sighted enough to perceive the whole of that which is and the parts within that whole in their essential relations to it. They did not confuse being with single existents, or believe that being is nothing more and nothing other than the sum total of single existents, the later view of metaphysicians whom Heidegger opposes. Moreover, their basic problem was to think this vision of totality adequately, to discover the integral relation of *physis* and *logos*, indeed to uncover the belonging-together of being and language. "It is in words and language," Heidegger asserts, "that things first come into being and are. For this reason the misuse of language in idle talk, in slogans and phrases, destroys our authentic relation to things."[9] Their thinking was prior to the scholarly separation of subject and object, hence prior to any separation of poetic and scientific thought. The pre-Socratics thought about the things of nature and man from the standpoint of the mighty spectacle itself, not the other way around. As he puts it in the *Introduction to Metaphysics*:

> The Greeks did not learn what *physis* is through natural phenomena, but the other way around: it was through a fundamental poetic and intellectual experience of Being that they

8. Manheim, pp. 11, 12.   9. Manheim, p. 11.

discovered what they had to call *physis*. It was this discovery that enabled them to gain a glimpse into nature in the restricted sense. Hence *physis* originally encompassed heaven as well as earth, the stone as well as the plant, the animal as well as man, and it encompassed human history as a work of men and the gods; and ultimately and first of all, it meant the gods themselves as subordinated to destiny. *Physis* means the power that emerges and the enduring realm under its sway. This power of emerging and enduring includes "becoming" as well as "being" in the restricted sense of inert duration. *Physis* is the process of a-rising, of emerging from the hidden, whereby the hidden is first made to stand.[10]

The above paragraph puts more clearly than any other I have been able to find the significance of the pre-Socratics for Heidegger. It also hints at the notion of what genuine thinking is, which he develops in later works. He does not want us to return to them for the sake of their discoveries, but to recover their stance as thinkers. This stance was one of simplicity, astonishment, and openness to the world as world. Only by returning to this stance will we be in a position to make a leap into the kind of thinking that will reveal our world to us as theirs was revealed to them. A thinker's task is to reveal being, according to him, and relate it to, and distinguish it from, single existents and their sum.

This task can be accomplished only by means of a poetic and intellectual experience, similar to that given to the pre-Socratics. In such still untranslated later works as *Was Heisst Denken? Holzwege,* and *Vorträge und Aufsätze* Heidegger has come to grasp this kind of experience in terms of man's learning to dwell rightly on earth. Dwelling and a capacity for dwelling rightly have come to have for him the ontological sense and weight that being in-the-world held for him in the earlier *Sein und Zeit* period.[11] If the fundamental characteristic of dwelling is care-taking, as he emphasizes in a key essay of the

---

10. Manheim, p. 12.
11. Compare Vincent Vycinas, *Earth and Gods, An Introduction to the Philosophy of Martin Heidegger* (The Hague: 1961). I am indebted to Vycinas for this point and at several other places in this essay. His scholarly study of the later Heidegger deserves to be known better than it is at present.

last-named volume, the activities that constitute care-taking are thinking and building. Let me first characterize briefly what he conceives to be the essence of thinking before I turn to his discussion of poets and poetry.

Thinking is called or bidden into existence by what there is to think about, and this, in the broadest sense, is being itself. Being, however, is not something that lies behind appearances, but *is* their face or countenance. The truth of things shines in their appearance; it is the elusive substance of appearance. We must look for the truth of being in the intricate structures and manifold phenomena of this motley world, of which man is so inextricably a part. In the phenomena of our cultural past the thinker must discover the unthought elements in every previous system if he is not to miss the essential and authentic. In the phenomena of nature he must seek to penetrate the disguises of appearance and come upon the necessary relations and abiding powers. Truth is an uncovering or revelation of what is, but there is always still another veil or cover concealing the essential. As Heidegger expresses it, being is always advancing toward man (who is, when authentic, open to its message), but it is retreating, too. Its uncovering is at one and the same time a covering up and obscuring of its essence. Words conceal as well as reveal it, whether the phenomenon in question be a philosophic system of the past, a technological civilization of today, or nature herself as yet untouched by human building or poetizing.

Hence the thinker must be at once receptive and assertive, fully focused on what is there to be perceived. He must know how to listen and to observe, for thinking in the first instance is not so much an activity that we initiate as it is something that is initiated by *physis* or being itself. He must learn how to be astonished by what he perceives, as the early Greeks were astonished. This implies an attitude of openness far more fundamental than the usual meaning of the word. It is not "a listening with the inner ear" or other such metaphorical ways of expression. Rather it is a belonging of the whole being to what is to be thought about and at the same time a collecting, or recollecting, in language of the abiding powers that inform our mortal natures. Man is in essence a pointer, as he reminds us in *Was Heisst Denken?*, a signpost which reveals this ever advancing and retreating phenomenon of the world whole.

Authentic thinking is far more simple than we complicated modern men imagine. We have not learned to think as yet because we do not know how to face the world as world, to understand the essence of a simple thing like a jug or a bridge, which assembles, focuses, this world for us. The difficulty, he seems to say, lies in us, in our inability to listen to what words in their primordial nature tell us about these objects. That is, we do not focus ourselves and our words rightly. For we possess in the immense power of language and in our primary inclination toward truth the necessary equipment by which to approach being. We do not know how to think or to build because of our lack of attunement and rootedness. To dwell close to things and approach them in their own nature involves a determination to let them be what they are—namely, the assemblage of the durable powers of the earth.

Heidegger is convinced that poets can come to the aid of thinkers now, when the latter are so out of touch with the sources of being. The importance of poetry has steadily grown in his estimation to the point where it appears to overshadow systematic philosophic analysis. In *Sein und Zeit* we read comparatively little of poets and art works. But with his Hölderlin essays of the thirties, references to poets and poetic utterances have increased so markedly that one wonders whether Heidegger has not discovered in poetry the way to overcome that "inadequacy" in the language of traditional philosophy which prevented him, as he claimed, from completing the second half of *Sein und Zeit*. According to reliable report, he has now written this second part, and it will be interesting to see when this work appears how much he has utilized poetic language to overcome the lack.

It should be emphasized, however, that turning to poetry does not signify that Heidegger is concerned with aesthetics per se. His interest in poets is for their ontological significance, the truths they can teach us about man's way of dwelling on earth.

Strictly speaking, he does not treat imaginative literature and other works of art *qua* literature and art, but as aspects of philosophy or meditative thought. In the last essay of the collection of lectures *Unterwegs zur Sprache* (1959), he puts this most succinctly: "All reflective thought is poetic: all poetry, however, is thought."[12] This progressive unity of function of poets and thinkers is an important development of his philosophy. At one time, following Hölderlin, he believed that "poets and thinkers dwell near to one another, on peaks farthest apart." The function of poets was to name the holy—that is, the essential powers of nature—and the function of thinkers was to think being. It would be fair to say that recently these peaks on which poets and thinkers dwell have come very close to each other.

Nevertheless, this sameness of function in poets and thinkers, Heidegger warns, must never be taken in the sense of identity, of an empty and mathematical oneness. The concept "identical" or "undifferentiated" is always quite different from the concept of "same." Things can be the same in the sense that they are inseparable from each other yet far from identical; there is a belonging-together of different qualities in an organic and primary unity. One can speak of the same, he writes, only when one thinks of the differences. So it is with poetry and thought. Poets and thinkers think the same but not the identical. Both are intent on discerning the powers of the earth and the sky, of mortals and gods, of *physis* and *logos*. Their differences lie in the way they conceive these powers and in the formulation of their thoughts.[13]

What specific role does poetry have for Heidegger in the task or mission of philosophy? Perhaps his most systematic statement of this role is to be found in the first long essay of *Holzwege,* entitled "Der Ursprung des Kunstwerkes."[14] In this

12. *Unterwegs zur Sprache* (Pfullingen: 1959), p. 267.
13. *Vorträge und Aufsätze* (Pfullingen: 1954), p. 193.
14. Translated by Albert Hofstadter as "The Origin of the Artwork" in *Philosophies of Art and Beauty,* ed. Albert Hofstadter and Richard Kuhns (New York: 1964).

essay he concentrates on the function of the work of art in assembling the world for us. Since my purpose here is more general and since the preceding essay by Professor Kaelin treats this work at length, I shall say no more about it except to note that Heidegger considers imaginative literature, that is, art using the medium of language, to be the primary form of the work of art.

The lines of Hölderlin that Heidegger most frequently quotes in his attempts to express man's relation to being are these:

> Voll Verdienst, doch dichterisch, wohnet
> Der Mensch auf dieser Erde.

These have been variously translated by Michael Hamburger[15] as

> Full of profit but poetically man
> Lives on this earth.

and by Douglas Scott[16] as

> Full of merit, and yet poetically, dwells
> Man on this earth.

As is his wont, Heidegger gives ontological weight to each of the words in these lines. He has even devoted an entire essay in *Vorträge und Aufsätze* to the portion of them that reads "poetically, dwells/Man on this earth." Perhaps the best way to reach the substance of his conception of the role of poetry in philosophy is to summarize his analysis of this line.

Poets teach us how to dwell on the earth because their language is concrete and exact. They are our teachers, as Homer was to the early Greeks, in the sense of keeping us near the earth and attentive to the real powers that dominate our lives. Far from being the irresponsible and arbitrary creatures that the Philistine imagines, they are according to Heidegger the model men of any epoch because they seek to catch in words the essence of appearance. They name the enduring powers in nature and culture and learn to sing and celebrate that which really is. Not only are they more "present" than the majority of men,

15. Michael Hamburger, *Hölderlin* (New York: 1952).
16. "Hölderlin and the Essence of Poetry," trans. Douglas Scott, *Existence and Being*, by Martin Heidegger (Chicago: 1949).

they are also more sensitive to the potentialities of language for revealing man to himself and for emphasizing his belonging to natural and social reality.

Moreover, poetry is "in a strict sense a measure or a standard by which man receives the measure for the width of his being."[17] Poets alone can teach us our limits, i.e., what we can and cannot do. By establishing in words man's capacities in relation to the immense forces of nature around him, they teach him his mortality and make him capable of death as death. When really poetic and genuine, their words are not simply arbitrary; they are neither subjective nor objective but a true standard of man's situation in time and in the midst of nonhuman realities. Such utterance is the voice of being itself. Poets are more open than the rest of us and under no illusion that they are masters of language. Rather, they allow language to speak through them. Heidegger quotes Hölderlin to the effect that "language, that most dangerous of possessions, has been given to man . . . so that he may affirm what he is."

In short, poets establish for us our human nature; they define us in relation to the earth and sky. They teach us to dwell rightly on earth, to make a home instead of merely inhabiting a series of houses; they teach us how to build properly, which is an activity of dwelling; and how to think instead of merely logicizing. And poets enable man to dwell by showing him how to be grateful and joyous for this possibility of dwelling. "Little knowledge, but much joy/Is given to mortals," sang Hölderlin, and Heidegger discovers that when one pursues thinking into its essential origin, thinking and thanking are much the same. If we can learn to dwell in the spirit of guarding and cherishing the earth, instead of exploiting and mastering it, we will learn that kind of gratitude which comes from "care," which Heidegger from the beginning of his career has conceived to be the most comprehensive essence of human nature. "The writing of poetry permits the act of dwelling initi-

17. *Vorträge und Aufsätze*, p. 196.

ally to enter into its own nature. Poetry is the original letting-dwell."[18]

If one could put in a few words what Heidegger is saying about poets it would run something like this: Men are initially given to dwelling poetically on earth—that is, to perceiving things as they truly are—but every age requires poets, who are the most innocent of beings, to see more deeply into the nature of things and to bring them close to the sources of their being. Far from being subjective or arbitrary in their utterances, they are able to sing of phenomena as phenomena. They teach us to see more exactly, to glimpse *physis* in its unity with *logos* in a way that scholars, scientists, and practical men are unable to glimpse it. They are not knowers but seers, and Heidegger is persuaded that such seers are the sanest men of any epoch.

Do all men dwell poetically? No, he answers, but all men are capable of it to some degree. And they can actualize these potentials by listening to and learning from poets, whether they write in verse or prose. In fact, it is best if they speak rather than write. Nor is Heidegger talking of all "poets," but only of the authentic few who are thinking and poetizing in the proximity of being itself.

It is evident that Heidegger's high estimation of the utterances of such selected poets is governed by two philosophical considerations: his conception of language and his theory of truth. To language Heidegger attributes a power that has rarely been accorded it by philosophers since the early Greeks. It was Aristotle who wrote that a thing is what it may be said to be. In the "Letter on Humanism" Heidegger calls language "the house of Being," which is, I take it, a contemporary expression of the Aristotelian position. *Logos* is not simply the way human beings reveal to themselves the appearances of *physis* or the world process, but in an ontological sense is the same (not to say identical) with it.

Man is under an illusion, Heidegger keeps repeating, so long as he imagines he is the master of language. Instead, language

18. *Vorträge und Aufsätze*, p. 202.

masters him. When a person is genuinely concerned with speaking rather than merely chattering, he does not really determine what he says, but his speech is determined for him by being, by the innermost essence of things. This faith in the powers of language to put us in touch with reality, not at the periphery but at its very center, has not been unexampled in the history of philosophic thought, but is, to say the least, uncommon in the modern world. In a climate of opinion where language is thought of as a tool or instrument of thought, Heidegger's conception testifies to the boldness and radicality of his philosophy. It is also testimony to the influence of the Greeks on him in an aspect of their thinking that has grown strange to us.

Sometimes it is said that Heidegger's philosophy can be understood only through his conception of truth as *aletheia*— uncovering or disclosure. This may well be so; in any event he has held without much change to this notion from his first works to his latest. Certainly this idea helps to explain the ever-closer relation between poetry and thinking which has undergone evolution in his philosophizing. Poetry, as we have seen, is of primary concern to him insofar as it reveals truth, that is, ontological truth or the truth of being. Such truth is not approached through a long process either of deduction or induction. It is not the result of the work of science and scientists. Heidegger does not, of course, deny the reality or importance of the correspondence theory of truth. Nor does he reject the work of scholarship and science in their principal concern with the notion of truth as adequacy between intellect and thing. In its own sphere this notion of truth is inevitable, necessary, and very fruitful. But in the quest of ontological truth, he insists that the conception of *aletheia*, revelation in its secular meaning, is all-important.

Man knows primary being not through the processes of logic or of scientific investigation. It is not a result either in the pragmatic sense or in that of sheer intellection. Empiricism and rationalism in their traditional roles are both inadequate. Truth is rather a kind of "seeing" reached by means of a leap out of man's habitual tendency to place himself as subject over against the world of objects. It is a leap into the midst of this world of things and a reading of the signs of the real displayed there, instead of an inventing of them as an outsider. Understood in this way, truth is more likely to reveal itself to innocent yet profound poetic natures than it is to highly sophisticated, self-conscious scholars or scientists. Hence for thinkers intent on ontological truth, poetry can be investigated more profitably than highly learned works. And nature herself can reveal the same truth when approached by thinkers without preconceptions. In his essay "Remembrance of the Poet," Heidegger writes of Lake Constance in a way that reveals how closely he equates poetry and truth.

> . . . Thus we still think of this water unpoetically. And how much longer are we going to? How long are we going to imagine that there was first of all a part of nature existing for itself and a landscape existing for itself, and that then with the help of "poetic experiences" this landscape became colored with myth? How long are we going to prevent ourselves from experiencing the actual as actual?[19]

How long, indeed? One might answer: Until we have recovered the perspective that the spectacular advances in knowledge of recent generations have served to becloud. Until we have become aware that the poetic eye is capable of seeing as deeply into nature and man as the scientific eye. Because poetry is "innocent" in not making demands on us—in "letting us be," to use a favorite Heideggerian phrase—we have been looking elsewhere, inquiring after truth in the more practical and theoretical realms, the more actionable kinds of knowledge. The sciences can never let us alone as poetry, and the arts in general, always do. Hence it is easily possible for us to "see" a primrose as simply a yellow primrose, a Lake Constance as merely a body of water. Seen this way poetry and imagination are embellishments on the actual. They simply adorn that which only the exact sciences can describe and detail.

Some of us find the greatest promise of the existentialist movement in this attempt to recover for thought the insights and

19. *Existence and Being*, p. 275.

visions of artists. Precisely because philosophers like Heidegger
are not approaching literature with the usual queries and concerns of aesthetics, there is hope that philosophers may once
again take seriously the discoveries of creative writers who are
not consciously seeking to "do" philosophy. Lately we have been
so occupied with the much-touted "two cultures" that we have
paid scant attention to a more serious estrangement, that between poets and thinkers, philosophy and literature. Even those
not interested in existentialism might well grant, for instance,
that real advances lately in ethics are more likely discoverable
in the writings of Dostoevsky or Camus than in most academic
moralists. Perhaps something of the same may be said for certain other traditional disciplines of philosophy. At least I find
Heidegger's investigation of poetic works highly suggestive in
this regard.

At the same time an important caveat is very much to the
point. Poetry may be the most innocent of occupations, as
Hölderlin has told us, but language, the poet's medium, is
"the most dangerous of possessions," as he has also reminded
us in the same poem. One senses that the older Heidegger is
becoming less and less critical of poetic utterances, less inclined
to apply the same standards of phenomenological analysis to
the art work that he applies to the history of thought. Heidegger
has a deeply religious nature, though it is surely not Christian
in any specific sense. There is a danger in his fascination with
language, in the almost irresistible impulse to play with it
which sometimes tends to divert him from his task. Though
this is a very innocent occupation, it is not less dangerous for
that reason.

We notice a similar tendency in Plato, but one of which
Plato was fully aware. Precisely because he loved poetry so
much, he was on guard against its seductions. In the *Metaphysics* Aristotle repeats what he calls a Greek proverb: "Bards
tell many a lie."[20] And Plato in the *Republic* speaks of the
ancient quarrel between philosophy and poetry and bids us be

20. Aristotle, *Metaphysics*, 983a.

on our guard against the enticements of the poets.[21] This ancient quarrel he, of course, detected as a quarrel within himself. While loving them, he distrusted poets and poetry because they were unable to distinguish truth from error in their gnomic utterances. One would like to see something of this same distrust in Heidegger, a heightened awareness that poets can lead us astray as well as lead us to truth.

Hölderlin's famous line begins with: "Full of merit, yet poetically, man dwells. . . ." Heidegger tends to neglect this opening phrase, *Voll Verdienst,* and to interpret only the part: "poetically man dwells on this earth." In the one place where he does take up the "full of merit" phrase, he makes it qualify the adverb "poetically." Hölderlin is not according to Heidegger contrasting "full of merit" with "poetically" or subordinating the latter to the former. Rather it is the other way around. The poet's "yet" means something like "to be sure."[22] He recognizes that Hölderlin means by "full of merit" man's civilizing capacities, such as building, planting, holding societies together by practical and political activities. But Heidegger tries to suggest that such prosaic activities are also poetical in Hölderlin's vision, that building and planting and the workaday world are poetical in essence.

Perhaps I can put this cautionary criticism of Heidegger's enterprise best by disagreement with this interpretation of his. I do not, of course, know what Hölderlin really intended by these cryptic lines. But I do believe that man should dwell prosaically on earth as well as poetically. He must first build a house in a very literal sense in order to dwell in it poetically as a home. Where there is no vision the people perish, as one of the proverbs in the Bible reminds us. But they will perish just as infallibly unless there is a kind of care-taking that centers on the prosaic functions of existence. Poetry can tempt a man to forget that he has a calling to provide the utilitarian means for imaginative "dwelling," by being first of all concerned with

21. Plato, *Republic,* Book 10, 607c *et passim.*
22. *Vorträge und Aufsätze,* p. 191.

the material conditions of existence in the sense of man's moral and social well-being.

It was Albert Hofstadter who recently pointed out in a brilliant article[23] that Heidegger's conception of truth as "unconcealment and lighting" leads him to forget that the concept of truth has long had a relevance and meaning in the ethical sphere as well. Truth means right as well as radiance. And Hofstadter suggests that this stress on light and radiance may well be a reason for the comparative absence of the ethical emphasis in Heidegger's thought. One should add that it was just this attentiveness to the ethical good which led Plato to reluctant criticism of poets and poetry.

In saying this I do not wish to be understood as criticizing Heidegger for placing primary emphasis on the power of imagination and poetry. Man is not first a prosaic being and then in his leisure able to live poetically. The prose of life is primary not in this Philistine sense that labor is more elemental and real to him than poetizing. That we tend to think so in advanced civilizations testifies, in my opinion, to a fundamental derangement in our true relations to our fellows and to the earth and sky. In this I agree with Heidegger. But I intend my criticism in a different sense. Man's first vocation is that of taking care of himself and his fellows in a moral and social way, and this, though not divorced from poetry, is frequently a prosaic task. Like Plato's cave dweller who escaped from the cave, it is necessary for men to return and take up the task of education, even though by preference they would live in the sun's rays. Man's first task, I think, is justice, and if we can make no conclusive progress on it without imagination, poetry alone is not enough. Poetry has a seductive power, as the Greeks understood far better than most of us do, and it must be controlled in the interests of the pursuit of the good.

The notion of morality in our specialist age is usually given a too limited scope. But it does mean something more concrete

23. "Truth of Being," *The Journal of Philosophy*, Vol. LXII, No. 7 (April 1, 1965).

than providing man with a love of the beautiful and the true in the sense of a vision of what is. It means also providing a sense for the political in the ancient and honorable meaning of that term as well as a capacity for friendship in the private sphere of life. *Physis* and *logos* may be more ultimate problems than are *politeia* and *philia,* but some of us believe that the latter are primary for mortals. In this respect Hölderlin's lines seem to put first things first, contrary to Heidegger's interpretation, in noting that men dwell "full of merit," and *yet* "poetically on this earth."

In affirming Heidegger's emphasis on the sameness of goal of poets and thinkers, I shall conclude with the hope that when philosophy discovers poetry it will not abandon the critical intelligence with which we are slowly learning to approach the deliverances of science.

The Existentialist Rediscovery of Hegel and Marx

GEORGE L. KLINE*

I

INTRODUCTION

The relation between phenomenology of the Brentano-Husserl type and existential philosophy of the Kierkegaard-Heidegger type is often held to be intimate and fruitful. Jean-Paul Sartre and Maurice Merleau-Ponty attempted to combine, and sometimes claimed to have succeeded in combining, the two tendencies. But the union was never perfect: Sartre remained a "phenomenologizing existentialist,"[1] Merleau-Ponty an "existentializing phenomenologist." From a sufficiently Olympian perspective, phenomenology and existential philosophy at midtwentieth century often appear to support each other—in Peirce's

* Department of Philosophy, Bryn Mawr College, Bryn Mawr, Pennsylvania.

1. From the beginning—in his essay "The Transcendence of the Ego," written in 1934 and published in 1936—Sartre was a "revisionist" Husserlian, rejecting the substantial self of Husserl's "egology" and the semi-Platonic essences of his *Wesensschau*. But Natanson overstates the contrast between Sartre and Husserl when he insists that Sartre's method "deserves the name 'phenomenological' only in so far as Hegel's phenomenology is intended, . . . it is quasi-phenomenological if we are referring to Husserl's variety of phenomenology" (Maurice Natanson, *A Critique of Jean-Paul Sartre's Ontology* [Lincoln, Neb.: 1951], p. 74; compare also p. 99). Mrs. Warnock seems to me to put the matter more equably, if more vaguely, when she says simply that "Sartre owes far more to Hegel than to Husserl" (Mary Warnock, *The Philosophy of Sartre* [London: 1965], p. 70).

113

earthy phrase—"like two drunken sailors," i.e., sincerely and warmly, but ineffectively.

The relationship between the two remains delicate and controversial. I shall not attempt to throw fresh light on it, except incidentally. My concern is mainly with existential philosophy of the Sartrean type. I shall refer less often to "phenomenology" than to *the* Phenomenology," meaning, of course, Hegel's *Phänomenologie des Geistes—Phenomenology of Mind* or *Spirit—*of 1807. I focus upon Sartre rather than upon Heidegger or Jaspers, because it was Sartre (and to a lesser extent Merleau-Ponty) who brought Hegel and early Marx into the mainstream of twentieth-century existentialism.

II

Hegel Rediscovered

The "rediscovery" of Hegel and Marx to which my title refers took place in Paris during the 1930's and 1940's. The French existentialists were highly selective in their appropriation of Hegelian and Marxist thought; indeed, their rediscovery verged on "intellectual re-creation," if not *creatio ex nihilo intellectualis!* In Sartre, for example, stress fell on specific themes drawn from specific works of specific periods in both Hegel and Marx. Sartre took over not only ideas that were there to be taken, but also at least a few ideas that were *not* there, or at least were not intended by their authors to be taken in the way that Sartre took them.

With minor exceptions, Hegel, for Sartre, meant *early* Hegel (through 1807) and above all the *Phenomenology*. The *Phenomenology* in turn meant two major themes: (a) the struggle for recognition among selves, and the master-slave dialectic; (b) alienation, including self-alienation; and two minor themes: (c) the "unhappy consciousness" and (d) "the death of God."

I shall sketch the historical background of (1) the rediscovery of Hegel, (2) the rediscovery of the *Phenomenology*, and (3) the rediscovery of the two major and two minor themes.

1. Until early in the twentieth century Hegel's thought was doubly eclipsed: in the middle of the nineteenth century by French positivism and toward the end of that century by neo-Kantianism and, to a lesser extent, the half-positivist, half-Kantian "empiriocriticism" of Mach and Avenarius. The movement "back to Kant" of the 1880's and 1890's was intended as a short-circuiting of Hegel himself as well as of post- and anti-Hegelian positivism.

The "rediscovery" of Hegel coincided with the discovery and publication of the long-lost early works. These works were quoted and discussed at length in Dilthey's commentary of 1905,[2] and mentioned in Croce's more general and critical commentary of 1906 (published on the seventy-fifth anniversary of Hegel's death).[3] The works themselves were published by Nohl in 1907 under the title *Theologische Jugendschriften* (Early Theological Writings). The title is misleading because many of the early works are nontheological, and some of them are antitheological.

However, this Hegel revival was not yet a rediscovery of the *Phenomenology*, even though the early works pointed toward it.

2. In both the mid-nineteenth century and the early twentieth century, the *Phenomenology* was generally eclipsed by Hegel's later works—especially the *Science of Logic* and the *Encyclopedia of Philosophical Sciences*. The *Phenomenology* was scarcely mentioned by serious commentators. (It had been taken very seriously indeed by the young Marx and by such neo-Hegelians as Cieszkowski,[4] but Marx's early works remained unpublished,

2. Wilhelm Dilthey, *Die Jugendgeschichte Hegels* (Berlin: 1905); reprinted in Dilthey, *Gesammelte Schriften,* Vol. IV (Leipzig and Berlin: 1921). Dilthey does not discuss the *Phenomenology*.

3. Benedetto Croce, *Ciò che è vivo e ciò che è morto della filosofia di Hegel: Studio critico seguito da un saggio di bibliografia hegeliana* (Bari: 1906). German translation by K. Büchler: *Lebendiges und Totes in Hegels Philosophie* (Heidelberg: 1909). Croce makes only brief and perfunctory references to the *Phenomenology*.

4. August von Cieszkowski, *Prolegomena zur Historiosophie* (Berlin: 1838).

and Cieszkowski was virtually unknown.) A partial exception was provided by the Russians, and this—curiously enough—may have a bearing on the French existentialist rediscovery of the *Phenomenology*. Alexander Herzen, in 1842, wrote of it (in a private letter not published until much later):

> Toward the end of the book it is as though you were plunging into the sea: profundity, transparency, the breath of *Geist* bears you along . . . *lasciate ogni speranza*—the shores disappear; salvation resides only in your own breast. And then a voice is heard: *Quid timeas? Caesarem vehis.* Fear dissolves, the shore appears; the fair leaves of fantasy are stripped away, but the sap-filled fruits of reality [*deistvitelnost* = *Wirklichkeit*] remain. The mermaids have vanished, but a full-breasted maiden waits for you. . . . Such was my impression. I read to the end with heart pounding, with a kind of solemnity. Hegel is Homer and Shakespeare together, and that is why respectable people find his Anglo-Greek dialect incomprehensible.[5]

Similarly appreciative if less lyrical comments were made by the Russian Slavophiles, especially Ivan Kireyevsky and Alexis Khomyakov, during the late 1840's and early 1850's. By the 1850's Herzen himself was calling the Hegelian dialectic (as exhibited in the *Phenomenology*) an "algebra of revolution."[6] In 1892, in a substantial and sympathetic article on Hegel in the standard Russian encyclopedia of the period, Vladimir Solovyov referred to the *Phenomenology* as Hegel's "best work."[7] One of the first translations of the *Phenomenology* into a foreign language was Gustav Shpet's Russian version of 1913. (Baillie's English translation had appeared in 1910.) It remains one of the best translations in *any* language. This early Russian interest found later French expression in the work of Alexandre Kojève (né Kozhevnikov), as we shall see in a moment.

5. Letter to A. A. Krayevski, written in Novgorod, February 3, 1842. In A. I. Herzen (Gertsen), *Sobraniye sochinenii* (Collected Works), XX (Moscow: 1961), 128.

6. A. I. Herzen, "Byloye i dumy," Part IV, chap. xxv, *op. cit.* (Moscow: 1956), IX, 23. Compare *My Past and Thoughts: The Memoirs of Alexander Herzen*, trans. Constance Garnett, II (London: 1924), 121.

7. V. S. Solovyov, "Gegel," *Entsiklopedicheskii Slovar Brokgaus-Yefron*, Vol. VIII (i.e., XV), 1892, p. 218.

The first serious twentieth-century European study devoted mainly to Hegel's *Phenomenology* was Jean Wahl's *Le Malheur de la conscience dans la philosophie de Hegel* (Paris, 1929). Here again there appears to be an underground link with non-French sources. Josiah Royce's posthumous *Lectures on Modern Idealism* (edited by his student, Jacob Loewenberg) had appeared in 1919 and included three chapters—over seventy-five pages—on the *Phenomenology* (pp. 136–212). Wahl, unlike most French philosophers of the interwar period, knew English well, had studied Royce, and had published a book on English and American philosophy in 1920.[8] Wahl's 1929 study of the "unhappy consciousness" lists Royce's *Lectures on Modern Idealism* in the bibliography (p. 202), quotes Royce twice, and refers to Roycean interpretations of Hegel several times.[9]

Of course by 1929 Wahl had also read Heidegger's *Sein und Zeit* (1927). But it should be emphasized that Hegel's *Phenomenology* is scarcely mentioned in Heidegger's long book. To be precise, it is cited twice; both references are to the final chapter, on "Absolute Knowledge," and have to do with Hegel's views of time. And these references are overshadowed in Heidegger's work by numerous references to Hegel's *Logic* and *Encyclopedia*.

Another stimulus to interest in Hegel generally and the *Phenomenology* in particular, for Sartre and Merleau-Ponty as well as for Kojève himself, was the special Hegel centennial issue of the *Revue de Métaphysique et de Morale* published in 1931. It was a large issue (233 pages) and an impressive one, with contributions by Croce, Nicolai Hartmann, and Charles Andler, among others.[10] Andler's article, which is devoted to

8. *Les Philosophies pluralistes d'Angleterre et d'Amérique* (Paris: 1920).
9. The quotations appear on pp. 34, n.1, and 73, the references on pp. 74, n. 2; 96, n. 2; 113, n. 2; 152, n. 1. Royce's *Spirit of Modern Philosophy* (1892), pp. 190–227 of which are devoted to Hegel, is also listed in Wahl's bibliography.
10. The contents of this issue are as follows: Benedetto Croce, "Un cercle vicieux dans la critique de la philosophie hégélienne," pp. 277–84; Nicolai Hartmann, "Hegel et le problème de la dialectique du réel," pp. 285–316; Charles Andler, "Le fondement du savoir dans la 'Phénoménologie de l'esprit' de Hegel," pp. 317–40; Victor Basch, "Des origines et des fondements de

the *Phenomenology*, discusses the importance of "the negative"[11] but makes no reference to alienation, the master-slave dialectic, or the unhappy consciousness.

However, Nicolai Hartmann's article,[12] although it refers to the *Phenomenology* only in passing, makes two significant points about it and a further relevant point about the *Logic*. First, Hartmann calls the *Phenomenology* Hegel's "first masterpiece" and says that it remains "a fundamental work";[13] second, he speaks of the "famous dialectic of master and servant" and devotes an extended passage to explicating it.[14] Presumably he called this dialectic "famous" or "well-known" in 1931—before the publication of Marx's Paris Manuscripts of 1844—on the basis of three serious earlier discussions: (a) that of Jean Wahl (1929), not referred to by Hartmann himself; (b) that of Richard Kroner, in Volume II of *Von Kant bis Hegel* (1924), which Hartmann refers to in the Preface to (c) Volume II of his own book, *Die Philosophie des deutschen Idealismus*, 1929, a long section of which (ch. 2: pp. 295–362) is devoted to the *Phenomenology*. This chapter includes several pages on the struggle for recognition among selves and the master-slave dia-

---

l'esthétique de Hegel," p. 341–66; René Berthelot, "Goethe et Hegel," pp. 367–412; M. Gueroult, "Le jugement de Hegel sur l'antithétique de la raison pure," pp. 413–39; Edmond Vermeil, "La pensée politique de Hegel," pp. 441–510. The possible significance of this special issue of the leading French philosophical journal of the period for Sartre's rediscovery of Hegel is noted by Klaus Hartmann in his *Grundzüge der Ontologie Sartres in ihrem Verhältnis zu Hegels Logik* (Berlin: 1963), p. 3.

11. Charles Andler, "Le fondement du savoir . . .," *Revue de Métaphysique et de Morale*, XXXVIII (1931), 319f.

12. The article was written in German and translated into French by R.-L. Klee. The German original, entitled "Hegel und das Problem der Realdialektik," was subsequently published in *Blätter für deutsche Philosophie*, 1935, and reprinted in Vol. II of Hartmann's *Kleinere Schriften* (Berlin: 1957), pp. 323–46.

13. Nicolai Hartmann, "Hegel et le problème . . .," *Revue de Métaphysique et de Morale*, p. 288.

14. *Ibid.*, pp. 308f. The French phrase—"la dialectique fameuse du maître et du serviteur"—is stronger than the original, which speaks only of "die bekannte Dialektik von 'Herr und Knecht'" (cf. *Kleinere Schriften*, II, 340).

lectic (pp. 332–35). The exposition is lucid and sympathetic; there are many quotations from Hegel's text. Hartmann makes clear his admiration for the master-slave dialectic, calling it "one of the finest things in the *Phenomenology*," concise and "plastic" in form, highly significant in content. He finds it the best example in Hegel of a dialectic that inheres in the subject matter itself.[15] Hartmann in 1929 also anticipated Kojève's lectures of 1933–39—and Marx's rediscovered Paris Manuscripts to be published in 1932—when he noted the "revolutionizing principle" in the master-slave relation, pointing out that the slave's work affects not only the *thing* worked on but the *man* who does the working, that the slave cannot shape (*bilden*) things without shaping himself. "This," Hartmann concludes, "may be regarded as the universal foundation for a philosophy of work."[16]

Finally, to round out the possible contribution that Nicolai Hartmann may have made to the existentialist rediscovery of Hegel, we note that he—or rather his French translator—uses the exact phrase that Sartre was to adopt as the title of his major philosophical work: he refers to the dialectic of "*L'Etre et le Néant*" at the beginning of Hegel's *Logic*.[17]

Alexandre Kojève was not only Russian-born; he had written a dissertation on Solovyov, stressing the latter's philosophy of history, a study which would surely have brought him into contact with Hegel in general and the *Phenomenology* in particular. Kojève was the first scholar in France to comment on the *Phenomenology* in detail—in a suggestive, often brilliant, sometimes eccentric, even perverse, study that has not yet found an equal in any language. This commentary was given to the public in lectures at the École des Hautes Études in Paris annually between 1933 and 1939 and distributed in mimeographed form during those years, although not published until 1947. Sartre

15. Nicolai Hartmann, *Die Philosophie des deutschen Idealismus*, II, 1929; cited from the 1960 Berlin edition, two volumes in one, p. 333.

16. *Ibid.*, p. 335.

17. *Revue de Métaphysique et de Morale*, XXXVIII (1931), 311.

and Merleau-Ponty attended some of Kojève's lectures[18] and doubtless read the mimeographed versions of those that they did not attend. It seems safe to assume that these lectures were the main direct source for the impact of Hegel's *Phenomenology* upon French existentialist thinkers during the 1930's. Kojève, in turn, was stimulated by Russian, German, and French sources. The Russian sources were his study of Solovyov and perhaps the Russian translation of the *Phenomenology*;[19] the German sources were doubtless those mentioned above—the commentaries of Nicolai Hartmann and, perhaps, Richard Kroner; the French sources included Jean Wahl's 1929 study of the unhappy consciousness and perhaps also Andler's 1931 article on the *Phenomenology* in the *Revue de Métaphysique et de Morale*.

During the late 1930's Jean Hyppolite, under Kojève's influence, began to publish articles on Hegel and the *Phenomenology*. His translation of the latter appeared in two volumes in 1939 and 1941; his detailed commentary followed in 1946.[20] Hyppolite's commentary, which remains the most careful and useful in any language, draws freely on both Wahl and Kojève and is, in a broad sense, "existentialist" in its orientation.

18. See Wilfrid Desan, *The Marxism of Jean-Paul Sartre* (Anchor Book edition; New York: 1966), p. 24. According to Desan, Hyppolite also attended Kojève's lectures. Desan erroneously dates the first lecture series in 1936; it was given in 1933.

19. Another possible Russian stimulus to Kojève's interest in Hegel is I. A. Ilyin's *Filosofiya Gegelya, kak ucheniye o konkretnosti Boga i cheloveka* [Hegel's Philosophy as a Theory of the Concreteness of God and Man] (2 vols.; Moscow: 1918). Abridged German translation: Iwan Iljin, *Die Philosophie Hegels als kontemplative Gotteslehre* (Bern: 1946).

20. Jean Hyppolite, *Genèse et structure de la Phénoménologie de l'Esprit de Hegel* (Paris: 1946). The need for a full-scale scholarly commentary on the *Phenomenology* was noted by Georg Lasson as early as 1907, in the preface to his centennial edition: "Gewiss ist ein ausführlicher Kommentar zur Phänomenologie ein wissenschaftliches Bedürfnis" (G. W. F. Hegel, *Phänomenologie des Geistes*, Jubiläumsausgabe [Leipzig: 1907], p. xv). In 1924 Richard Kroner repeated the point with greater emphasis: "Ein Kommentar zur Phänomenologie ist eine heute dringend geforderte Aufgabe, die ... nur in einem selbständigen Buche gelöst werden kann" (*Von Kant bis Hegel* [Tübingen: 1924], II, 382n). Kojève and Hyppolite between them have supplied a more useful and comprehensive commentary than any of the numerous German scholars who have written on Hegel's philosophy.

3. As we have already noted, Heidegger in *Sein und Zeit* makes no reference to the master-slave dialectic, to alienation (in Hegel), to the unhappy consciousness, or to the "death of God."

It seems fair to assume that Sartre and Merleau-Ponty derived their interest in these themes from other sources. The sources, in fact, are fairly obvious: (a) Wahl's 1929 study;[21] (b) Kojève's lectures of 1933–39; (c) the rediscovery of Hegel by such Marxists as Lukács (especially in his controversial and subsequently disavowed work, *Geschichte und Klassenbewusstsein,* 1923); (d) Sartre's and Merleau-Ponty's direct study of Marx's 1844 *Economic and Philosophic Manuscripts*—the "Dead Sea Scrolls of Marxism," as Lewis Feuer has called them. Mention of these last two sources brings us to the existentialist rediscovery of *Marx.*

III

YOUNG MARX REDISCOVERED

In the case of Marx there was no need, as there had been with Hegel, for near-total rediscovery. All of Marx's works from the *Manifesto* of 1848 on had been readily available since their publication and widely influential at least since the 1880's. Most of Marx's mature works had been translated into French, although thinkers like Sartre and Merleau-Ponty, to say nothing of Wahl, Hyppolite, and Kojève, did not need translations, being entirely at home in German. The "mature" Marx of 1848–83, like the "mature" Engels of 1848–95, had no appeal for existentialists in either Germany or France.[22] *Sein und Zeit*

21. Wahl discusses the theme of "the death of God" at some length, with reference to Hegel rather than Nietzsche. The first two chapters in Pt. II of his book are entitled, respectively, "La mort de Dieu" and "La double signification de la mort de Dieu" (*Le Malheur de la conscience,* pp. 69–91).

22. In his postexistentialist treatise of 1960, *Critique de la raison dialectique,* Sartre enthusiastically appropriates both Engels and "mature" Marx, stopping short only of the Engelsian universalization of the dialectic to include all of (nonhuman and nonhistorical) nature. Here, as Mrs. Warnock remarks, "it is the fully grown Marx-Engels doctrine of dialectical materialism which has taken over—the very doctrine which, in 1946 [i.e., in the essay, "Materialism and Revolution"] Sartre claimed to find actually [self-] contradictory" (*op. cit.,* p. 156; compare p. 164).

makes no reference at all to Marx. It is doubtful that any existentialist work published before 1932 showed sympathy for, or interest in, Marx's thought. The earliest works to show such sympathy are from the pen of another Paris-based Russian émigré—Nicolas Berdyaev, who as a young man in Kiev and St. Petersburg had flirted briefly with a "Kantian" revision of Marxism and who later, in works published in Russian in Paris during the 1930's and quickly translated into the major Western languages, including French, embraced the young Marx as a congenial critic of both alienation and objectification. (On the second point, Berdyaev, like Sartre later, misinterpreted Marx, who in fact attacked alienation but defended objectification [*Vergegenständlichung*].)

During the years of the Nazi occupation of Paris, and perhaps earlier, Sartre turned to a serious study of Marx's Paris Manuscripts of 1844.[23] He was drawn to them for a variety of reasons: by a general sympathy with Communism, hence with Marxism; by the Hegelian "young-Marx" Marxism of Kojève's lectures; possibly by some of Berdyaev's writings of the 1930's; probably by his study of early Lukács, which in turn was stimulated by Lukács' Rumanian-born disciple, Lucien Goldmann, who had settled in Paris and whom Sartre knew well. Sartre was responsive to the echoes of Hegel's *Phenomenology* in the young Marx, especially the stress on the master-slave dialectic (reformulated by Marx as the dialectic of non-worker and worker) and the theory of alienation and self-alienation. In turn, Sartre was led by his study of Marx (and by Lukács and Kojève) to look more closely and "existentially" at Hegel's own formulations of these themes.

23. Sartre has told us something about his early encounters with Marx's writings, especially the *German Ideology* and *Capital*. Since he took them as theoretical statements rather than incentives to revolutionary *praxis*, he claims to have missed their main point. Compare *Critique de la raison dialectique* (Paris: 1960), pp. 22f. Partial English translation by Hazel Barnes: *Search for a Method* (New York: 1963), pp. 17f. (Hereafter references to the *Critique* will be given as *CRD* with page number.)

IV

HEGEL AND MARX EXISTENTIALIZED

I suppose that everyone is entitled to his own Hegel and his own Marx. But Sartre's philosophical appropriation and "possession" of both Marx and Hegel are quite extraordinary. Following the lead of Lukács, he Hegelianizes Marx (interestingly enough, Lukács had done this in 1923, nine years before the Paris Manuscripts were published—although there have been rumors that he had access to some of them prior to their publication). Following the lead of Kojève, he Marxianizes Hegel, although in *Being and Nothingness* (1943) he does this less drastically and systematically than Kojève. What Sartre does to both Marx and Hegel, and to his own "vintage" existentialism (the vintage year being 1943), in the huge and difficult first volume of his *Critique de la raison dialectique* (1960) is a question to which I shall recur briefly in Section VI.

Being and Nothingness, as Marcuse has said, "is in large parts [sic] a restatement of Hegel's *Phenomenology of Mind* and Heidegger's *Sein und Zeit.*"[24] *Being and Nothingness* is closer to the *Phenomenology* than to *Being and Time.*[25] The two books are of about the same length; both aim at unusual comprehensiveness; both include much material of a kind not usually found in philosophical works of their respective periods. Perhaps most striking is the inclusion in both of historical as well as literary materials: Sartre follows Hegel in discussing the French Revolution of 1789 and in making several excursions into ancient history. He rivals Hegel in the number of writers whom he discusses at some length.[26]

24. Herbert Marcuse, "Existentialism: Remarks on Jean-Paul Sartre's *L'Etre et le Néant,*" *Philosophy and Phenomenological Research,* VIII (1947–48), 311.

25. By a curious coincidence, Heidegger and Sartre were exactly the same age (thirty-eight) when they published their respective *opera magna.* Hegel was a year younger when he published the *Phenomenology.*

26. The *Phenomenology* includes discussions—sometimes without explicit identification of the author in question—of Homer, Sophocles, Shakespeare, Cervantes, Rousseau, Diderot, Goethe, and Schiller; *Being and Nothingness*

Being and Nothingness, like the *Phenomenology,* sets forth "forms or shapes of human consciousness" (*Gestalten des Bewusstseins*). Indeed one might consider Sartre's detailed analysis of *mauvaise foi*—bad faith or self-and-other deception—as an attempt to add a new "form of consciousness" to the Hegelian galaxy.[27] The same might be said of the Sartrean treatment of sadism in interpersonal relations—a theme not touched upon by Hegel. In *Being and Nothingness,* as in the *Phenomenology,* such *Gestalten* as *mauvaise foi,* "the unhappy consciousness," (*das unglückliche Bewusstsein*), and "spirit alienated from itself" (*der sich entfremdete Geist*) are personified, acquiring almost mythological status.[28] In both cases the result is impressive. "Sartre's great inexact equations," as Iris Murdoch has put it, "like those of his master Hegel, inspire us to reflect."[29]

In *Being and Nothingness* Sartre's basic categories are Hegelian; they are taken mainly from the *Phenomenology,* with important supplementation from the *Logic:* for-itself and in-itself,

---

includes discussions of Sophocles, Rousseau, Balzac, Flaubert, Dostoyevsky, Kafka, Gide, and Faulkner. This common concern with literary expression of "forms of consciousness" is related to the assumption, noted by Wahl (with special, but not exclusive, reference to stoicism, skepticism, and the unhappy consciousness): ". . . ce que Hegel considère dans la *Phénoménologie,* ce ne sont pas des philosophies mais des façons de vivre; ou plutôt les deux ne sont pas séparés" (Wahl, *op. cit.,* p. 7). But the *Phenomenology* is much more than cultural history plus philosophical anthropology. It also deals—as does Heidegger's *Sein und Zeit*—with the traditional problems of being, certainty, truth, law, the order of nature, etc., none of which seems to have interested Sartre in 1943. Compare the comments by William Barrett in *Irrational Man* (New York: 1958), pp. 221f.

27. Klaus Hartmann has suggested that Sartrean *mauvaise foi* may be derived from that "shape of consciousness" which Hegel in the *Phenomenology* calls *Verstellung* (dissemblance), as well as from the Kierkegaardian concept of dread. (Compare K. Hartmann, *op. cit.,* p. 55.)

28. *Ibid.,* pp. 55f.

29. Iris Murdoch, *Sartre: Romantic Rationalist* (2d ed.; New Haven, 1959 [first ed., 1953]), p. 114. Of course, Hegel's "inexact equations" are dynamic, his dialectic cumulative and "progressive," whereas Sartre's "equations" are static, his "dialectic" noncumulative and, in a sense, circular.

consciousness and self-consciousness, being and nothingness.[30] Sartre's fundamental themes—negation as an ontological factor and the negativity of consciousness—are entirely Hegelian.[31]

However, the use to which Sartre puts his Hegelian categories is radically un- and even anti-Hegelian. His is a truncated dialectic, a dialectic without synthesis, without reconciliation, oddly reminiscent in this respect of the nihilistic dialectic of Bakunin and Lenin. For Hegel, the in-itself and the for-itself are *abstrakte Momente*,[32] that is, one-sided and partial phases

30. Each of Sartre's key philosophical terms corresponds to a Hegelian term. The terminological transposition of Hegel from German into French had been substantially completed—by Wahl, Kojève, and Hyppolite—when Sartre began his *magnum opus*. Here is a partial list: *für sich = pour-soi; Für-sichsein = être-pour-soi; an sich = en-soi; Ansichsein = être-en-soi; an-und-für sich = en-soi-pour-soi; An-und-fürsichsein = être-en-soi-pour-soi; Bewusst-sein = conscience* (occasionally *Gewissen = conscience*—since the notoriously ambiguous French term *conscience* means both "consciousness" and "conscience"); *Selbstbewusstsein = conscience (de) soi* (the parenthetical "de" in Sartre's words, "ne répond qu'à une contrainte grammaticale" [*L'Etre et le Néant* (Paris: 1943), p. 20; hereafter *EN*]; for the remaining 700 pages of the book, Sartre follows this grammatically unorthodox usage) ; *das Andere = l'autre; der Andere = autrui; aufheben = supprimer et sublimer; Auf-hebung = suppression et sublimation; Sein = l'être; das Nichts = le néant.* Sartre occasionally introduces German terms directly into his French text, e.g., Husserl's *Abschattung*, Hegel's *selbständig, unselbständig, Selbständigkeit,* and *Unselbständigkeit.* As Joseph Fell has pointed out, Sartre follows Hegel in using *conscience (Bewusstsein)* and *conscience (de) soi (Selbstbewusstsein)* to designate not states but activities and even agents—as in the "struggle of self-consciousnesses." Compare Joseph P. Fell, III, *Emotion in the Thought of Sartre* (New York: 1965), p. 156. Of course, Sartre's exotic term *ek-stase,* used in the special sense of "a (futile) gesture of self-transcendence," derives, via Heidegger, from the Greek *ekstasis.*

31. Compare *EN* 47–52, 511. *Being and Nothingness,* trans. Hazel Barnes (New York: 1956), pp. 12–16, 436. (Hereafter cited as *BN.*) See also K. Hartmann, *op. cit.,* p. 4.

32. In Hegel *das Moment* (= phase or aspect of a cumulative dialectical process) is clearly distinguished from *der Moment* (= moment of time). In French *le moment* is used indiscriminately for both. English translators of Hegel and of Sartre have used 'moment' in the two different senses, without distinguishing them. *Das Moment* should be rendered either as "dialectical phase" or, more precisely if less elegantly, as 'moment$_H$'. Similarly with Hegel's special senses of 'abstract' and 'concrete'. In Hegelian usage 'abstract' means "one-sided, inadequately related, deficiently mediated"; 'concrete' means "many-sided, adequately related, complexly and fully mediated." Unfortunately, Sartre regularly confuses these senses ('abstract$_H$'

of a dialectical whole, which will be *aufgehoben*—canceled, preserved, and raised to a higher level—and thus reconciled in the concrete_H synthesis of the "in-and-for-itself." For Sartre, the in-itself and the for-itself are irreconcilable; their opposition is unmediatable.[33] Similarly with self and other, and with being and nothingness.[34] In Hegel the self returns to itself out of otherness, including and reconciling the other within itself. For Sartre self and other stand permanently hostile and unreconciled. His doctrine of the *néantisation* ("nothingizing" or nihilation) of the *en-soi* by the *pour-soi,* whatever sense one may make of it (see below), is certainly not a doctrine of dialectical reconciliation. The result is a distorted Hegelianism; it retains the harsh action of contradiction without the soothing balm of synthesis. And Sartre's is a deeply pessimistic view: every *ekstase* must fail, every effort by an existing individual to become God, to conquer another's freedom, to assimilate the "massive, viscous, and sickening" *en-soi* is doomed to frustration.[35]

In general, the defective, destructive, or frustrating aspects of human existence which in the *Phenomenology* are only *abstrakte Momente*—one-sided and partial stages in the dialectical development of the human spirit, destined to be definitively *aufgehoben*—are for Sartre permanent, uneliminable, and unmediatable features of *la condition humaine.* Thus, for example, the "unhappy consciousness," which for Hegel is a defective

---

and 'concrete_H') with the quite different Kierkegaardian and even Humean-empiricist senses ('abstract_K' and 'concrete_K'; 'abstract_E' and 'concrete_E'). Often he falls into an "ordinary-language" usage, according to which "concrete" means simply "specific" or "particular." For details see my article, "Some Recent Reinterpretations of Hegel's Philosophy," *The Monist,* XLVIII (1964), 40–44.

33. See the perceptive article by Joseph P. Fell, III, "Sartre as Existentialist and Marxist," *Bucknell Review,* XIII, No. 3 (1965), pp. 63–74, esp. p. 68.

34. In the dialectical movement of Hegel's *Logic,* being *(Sein)* and nothingness *(Nichts)* are *aufgehoben* in becoming *(Werden).*

35. There is a kind of subdued and stoical Prometheanism about the Sisyphus of Camus; Sartre's Sisyphian *pour-soi,* in contrast, carries no touch of Prometheus. The postexistenialist Prometheanism of Sartre's *Critique* is essentially Marxist-Leninist.

form of the religious consciousness, is for Sartre an ultimate: "The being of human reality is suffering. . . . Human reality therefore is by nature an unhappy consciousness with no possibility of surpassing its unhappy state."[36] Similarly with the struggle of self against self, the striving to gain recognition or respect (*Anerkennung*). This is a stage or moment$_H$ which gives way to the master-slave relation, that in turn giving way to the stoic consciousness, skepticism, the unhappy consciousness, etc. But for Sartre, "Conflict is the original meaning of being-for-others."[37] Rejecting Heidegger's category of *Mitsein* (being-with), Sartre asserts: "The essence of the relations between consciousnesses is not the *Mitsein;* it is conflict."[38] In his philosophical play *No Exit*, the celebrated aphorism: "L'enfer c'est les autres" (Hell is the others) makes the same un-Hegelian point.

Miss Murdoch puts this point vividly when she describes Sartrean "love" as "a battle between two hypnotists in a closed room," adding that "other people" enter Sartre's solipsistic universe "one at a time, as the petrifying gaze of the Medusa, or at best as the imperfectly understood adversary in the fruitless conflict of love."[39]

Sartre *begins* with Hegel: each self-consciousness seeks to be truly *pour-soi* by eliminating all competitors, by reducing each claimant to selfhood to the status of a mere *en-soi*, a thing or object. But whether in the short run it suceeds or fails in this

36. *BN* 90. "La réalité-humaine est souffrante dans son être. . . . Elle est donc par nature conscience malheureuse, sans dépassement possible de l'état de malheur" (*EN* 134). Wahl makes Hegel sound, in anticipation, rather close to Sartre when he writes: ". . . comme en chacun de ces aspects [of human consciousness] il y a un conflit, on peut dire qu-*en chacun d'eux nous trouverons cette conscience malheureuse* qui s'est manifestée sans doute plus nettement à telle ou telle époque, mais qui se renouvelle sous une forme ou sous une autre *à toutes les époques de la vie de l'humanité*" (*op. cit.*, p. 94; italics mine).

37. *BN* 364. "Le conflit est le sens originel de l'être-pour-autrui" (*EN* 431).

38. *BN* 429. "L'essence des rapports entre consciences n'est pas le Mitsein, c'est le conflit" (*EN* 502).

39. Murdoch, *op. cit.*, pp. 96, 72.

attempt, it must ultimately fail. If it fails in the short run, and other selves remain as *pour-soi,* they pose a continuing threat to its selfhood. On the other hand, if it suceeds in reducing all other selves to things (by killing them), no self will be left to recognize or respect it.[40] Self-respect requires the respect of others whom the self in turn respects as selves.

This impasse leads to the master-slave dialectic. I shall not enter into its details, since Sartre—unlike Kojève—is not interested in them. He is concerned only to assert, with Hegel— but twisting Hegel's meaning by universalizing and eternalizing what for Hegel was particular and transitory—that the relation of self to self is marked by hostility, conflict, the attempt to destroy and enslave.[41] Sartre agrees with Hegel that the attempt to enslave must founder—but not quite for Hegel's reasons. In Sartre the foundering is, in a clear sense, nondialectical. In Hegel it is dialectical: the master becomes other than himself, becomes his own other, becomes nonmaster and ultimately slave (of his slave). The slave in turn becomes master of his master; and the point at which each becomes his own "other" marks the transition to the new dialectical phase (moment$_H$) of stoicism, in which the master-slave distinction is *aufgehoben.*[42] The good stoic can be indifferently either a master (e g., Marcus Aurelius) or a slave (e.g., Epictetus), because he is not seriously committed to either role. In the absence of such a dialectical *Aufhebung* of the master-slave relation in stoicism, the slave's mastering of his master would generate a "bad," i.e., merely reiterative, infinity.[43]

40. Sartre sees a further, quite clearly neurotic, level of frustration: killing the rival self does not eliminate him completely, for it fails to destroy his pastness, to make him "never to have been." His memory remains to haunt and taunt the "victor."

41. Compare, e.g., ". . . while I seek to enslave the Other, the Other seeks to enslave me" (*BN* 364). (". . . pendant que je cherche à asservir autrui, autrui cherche à m'asservir" [*EN* 431].) At this point, too, Wahl appears to want to build a bridge from Hegel to Sartre. He sees the tendency to "concevoir les choses sous la catégorie 'domination et esclavage' " as a "trait fondamental de la conscience humaine" (*op. cit.,* p. 126).

42. This whole process is lucidly described by Wahl, *op. cit.,* pp. 119f, 124.

43. Cf. Jan van der Meulen, *Hegel: Die gebrochene Mitte* (Hamburg: 1958), p. 305.

The question of the role of work in the master-slave dialectic and in what Lukács and Kojève have called—following Marx— the "emancipation of mankind" is a theme not pursued by Sartre in his existentialist writings. So I shall not pursue it here; it belongs in the story of Marxist interpretations and misinterpretations of Hegel, including the "existentialist-Marxist" interpretations and misinterpretations of Hegel in Sartre's *Critique de la raison dialectique*, to which I shall return briefly in Section VI.

On another central point Sartre remains somewhat closer to Hegel; yet he manages to twist the Hegelian position into something that Hegel would surely have repudiated. I think that Hegel would have welcomed Sartre's stress on actuality—"whatever is is actual"[44]—and accepted his concomitant denial of possibility or potentiality as an ontological category. But I think that Hegel would *not* have accepted Sartre's replacement of possibility by "nothingness."

Sartre confuses nonactuality with nonbeing: possibilities are obviously not actual, therefore they are not.[45] Expressed positively, what is merely possible is nothing, a nothingness. For Aristotle's potency (*dynamis*), Sartre substitutes nothingness (*le néant*); for his actualization (*energeia*), nihilation or "nothingizing" (*néantisation*); and for the product or outcome of this process (*ergon*), the "negated" or "nothingized" (*négatité*). This bouquet of neologisms would, I suspect, have a fresher *parfum*

44. "Tout est en acte" (*EN* 12). Hazel Barnes mistranslates this sentence as "The act is everything" (*BN* xlvi). In this passage Sartre explicitly repudiates any "duality of potency and act" ("la dualité de la puissance et de l'acte"), insisting that "behind the act there is neither potency, nor 'hexis'. . . " (Derrière l'acte il n'y a ni puissance, ni 'exis'. . . ."). Mrs. Warnock comments: "Beings-in-themselves have no possibilities; or, rather all their possibilities are realized at once at the moment of creation" (*op. cit.*, p. 62) .

45. I am not persuaded by James Edie's contention that " 'pure potency' in the language of Aristotle can be translated into good English as 'nothingness' " (see his contribution to this volume, "Sartre as Phenomenologist and as Existential Psychoanalyst," n. 37). Pure potency or potentiality is nonactual, but it is not nonexistent—not a sheer nonbeing or nothingness. On this point, Kierkegaard, who prized free choice and decision at least as much as Sartre did, remained Aristotelian, analyzing free choice as the actualizing of one among a plurality of possibilities.

in Latin: for *néant* read *nihil;* for *néantisation, nihilatio;* for *négatité, nihilatum.*

Sartre's curious doctrine derives from Heidegger ("Das Nichts nichtet," etc.) at least as much from Hegel. It is reminiscent of Berdyaev's existentialist doctrine of freedom as rooted in the *Ungrund* or "void of non-being (in Greek *me-on*)." Human freedom, in Berdyaev's words, is "not ontal but meonic."[46] Sartre *may* have been familiar with Berdyaev's position, but his immediate sources were (a) Heidegger and (b) Hegel, as filtered through the Heideggerianizing Hegel-commentaries of Wahl and Kojève. Wahl had said that "for Hegel negativity, freedom, subjectivity, and the process of *Aufhebung* are united."[47] Kojève explicitly "existentialized" Hegel's remarks about the negativity of free human action: "Man," he declared, "is not a being who *is*; he is *nothingness* which *nothingizes* [or *nihilates*] by negating being. Now the negation of being is action." Kojève adds that negativity, as "pure nothingness," is "a real freedom which manifests itself in the form of action."[48]

46. "Freedom," Berdyaev declares, "is rooted in non-being or nothingness" *(Dream and Reality,* trans. Katharine Lampert [New York: 1951], p. 213). The Russian text reads: "svoboda vkorenena v nebytiye ili v 'nichto'" *(Samopoznaniye: opyt filosofskoi avtobiografii* [Self-Knowledge: An Essay in Philosophical Autobiography], [Paris: 1949], p. 232).

47. "Pour Hegel, negativité, liberté, subjectivité, processus de l'*Aufhebung* sont unis" *(op. cit.,* p. 95, n. 1).

48. "L'Homme n'est pas un Etre qui *est*: il est *Néant* qui *néantit* par la négation de l'Etre. Or, la négation de l'Etre—c'est l'Action. " Negativity, as "néant pur," is a "*liberté* réelle qui . . . se manifeste . . . en tant qu'*action*." (Alexandre Kojève, *Introduction à la lecture de Hegel: Leçons sur la Phéno-ménologie de l'Esprit professées de 1933 à 1939 à l'École des Hautes Études* [réunies et publiées par Raymond Queneau; Paris: 1947], pp. 181, 493.) Kojève also speaks of action as being "négatrice du donné" *(ibid.,* p. 497). It may be worth noting that Kojève—like Nicolai Hartmann (see n. 10)—uses the exact phrase which Sartre was to make the title of his major work: "L'Etre et le Néant" *(ibid.,* p. 493n). Kojève makes Hegel sound very much like Sartre when he writes: "Sur le plan 'phénoménologique' la Négativité n'est donc rien d'autre que la *Liberté* humaine. . . ." And again: "La liberté ne consiste pas dans un *choix* entre deux *données:* elle est la *négation* du donné . . ." *(ibid.,* p. 494). All of this, I submit, is much closer to French existentialism than it is to Hegel's own doctrine.

Sartre's way of putting the point is even more paradoxical: "Freedom is precisely the nothingness which *is made-to-be* [literally "is be'd"] at the heart of man and which forces human-reality to *make itself* instead of *to be.*"[49] Again: "The for-itself is defined ontologically as a *lack of being,* and possibility belongs to the for-itself as that which it lacks. . . . Freedom is the concrete mode of being of the lack of being."[50]

Sartre's position may be seen as a radicalization of Bergson's view (Sartre refers to Bergson more than a dozen times in *Being and Nothingness*): Bergson had denied the ontological status of possibilities as (timeless) structures of nonactuality, asserting that men create their own possibilities and subsequently actualize (some or all of) them.[51] Sartre appears to share Bergson's insensitivity to the *aporiai* generated by such a denial of the "objective" or "structural" character of possibility or potentiality. But it must be admitted that in this denial the two Frenchmen have eminent philosophical company—no less than that of Parmenides, Spinoza, and Hegel!

49. *BN* 440. "La liberté, c'est précisément le néant qui *est été* au coeur de l'homme et qui contraint la réalité-humaine à *se faire,* au lieu *d'être"* (*EN* 516). Further on Sartre adds that "Freedom . . . is strictly identical with nihilation" (*BN* 567). ("La liberté . . . est rigoureusement assimilable à la néantisation" [*EN* 655].)

50. *BN* 565. ". . . le pour-soi se décrit ontologiquement comme *manque d'être* et le possible appartient au pour-soi comme *ce qui lui manque.* . . . [La liberté] est le mode d'être concret du manque d'être" (*EN* 652). Sartre adds, punningly, that the possible "has the being of a lack and as a lack, it lacks being. The Possible is not, the possible is possibilized . . . : the possible determines in schematic outline a location in the nothingness . . ." (*BN* 102). (The possible "a l'être d'un manque et, comme manque, il manque d'être. Le Possible n'est pas, le possible se possibilise . . . ; il détermine par esquisse schématique un emplacement de néant . . ." [*EN* 147].)

51. Bergson attacks those philosophers who consider "freedom a choice between possibles,—as if possibility was not created by freedom itself!" (Henri Bergson, *The Creative Mind,* trans. Mabelle L. Andison [New York: 1946], p. 123). (". . . par liberté un choix entre les possibles,—comme si la possibilité n'était pas créée par la liberté même!" [*La Pensée et le mouvant* (Paris: 1934), p. 132].) Compare Sartre's characterization of freedom as "a choice which creates for itself its own possiblities" (*BN* 566)—". . . un choix que se crée ses propres possibilités" (*EN* 654).

V

ALIENATION AND OBJECTIFICATION

I shall not treat the topic of alienation, or the related sub-topic of objectification, in detail; it is being treated separately in this volume.[52] I wish only to indicate briefly what Hegel meant by alienation (*Entfremdung* or *Entäusserung*) and by objectification (*Vergegenständlichung*), and the relation between the two; what, in turn, Marx meant by these terms and how he understood their relation; and, finally, what an existentialist like Sartre understands by the terms and their relation.

Hegel in the *Phenomenology* treats alienation in a section entitled "Der sich entfremdete Geist; die Bildung" ("Spirit Alienated from Itself; Culture—[or Education, Formation, "Shaping"]"). The phenomenological reference is not to *absoluter Geist* (Absolute Spirit) but rather to *daseiender Geist* (existing, finite spirit); the historical reference is to seventeenth-century France, a period of extreme cultural formalism, universalism, and sophistication.

Hegel asks how the individual can develop his "natural" powers and gifts, coming to be what he intrinsically and uniquely is. And he answers: by being *gebildet,* shaped and formed by culture—i.e., by acquiring a language, a *"formation littéraire,"* manners, mores, etc. To actualize himself as a *particular* individual, a man must, paradoxically, take on *universal* forms. Moreover, these forms are not his creation, indeed are alien to him. Yet historical culture is a wholly human product. Thus men's own historical, collective creations stand massively over against, and alienated from, individual men.

In the *Paris Manuscripts* Marx adds to this account of cultural alienation motifs from Hegel's own dialectic of work (taken from the much earlier master-slave stage of the *Phenomenology*); but he simplifies and distorts Hegel's account by omitting the cultural, literary, and linguistic dimensions of alienation, con-

52. See Albert William Levi, "Existentialism and the Alienation of Man," Essay Ten.

centrating exclusively upon the economic, social, and—to a degree—psychological aspects of "alienated work" (*die entfremdete Arbeit*). Sartre's version is equally one-sided: it omits the cultural and literary dimensions of alienation, concentrating upon the psychological, and—to a degree—social aspects of "being for others."

As Mrs. Warnock has observed, Sartre's description of bad faith (as a sociopsychological phenomenon) partly echoes the description of alienation in early Marx.[53]

Marx had charged that Hegel confused alienation with objectification and, while praising Hegel's attempt to overcome human alienation, had rejected his parallel effort to overcome objectification.[54] For Marx, every significant action or production (*praxis*) must be an objectification, leaving its permanent, external, objective mark on nature and history. Only under capitalism, with its private ownership of the means of production, is productive objectification an alienation. Beyond capitalism alienation will disappear, but objectification will remain as a necessary and permanent aspect of all production.

It should be stressed that existential inwardness, decision, passion—so long as they lack objective expression, so long as they remain unobjectified (*unvergegenständlicht*)—are of no interest or value in Marx's eyes. The process of objectification, the act of objectifying, is incomplete so long as it has not issued in an *objectificatum*, a thing objectified, a product, an *ergon*, in one of Aristotle's senses of that term, namely, the sense in which *ergon* is related to *energeia* as product to process of actualization—as what Hegel and early Marx called *Werk* is related to what they called *Verwirklichung*. For Marx *praxis*

53. Warnock, *op. cit.*, pp. 157f. In his "phenomenology of shame" Sartre interprets "the alienation of myself" as (the effect of) an "act of being-looked-at," the result of which is that "I cause myself to learn from outside what I must be" (*BN* 263, 290). (". . . l'aliénation de moi qu'est *l'être-regardé* . . . .'"; "je me fais prendre par mon dehors ce que je dois être" [*EN* 321f, 350].)

54. Sartre alludes to Marx's critique of Hegel on this point at *CRD* 20 (English translation: *Search for a Method*, p. 13).

stands beyond existence (*hexis*) in virtue of its collective, historical, and objectifying action.

Thus, to Montaigne's question: "What have I done [i.e., made, objectified] today?" Sartre, but not Marx, can reply, with Montaigne, "What, have I not lived [i.e., existed]?" To exist, for Marx—even young Marx—is not enough. To be human, or rather to become human, one must make, must produce—which means that one must objectify, impose an enduring human shape on what is nonhuman.

In *Being and Nothingness* Sartre rejected the positive Marxist evaluation of objectification. (In the *Critique* he accepts it in a vulgarized form that equates objectification with "materialization." See Section VI.) To be sure, for Sartre objectification was never the *bête noir* that it was for Berdyaev, who saw in it a prime threat to freedom, creativity, and the "spirit." What is objectified, for Berdyaev, is alien, hostile, "intolerably banal." Still, Sartre would agree with Berdyaev's claim that "every outward action" is doomed to "tragic failure" because it necessarily involves objectification.[55] In Sartre, as in Berdyaev, the realm of the objectified is the realm of the given—of facticity, inertness, determination.

On Hegel's view, both alienation and objectification must and will be overcome through the dialectical movement of spirit; on Marx's view, alienation, but not objectification, should and will be overcome through the dialectical movement of history; for Sartre, neither alienation nor objectification can be overcome, which is another way of saying that every *ek-stase* is doomed to failure and that, in consequence, man is a "useless passion."[56]

55. Berdyaev, *Dream and Reality*, p. 39 (*Samopoznaniye*, p. 51).
56. *BN* 615. (". . . nous nous perdons en vain; l'homme est une passion inutile" [*EN* 708].) James Edie has argued that *inutile* in this context means not "useless" but noninstrumental—the sense in which Baudelaire called a poem an *objet inutile* (compare Edie's contribution to this volume, n. 41). However, it seems clear from many passages in Sartre that *inutile* means "(necessarily) unsuccessful." A *passion inutile* is one that cannot attain its object. Christ's passion—the effort, through suffering, to become human: temporal, finite, etc.—succeeded; man's parallel passion—the effort, through suffering, to become divine: eternal, infinite, etc.—must fail, since the concept of a divine Being, an *ens causa sui*, is self-contradictory. See also Sartre's

VI

SARTRE AS MARXIST

Sartre's "radical conversion"[57] from existentialism to Marxism—a doctrine which he now calls "Knowledge" (*le Savior*, always with a capital letter) and "the inescapable philosophy of our time"—is not strictly the concern of this paper. However, since I have been examining the relation of Sartre's existentialism to Hegel and Marx, and since the "conversion" might be described as a shift from the position of Husserl and Kierkegaard-Heidegger to that of Hegel and Marx-Engels, I shall comment briefly on the main doctrinal changes between *Being and Nothingness* (1943) and the *Critique de la raison dialectique*, I (1960).

Sartre has always been pro-Communist;[58] his conversion is not political but philosophical—a move from subjectivism to objectivism, from individualism to collectivism, from a theory of individual consciousness to a theory of sociohistorical *praxis*. Sartre has swung from one extreme to another; his new Marxist extreme is reductionist and often vulgarized. Despite a ponderous and complex terminology ("totalized totality"—*totalité totalisée*, the "practico-inert"—*le pratico-inerte*, "dialectic in [sociohistorical] situation"—*la dialectique située*, etc.), his position comes close to old-fashioned materialism. The individual

---

assertion that those who believe that they can reconcile or synthesize the *en-soi* and *pour-soi* are "condemned to despair," since "all human activities . . . tend to sacrifice man in order that the self-cause [i.e., God] may emerge and . . . all are on principle doomed to failure" (*BN* 627). (". . . ils sont condamnés au désespoir, car . . . les activités humaines . . . tendent toutes à sacrifier l'homme pour faire surgir la cause de soi et . . . toutes sont vouées par principe à l'échec" [*EN* 721].)

57. After graphically portraying the bitter struggle and frustration involved in all interpersonal relationships, Sartre adds enigmatically, "These considerations do not exclude the possibility of an ethics of deliverance and salvation. But this can be achieved only after a *radical conversion* which we cannot discuss here" (*BN* 412n; italics mine). ("Ces considérations n'excluent pas la possibilité d'une morale de la délivrance et du salut. Mais celle-ci doit être atteinte au terme d'une *conversion radicale* dont nous ne pouvons parler ici" [*EN* 484n; italics mine].)

58. Iris Murdoch shrewdly notes that Sartre is "infected . . . with a certain Trotskyite romanticism, the nostalgia for the perpetual revolution" (*op. cit.*, p. 41).

is no longer an agent, or *Dasein*, or *réalité-humaine*,[59] but an "organism"—an organism that suffers, runs risks, acts dialectically, "interiorizes" inorganic structures, "materializes itself," etc. Man is now a "material being" (*être matériel*), member of a "material group" (*ensemble matériel*) (*CRD* 166). The world is entirely material; "matter alone holds meanings" ("la matière seule compose les significations") (*CRD* 245).[60] Sartre expresses complete agreement with Marx's statement that the "ideal" (i.e., the "mental" and/or "conceptual") is nothing but the "material, inverted and translated in the human head."[61]

Marx himself was *not* an ontological materialist, as I have argued elsewhere; rather, he was an "economic objectivist," who often confused the terms and concepts 'economic' and 'material'. Sartre as a Marxist materialist comes close not to Marx himself, whether "old" or "young," but rather to Engels, Plekhanov, and Lenin.

Sartre's version of economic theory is almost a caricature, not so much of Marx as of Adam Smith and Ricardo. What sets human history in motion, generating conflict among individuals and groups, is the "contingent but ineluctable [!]" fact of "material [i.e., economic] scarcity."[62] However, the main thrust of the *Critique* is not economic but sociological. Sartre offers an

59. Robert Cumming considers *réalité-humaine* (a much-used term in *EN*) to be Sartre's rendering of Heidegger's *Dasein*. Compare Robert D. Cumming (ed.), *The Philosophy of Jean-Paul Sartre* (New York: 1965), p. 115n.

60. The bulk of the *Critique* remains untranslated. *Search for a Method*, trans. Hazel Barnes (New York: 1963), contains only the introductory essay (181 pp. in English). The Cumming volume includes sixty-two additional English pages (*op. cit.*, pp. 421–83), translated by Starr and James Atkinson. Aside from its turgid, prolix, and repetitive style, the *Critique* is visually forbidding: the type is small, and the pages crowded (fifty lines per page); there are few divisions in the text, relatively few paragraph divisions. Many "paragraphs" are three or four pages long; at least one is more than six pages long (*CRD* 218–24)!

61. Marx wrote: "Bei mir ist . . . das Ideelle nichts andres als das im Menschenkopf umgesetzte und übersetzte Materielle (*Das Kapital*, I: in Karl Marx, Friedrich Engels, *Werke*, XXIII [E. Berlin: 1962], 27). Sartre quotes a rather free French translation: "Pour moi, le monde des idées n'est que le monde matériel transposé et traduit dans l'esprit [sic] humain" (*CRD* 239, n. 3).

62. "Instead of the metaphor of indigestion in *Nausea*, we are faced with actual hunger" (Cumming, *op. cit.*, p. 41).

involved theory of (atomic, disintegrated, merely "serial") *collectives*—characteristic of capitalist society—and of their supersession by (cohesive, integrated, "nonserial") *groups*—under "socialism." Sartre's position seems to be a synthesis of Tönnies and Marx: *Gemeinschaft* succeeds *Gesellschaft* through the historical struggle of classes!

Sartre's attitude toward objectification is now close to that of Marx, both young and old (see Section V), and thus close to the position which in *Being and Nothingness* he had repudiated, as entailing the "dogma of the serious [i.e., of the self-righteous and pompous]": "Marx," he wrote then, "proposed the original dogma of the serious when he asserted the priority of object over subject."[63] Like the appeal to determinism, the "spirit of seriousness" involves bad faith. (Cf. *BN* 626; *EN* 721.)

Feasting on historical humble pie, Sartre declares the existential position that he had elaborated in *Being and Nothingness* to have been only an "ideology," in the special and pejorative sense of "a parasitical system living on the margin of Knowledge [i. e., of Marxism], which at first it opposed but into which today it seeks to be integrated."[64]

In fact, what we see in Volume I of the *Critique* is not an "integration" of existentialism into Marxism. Rather, the doctrinaire position of Engels and late Marx—*le Savoir*—has simply "swallowed up existentialism."[65]

VII

CONCLUSION

My conclusions may be summarized briefly under three heads:

(1) Although Sartre was stimulated by Hegel's *Phenomenology* and by Marx's 1844 *Manuscripts*, he both modified and

---

63. *BN* 580. ("Marx a posé le dogme premier du serieux lorsqu'il a affirmé la priorité de l'objet sur le sujet . . . " [*EN* 669].)

64. *Search for a Method*, p. 8. ("C'est un système parasitaire qui vit en marge du Savoir qui s'y est opposé d'abord et qui, aujourd'hui, tente de s'y intégrer" [*CRD* 18].)

65. Warnock, *op. cit.*, p. 176.

misinterpreted key points in Hegel's and Marx's thought—perhaps deliberately, certainly not without precedent (especially the precedent of Kojève's Hegel-commentary). Sartre's is a truncated dialectic; it lacks synthesis and reconciliation and is thus fundamentally un-Hegelian even though it is formulated in explicitly Hegelian categories and concepts.

(2) Sartre takes what for Hegel were low-level, partial, one-sided, abstract$_H$ phases of a continuing dialectical process and lifts them into permanent universality—e.g., alienation, self-alienation, the struggle with the "other," the project of mutual enslavement.

Like Marx, Sartre omits the *cultural* dimension of alienation, which had been central in Hegel's own account, in the *Phenomenology*, of "spirit alienated from itself."

(3) In attempting to assimilate young Marx's theory of alienation, Sartre effected two distortions: first, as he did with Hegel, Sartre treated alienation not as something phenomenologically or historically mediatable and overcomable, but as a fixed and uneliminable feature of *la condition humaine*. Second, he overlooked Marx's insistence on the positive, trans-historical character of objectification, a theme radically incompatible with Sartrean (or any other) existentialism. He tended, as many Marxists have tended—especially among the contemporary existentializing revisionists in Poland, Czechoslovakia, and Yugoslavia—to convert the young Marx into a protoexistentialist. But the youngest possible Marx was in fact no more of an existentialist than the Hegel of the *Phenomenology*—which is to say, he was not an existentialist at all in any meaningful sense of that term.

Since his conversion of Marxism, Sartre, in stressing the (externalizing) objectification of sociohistorical *praxis*, has been forced, in effect if not in so many words, to renounce his earlier existentialist emphasis on the subjectivity of free individuals. His own existentialism has been organically absorbed into his Marxism.

Essay Six

Sartre as Phenomenologist and as Existential Psychoanalyst

JAMES M. EDIE*

There is some question about the place to which Jean-Paul Sartre is entitled in contemporary philosophy. He is a scandalous man, a "Communist," an advocate of violence, an anti-American, a man possessed of a white hot hatred for the bourgeoisie, apparently (on the testimony of his enemies) a disagreeable and inconstant friend, a "litterateur" who mixes a highly idiosyncratic theory of society and history into his philosophical deductions and who seems to confuse his remarkable gift for illustrating the "viscosity," the meaninglessness, the obscenity, the pettiness of human life, with philosophical insight. As Philip Thody has pointed out,[1] his continual injection of descriptions of "physical

* Department of Philosophy, Northwestern University, Evanston, Illinois.

1. Philip Thody, *Jean-Paul Sartre, A Literary and Political Study* (London: 1960), p. 17. This very legitimate and restrained observation is, however, followed by an incredible passage, written with a straight face and without irony: "Voltaire criticized Pascal's arguments in favor of Christianity by pointing out that they were based upon the experience of a desperately sick man. On a much lower level, it is possible to do the same thing in the case of Kierkegaard and Sartre. If Kierkegaard had been brought up by a moderately reasonable father with intelligent ideas on religion, his whole attitude to God and to his own sense of sin would have been radically different, and his attitude towards life much less a philosphy of despair. If Sartre—for reasons which are at the moment impossible to ascertain—did not at one period of his life experience existence as physically nauseating, his early philosophy would likewise have been much closer to the conclusions of common-sense." It is one thing for Professor A. J. Ayer to make the rather pompous observation that Sartre's examples "do not correspond empirically

obsessions" into philosophical discussion makes it difficult for the English or American reader either to follow his arguments or to sympathize with his conclusions. This is remarkably illustrated by the reaction of many contemporary British and American philosophers to the works of Sartre. They see in Sartre a "major," if rather too morbid and personally objectionable, novelist *and playwright but *not a philosopher,* at least in the commonsensical British sense of the term. At best he is recognized as a "moralist," a twentieth-century Voltaire, even as a "man of good will," but, after all, as a writer who cannot on the whole distinguish rhetoric from logic and who is too obsessed and tormented by the "human condition" to think clearly or to achieve the kind of impartial rational lucidity that is the union card of philosophers.

On the other hand it is a fact of contemporary history that Sartre is the person who more than any other has "domesticated"

---

to the way most people behave" (*Horizon,* August, 1945, pp. 101–10). It is another thing for a perceptive critic like Philip Thody to give way to such pontifical banalities of British "common-sense" as these. We are again brought back to the observation that the moral experience of British philosophers—or at least that portion of it which they consider fit to examine—is excessively narrow. Is it really *evident* that the thought of Kierkegaard and Sartre can be explained by certain hypothetical obsessional traits read into them in this manner? What are, in fact, the "intelligent ideas on religion" which would have saved Kierkegaard from despair? What, indeed, are the experiences that Sartre ought to have had to save his philosophy for British common-sense? American writers are more likely to conclude their summaries of Sartre's ideas with a piece of vapid moralizing such as: "Incidentally, the kind of experiences with which [Sartre's analysis] are concerned should not be overlooked in an admittedly crazy world." (Quentin Lauer, *The Triumph of Subjectivity* [New York: 1958], p. 179.) In his book *Jean-Paul Sartre* (New York: 1962), p. 24, Maurice Cranston warns us that the English translations of Sartre's short stories and novels have been "carefully bowdlerized out of respect for Anglo-Saxon sensibilities." But the question is: What precisely is the *evidential value* of these "Anglo-Saxon sensibilities" which require that we be spared a direct exposure to Sartre's prose and which force us, if we are to follow his thought, to return to the original French? Is there some intrinsic reason why "Anglo-Saxon" philosophers of moral experience must restrict themselves to the world "in which people play cricket, cook cakes, make simple decisions, remember their childhood and go to the circus" and exclude the adult world "in which they commit sins, fall in love, say prayers or join the Communist Party" (Iris Murdoch, *Sartre, Romantic Rationalist* [New Haven: 1959], p. 42)?

the German phenomenology of Edmund Husserl and created what is now called the "second school of phenomenology," i. e., French phenomenology; that he is not an irrationalist at all but a "rationalist" fully in the tradition of Descartes and the entire French tradition of "reflexive analysis"; that though there is a continuity of themes and even of terminology which binds his literary productions to his more strictly philosophical works, these latter stand apart as highly original and highly technical discussions of otherwise distinguishable philosophical problems. Very few personages in the history of philosophy have been both major playwrights and technical philosophers as well; Sartre's very versatility is a cause of suspicion to contemporary academic philosophers.[2]

The purpose of this study is to present Sartre as a "phenomenologist" and as an "existential psychoanalyst." Though I believe him to be an authentic philosopher, we must put both of these titles in quotation marks, because on the one hand Sartre is a phenomenologist like no other[3] and bases his own phenomenological investigations on a rather personal reading of Husserl while on the other hand the method that he calls "existential psychoanalysis" was invented by himself, and, up to now, he has been its only practitioner. There is even some question as to whether the method is not so highly idiosyncratic as to be unemployable by anyone but himself. But this is not to question his results or to ascribe to them a merely autobiographical value. It is to determine their wider value that we propose to examine them in some detail. In this paper I intend to illustrate Sartre's method and results by an examination of his theory of consciousness, first as he establishes it in a general way through a phenom-

2. Of course, not everything that Sartre has written can be characterized as "great" literature, and though his early short stories are remarkably successful, his novels are not. However, among his plays there are several that clearly rank with the "great" literature of the twentieth century, chiefly: *The Flies, Dirty Hands, The Devil and the Good Lord,* and *The Condemned of Altona.*

3. Herbert Spiegelberg in *The Phenomenological Movement* (The Hague: 1960), II, 445ff., gives a judicious account of the sense in which Sartre can and cannot be called a "phenomenologist."

enological investigation of typical behaviors and activities of
consciousness and, then, as he makes a more concrete application
of his general theory of consciousness in existential psychoanalysis.

I

SARTRE AS PHENOMENOLOGIST

Up to Merleau-Ponty there is almost no French philosopher of
the modern period who was not, in the most fundamental sense,
"Cartesian." Sartre is no exception. In his literary works he
stands out for the acuity and subtlety of his psychological descriptions. In the philosophical themes with which he is concerned, in his distrust of the body and the emotions, in his very
style, and even in his metaphysical system with its radical
dichotomization of being into the for-itself and the in-itself, we
find a unifying strand of Cartesian rationalism. Taken globally,
it has been characteristic of French philosophy since Descartes, of
the school of "reflexive analysis," and of French literature in
general to be centered on the experience of the *cogito*, on psychological experience in all its manifestations and in all its vagaries.
Hence the psychological richness and depth which distinguish
French philosophical speculation from other schools of thought
and give it its distinctive flavor. Unlike Kant, for instance, who
approached experience from the aspect of its general validity and
necessary conditions, French philosophers from Descartes to
Sartre have been concerned mainly with questions of fact—not
with the transcendental conditions of thought, but with the actually thinking and experiencing *cogito*; not with the necessary
but with the sufficient conditions; not with the formal but with
the "material" structures of consciousness. Any such generalization as this is of course subject to correction as applied to individual cases and, like all generalizations, becomes more and more
dubious as we descend from the general characterization to the
particular instances—in this case the particular French philosophers. Yet it seems to have a general validity, and quite likely
the success of Husserl's thought in France and its influence

on Sartre in particular are due to the fact that Husserl is the most "French" of all German thinkers. Like Descartes, he begins with *Die Urtatsache, Das Wunder aller Wunder: that conscious-ness is.* And, as is well known, he at one point reformulated his entire philosophical enterprise as a meditation on the medita-tions of Descartes and admitted that one might fairly call his phenomenology a "neo-Cartesianism."[4]

Sartre's reflections on the *experience of consciousness* gravitate around two central poles, both of which he derives from Descartes and Husserl and both of which he colors with his own personal experience: (a) the experience of radical autonomy from being, of freedom, a personal escape from the threat of being or becom-ing a determined and determinate "thing" and (b) the recogni-tion that consciousness has no single essence, that it cannot be defined like other realities but only described in its polymorphous variety.[5]

a. THE EXPERIENCE OF NOTHINGNESS (I.E., OF BEING CONSCIOUS).

To begin on the autobiographical level—that is to say, on the level of the description of immediate experience—it seems true to say that Sartre was haunted by the problem of Being and Nothingness from early in life. He describes very well the "threat of being" (which for him is a peculiar form of the threat of *determinism*) for his consciousness. He is not, of course, the only philosopher who reached his maturity through anguished reflection on the problem of freedom and determinism,[6] but in

4. Edmund Husserl, *Cartesian Meditations,* trans. Dorion Cairns (The Hague: 1960), p. 1: "Accordingly one might almost call transcendental phenom-enology a neo-Cartesianism, even though it is obliged—and precisely by its radical development of Cartesian motifs—to reject nearly all of the well-known doctrinal content of the Cartesian philosophy."

5. The chief philosophical value of Iris Murdoch's short book on Sartre (*op. cit.,* pp. 79ff.) is to have called attention to this similarity between Sartre's phenomenology of consciousness and Ryle's theory of mind. It might be remarked that Descartes himself conceived of consciousness as being polymorphously diverse when he said that he understood a "thinking thing" to be one which doubts, understands, conceives, affirms, denies, wills, re-fuses, imagines, as well as feels. It is evident, however, that this is not yet Sartre's own conception of the "behaviors" of consciousness.

6. I have in mind chiefly William James. Compare "Notes on the Philo-sophical Anthropology of William James" in *Invitation to Phenomenology,* ed. James M. Edie (Chicago: 1965), pp. 130–31.

him it takes the form of an obsessional fear that he could be
turned into a thing and thereby lose freedom, that he was, perhaps, ultimately only a "thing." This threat occurs on two levels:
on the level of bodily existence in which we exercise our consciousness as a nature in the midst of nature and on the level of
social existence in which we attempt to identify our consciousness
with our emotions, our ideas, our social roles, and thus reduce
ourselves to the thinglike and determined reality (the "facticity")
of our particular egological situation.

The first, or more physical, form of this threat to the autonomy
of consciousness was first described by Sartre in *Nausea*.
"Nausea," for Sartre, designates the everpresent feeling I have,
as a consciousness, of being embedded in being through my
body; it is the sickening awareness of my existence as a part of an
impersonal, unconscious nature. It also designates, like "boredom," "ennui," etc., a route of privileged access to the experience
of the brute facticity of pure *being-in-itself*. Sartre's description is
worth recalling:

> The chestnut tree pressed itself against my eyes. Green blight
> covered it halfway up; the bark, black and swollen, looked like
> boiled leather. The sound of the water in the Masqueret Fountain
> trickled in my ears, made a nest there, filled them with sighs; my
> nostrils overflowed with a green, putrid odor. All things, tenderly,
> were letting themselves exist like weary women . . . they were
> sprawling in front of each other, abjectly confessing their exist-
> ence. I realized there was no mean between non-existence and
> this swooning abundance. If you existed, you had to exist to
> excess, to the point of moldiness, bloatedness, obscenity. . . . We
> were a heap of existences, uncomfortable, embarrassed at ourselves,
> we hadn't the slightest reason to be there, none of us, each one
> confused, vaguely alarmed, felt superfluous in relation to the
> others. . . . And I myself—soft, weak, obscene, digesting, jug-
> gling with dismal thoughts—*I, too, was superfluous*. . . . I dreamed
> vaguely of killing myself to wipe out at least one of these super-
> fluous existences. But even my death would have been *super-
> fluous*.
> . . . I was *superfluous* for eternity.
>
> . . . The trees were floating. Gushing toward the sky? Rather
> collapsing. At any moment I expected to see the tree trunks shrivel
> up, like weary penises, crumple up, fall on the ground, softly

folded in a black heap. They didn't want to exist, only they could not help themselves. . . . Tired and old, they kept on existing, reluctantly, simply because they were too weak to die, because death could only come to them from the outside. . . . Every existing thing is born without reason, goes on living out of weakness, and dies by accident. . . . I hated this ignoble messiness. Piling up to the sky, spilling over, filling everything with its gelatinous slither . . . I choked with rage at this gross absurd being. . . . I felt with weariness that I had no way of understanding. . . . I had learned all I could about existence.[7]

In *Being and Nothingness* Sartre describes "being-in-itself" as absurd, unjustifiable, unfounded, meaningless, opaque, massive, nontransparent: like the well-rounded sphere of Parmenides it has no emptiness or holes, no negativity; it is pure positivity. *It is what it is* and that is about all that can be said about it. Except that it is a threat to consciousness. Consciousness tends to get bogged down in being. There is *too much* of it. It is soft, warm, sticky, sweet, suffocating, viscous, corpulent, flabby, excessive. We cannot com-prehend it; it stands there dumb, in bad faith.

Thus, Sartre likes to describe the activity of consciousness as an effort, a *conatus*, to become unstuck, unglued from this sticky mass and to take its distance, to assert its independence of being. Consciousness alone, though embedded in being through its body, experiences itself to be not a thing but the consciousness of things, not a being but consciousness of being, i. e., a *no-thing*, separated from being by *nothing* but itself. Sartre sees both Descartes and Husserl as his predecessors in this theory of consciousness, and he has not the least scruple over interpreting their thought in his own sense. In 1946 he edited a selection from the writings of Descartes[8] which is highly instructive, not as an historical introduction to the thought of Descartes, to be sure, but as a synopsis of the "Sartrean passages" in his thought. To this collection he prefaced an essay entitled "Cartesian Freedom" in which he discusses Descartes' "splendid

7. *Nausea*, as given in Robert D. Cumming's improved translation, *The Philosophy of Jean-Paul Sartre* (New York: 1965), pp. 60–68.
8. *Descartes*, Introduction et choix par Jean-Paul Sartre (Paris: 1946).

humanistic affirmation of creative freedom."[9] It was the merit of Descartes, according to Sartre, to have discovered that meaning ("truth") and value enter the world only through man and are not there "as things" independently of human consciousness: "No one had shown that freedom does not come from man as he is, as a fullness of existence among other fullnesses in a world without lacunae, but rather from man as he is *not*. . . ."[10]

Descartes realized that the experience of freedom does not result from acts of an "indifferent" will but, more fundamentally, from the consciousness of "autonomy" and "solitude" in the face of the positivity of essences, of objective truth, of the universe created by God. Man alone has the ability to say *yes* or *no* in and to the universe. Heidegger, says Sartre, thought he was being original when he said that no man can die for another, but Descartes had said, earlier, that no man can understand for another. We will return later to Sartre's consideration of consciousness as freedom. Here let us dwell momentarily on the preoccupation with the "negativity" or "nothingness" of consciousness which seems to have preoccupied Sartre enormously from early in life and in which he finds the root phenomenon of freedom.

There is a passage in one of Sartre's early short stories, *The Childhood of a Leader,* which describes a youthful preoccupation:

> Lucien, who had been given an "A" for his dissertation on "Morality and Science" dreamed of writing a "Treatise on Nothingness" and he imagined that people, reading it, would disappear one after the other like vampires at cockcrow. Before beginning this treatise, he wanted the advice of the Baboon, his philosophy prof. "Excuse me, sir," he said at the end of a class, "could anyone claim that we don't exist?" The Baboon said no. "Goghito," he said, "ergo zum. You exist because you doubt your existence." Lucien was not convinced but he gave up his work.[11]

9. From the English translation of "Cartesian Freedom" in *Literary and Philosophical Essays* (New York: 1962), p. 185.

10. *Ibid.,* p. 191.

11. "The Childhood of a Leader" in *The Wall and Other Stories,* trans. Lloyd Alexander (New York: 1948), pp. 187–88.

The heavy-handed irony of this passage, which does not even spare the professor's pronunciation of Latin, gives it an almost autobiographical flavor. Lucien had for months been preoccupied with the question of whether he really existed, of what he was, and of why he was what he was. His father had told him he was the son of a boss and that he would grow up to be a boss, but Lucien didn't *feel* like a boss, he didn't feel like *anything*, and he wondered. Eventually he does choose to be *something*, and his choice is one that Sartre finds execrable, but before this development his experience is one of emptiness, aimlessness, nothingness, the experience of not being *any* determinate *thing*; consequently, he wondered if he really existed.

On the one hand we are immersed in being, but through consciousness of being we distinguish ourselves from being and put being at a distance from us. Sartre says that he owes to Husserl the full realization of the nature of the *absolute difference* that simultaneously distinguishes and unites the two regions of consciousness and being.[12] According to Husserl all consciousness is consciousness *of* something, and Sartre emphasizes the transitive value of the "of." "This means," he writes, "that transcendence is the constitutive structure of consciousness; that is, that consciousness is *born oriented towards* a being which is not itself."[13] In an early article on Husserl[14] Sartre describes his

12. This is not, strictly speaking, Husserl's own theory of intentionality but Sartre's "realistic" interpretation of it. He is aware of this alteration and already in *The Transcendence of the Ego* (originally published in 1936, English translation by Forrest Williams and Robert Kirkpatrick [New York: 1957], p. 41) accuses Husserl of abandoning and destroying "the fruitful definition of intentionality"—i. e., the one Sartre accepts—in favor of an idealistic philosophy of immanence. Compare Spiegelberg, *op. cit.*, pp. 451ff.

13. *Being and Nothingness*, trans. Hazel Barnes (New York: 1956), p. lxi. Note here one of the rare mistranslations in the Barnes translation; I have followed the correction suggested by Spiegelberg, *op. cit.*, p. 488.

14. "Une idée fondamentale de Husserl" (1939) in *Situations I* (Paris: 1947), pp. 31–35. "Against the digestive philosophy of empirio-criticism," he writes, "of neo-kantianism, against all 'psychologism,' Husserl never tires of repeating that we cannot dissolve things in consciousness. . . . Husserl sees in consciousness an irreducible fact which cannot be rendered by any physical image, except, perhaps, the rapid and obscure image of bursting forth. To

discovery of the doctrine of the intentionality of consciousness as a liberating experience: it enabled him, finally, to escape the threat of thinghood and to "eject" literally everything from consciousness—to see that consciousness is neither a thing nor a container of things.[15] Such a notion both safeguards the uniqueness of the *for-itself* as independent of all modes of being, as a *nonsubstantial absolute,* and at the same time guarantees the reality of things independent of all consciousness. "To say that consciousness is consciousness of something means that for consciousness there is no being outside of that precise obligation to be a revealing intuition of something, i.e., of a transcendent being.... It can be qualified only as a revealing intuition or it is nothing."[16] The two realms are utterly distinct: neither can be reduced to the other, neither can be derived from the other, each is its own justification. And yet there is a *de facto* dialectical relationship between the two. All being is *relative* to consciousness, not *as being,* but *as known,* and all consciousness is intentional, i.e., is consciousness *of* being. Of itself consciousness is "nonsubstantial"; its only "substance" and "content" come from its objects; it is a pure intentionality.

Sartre's major work, *Being and Nothingness,* is an attempt to "reconcile" being (the object) and consciousness (the subject) by describing the dialectical relationships that in fact pertain between these two regions. Sartre uses the word "being" to designate these two distinct yet inseparable realities, but it is clear that *being* "in the strong sense of the term" is wholly on the side of the *in-itself.* The being of consciousness is "the being

---

know, is 'to burst out towards,' to tear oneself away from the clammy gastric depths to slip outside of oneself over there, towards what is not oneself. . . . Now, consciousness is purified, it is as clear as a strong wind, there is nothing left in it, except a movement of escaping itself, a slipping outside of itself. If, by an impossible chance, you were to get 'inside' a consciousness, you would be seized by a whirlwind and thrown back outside . . . for consciousness has no 'inside.' . . . Here we are delivered from Proust. Delivered at the same time from the 'interior life. . . .' "

15. Compare Spiegelberg, *op. cit.,* p. 451, and Francis Jeanson, *Sartre par lui-même* (Paris: 1956), p. 187, also cited by Spiegelberg.

16. *Being and Nothingness, op. cit.,* p. lxi.

of nothingness." Consciousness must be defined as the reality that "is not what it is and is what it is not."

To understand the meaning of this paradoxical definition it is necessary to recapitulate Sartre's progressive "ejection" of all beings from consciousness. When we reflect on the *cogito*, what do we find? he asks. Descartes and Husserl found both an *ego* and *objects of thought* (*ego cogito cogitata*). But, clearly, says Sartre, we *are* not our objects of thought, nor are they "within" us as the ancient alimentary epistemologies claimed. The first step in Sartre's purification of the *cogito* is not dissimilar in intent and in results to Gilbert Ryle's criticism of theories of mind which see the mind as constituted of an "inner world." Sartre says there is no "interior life"; consciousness is entirely *voué au monde*. It does not assimilate objects but passes over them like a "clear wind" without contaminating, changing, or even touching them. Being remains exactly what it was without consciousness; consciousness adds *nothing* to being, only a relationship to itself. There are neither pictures nor images nor forms in the mind; all its objects are outside it.

Secondly, Sartre ejects the *ego* itself from consciousness. Descartes' reflection had revealed a *res cogitans*; Husserl discovered a "transcendental ego." But again, like Ryle, Sartre ejects all these "ghosts in the machine" from consciousness. What is *new* in Sartre's interpretation of Husserl is his conception of a consciousness that is not a *me*, that is transphenomenal, prepersonal, prereflexive. He accuses Husserl of not operating the phenomenological reduction on the ego, and this, he says, is the reason for Husserl's ultimate "idealism." The ego is not the source and producer of intentionality; it is consciousness that produces the ego. My ego is an object to my consciousness just like any other (though it is more "intimate"). It appears only in fully reflexive or thematic states of awareness *as a new object*.

> My reflecting consciousness does not take itself for an object when I effect the *Cogito*. What it affirms concerns the reflected consciousness. Insofar as my reflecting consciousness is consciousness of itself, it is *non-positional* consciousness. It becomes positional only by directing itself upon the reflected consciousness

of itself before being reflected. Thus the consciousness which says *I think* is precisely not the consciousness which thinks.[17]

In short, when we reflect on consciousness we discover (1) an experience of things and (2) an experience of self. Descartes and Husserl took the latter in a personal and more or less "substantial" sense. Sartre distinguishes two levels of self-consciousness: the fully thematic consciousness *of* self, in which the ego is grasped as an object for consciousness, and the more fundamental, prethematic consciousness that never objectifies itself, that is an "operating intentionality," an impersonal spontaneity, always ahead of its own self-objectification. Such a consciousness can take itself as an object only through "retrospection"; the reflecting consciousness itself is never grasped.[18] This prepersonal consciousness *is not* anything. Its only unity comes from its continual and temporal self-appropriation of its just-completed intentional acts, which it claims as its own and designates, reflexively, with the word "me."

But even this discovery of the "transcendence of the ego" is not, for Sartre, sufficient to desubstantialize consciousness. We could still identify consciousness with its acts, its roles, its psychic states, with its emotions perhaps. Sartre wants to show that even these are "essences" or "objects" of consciousness and are not *me*, that I am cut off even from my own essence "by the nothing that I am."[19] By its very intentionality, its directedness towards a world of being which it is not, consciousness is tempted, ensnared, persuaded, to give itself a substance, to take itself for a thing. This universal tendency of consciousness to reify itself Sartre terms "bad faith." His analyses of this constant and ineluctable tend-

17. *The Transcendence of the Ego, op. cit.*, p. 45.
18. Compare Gilbert Ryle, "The Systematic Elusiveness of *I*," *The Concept of Mind* (New York: 1949), pp. 195ff; and Iris Murdoch, *op. cit.*, p. 84. Like Sartre, Ryle also relates the impossibility of self-objectification to the phenomenon of freedom.
19. *Being and Nothingness, op. cit.*, p. 39. The whole passage reads: "I do not have nor can I have recourse to any value against the fact that it is I who sustain values in being. Nothing can ensure me against myself, cut off from the world and from my essence by this nothingness which I am. I have to realize the meaning of the world and of my essence; I make my decision concerning them—without justification and without excuse."

ency are well known: Daniel in *The Age of Reason* wishes "to *be* a pederast, as an oaktree is an oaktree." Brunet says he is a Communist without reason or justification—he just *is*—he acts like a Communist, he talks like a Communist, he walks like a Communist, he looks like a Communist, he thinks Communist thoughts, he even makes love like a Communist. But Daniel is unable to coincide with his vice and Brunet is unable to coincide with his virtue. A consciousness is never a thing or the role that it plays; it is forever ahead of its past, *more* and *other than* it is, condemned to be free. A consciousness is an emptiness of being, a void, a hole in being which dreams of making itself into a thing, whose highest ambition is to become god (the perfect reconciliation of the in-itself and the for-itself in a perfectly determined state of being-what-it-is under the mode of a pure, spontaneous consciousness). But a man, on this side of the divine, must remain free and can never *be* what he *is*.[20] Consciousness "creates and supports its essence—that is, the synthetic order of

---

20. This is one of the major themes of two of Sartre's most important plays, *The Flies* and *The Devil and the Good Lord*. *The Flies*, which is in large part a debate between God (Jupiter) and Man (Orestes), reaches its climax in Orestes' defiance: "Alien to myself, I know it. Outside of nature, against nature, without excuse, without recourse save myself. But I shall not return under your law; I'm condemned to have no other law but my own. Nor shall I return to nature, where a thousand paths are marked out, all leading up to you. I can only follow my own path. For I'm a man, Jupiter, and each man must find his own way" (as cited in Cumming, *op. cit.*, p. 240). In *The Devil and the Good Lord* Goetz begins by "doing evil" because it is the only avenue of creation left open to man—"the good has already been done by God the Father"—but, towards the middle of the play, he converts and tries his hand at "doing good" and entering into an alliance with God as a "saint." Throughout both these attempts God remains silent and utterly indifferent to everything which is happening on earth. Goetz finally understands that there is neither absolute evil nor absolute good for man and that in whatever finite project he undertakes he will always be alone and without help from on high. "I killed God because he divided me from mankind," he says, ". . . I shall not allow this huge carcass to poison my human friendships; I shall tell the whole truth, if necessary. . . . The kingdom of man is beginning. . . . I shall remain alone with his empty sky over my head, since I have no other way of being among men. There is a war to fight, and I will fight it" (*The Devil and the Good Lord*, trans. Kitty Black [New York: 1960], pp. 147–49).

its possibilities."[21] If only I were what I *am*, writes Sartre, I could avoid any responsibility or censure for my actions, I could escape my freedom, but "human reality" cannot escape because it is precisely that "being which is what it is not and is not what it is."[22]

> I never am any one of my attitudes, any one of my actions. The good speaker is the one who *plays* at speaking, because he cannot *be speaking*. . . .I cannot say either that I *am* here . . . in the sense that we say "that box of matches is on the table". . . . Nor that I *am* standing, nor that I *am* seated; this would be to confuse my body with the idiosyncratic totality of which it is only one of the structures.[23]

In short, I am not being because I am always consciousness of being. I am separated from what I am precisely *by nothing*, by the abyss that consciousness inserts between my being and myself.

Finally, and in a similar way, Sartre empties consciousness of even its most intimate emotional states, moods, affections; consciousness, he says, is no more a psychological process than it is a biological process. We are sometimes caught up by feelings such as sadness, dislike, love, etc. They seem to come "from within" and define and polarize our entire relationship with the world and other persons. But Sartre shows that whenever and as soon as I can reflexively say to myself, "I am sad," or "I hate," or "I love," for instance, I have *ipso facto* operated the transcendental reduction and *am* no longer sad or hateful or in love, because I have become the consciousness of a state of being sad, of a state of being in love, and so on. My consciousness cannot *be* sad, since sadness is a state that affects the being (in this case myself) of which I am conscious.

> Phenomenology has come to teach us that *states* are objects, that an emotion as such (a love or a hatred) is a transcendent object and cannot shrink into the interior unity of a "consciousness." Consequently, if Paul and Peter both speak of Peter's love, for example, it is not true that the one speaks blindly and by analogy of that which the other apprehends in full. They

21. *Being and Nothingness, op. cit.,* p. lv.
22. *Ibid.,* p. 58.
23. *Ibid.,* p. 60.

speak of the same thing. Doubtless they apprehend it by different procedures, but these procedures are equally intuitional. And Peter's emotion is no more *certain* for Peter than for Paul.[24]

What Sartre attempts to achieve on the basis of his interpretation of Husserl's theory of intentionality is thus to "purify" consciousness of "all egological structure." He calls it a "nothing" because all physical, all psychophysiological, all psychic objects, all objective truths and values are transcendent to it.[25] There is no longer an "inner life," and consciousness is wholly a self-transcending, spontaneous activity that intends a world of meaning and value for itself.

It is at this point that we see how such a doctrine could be Sartre's answer to determinism: consciousness is so independent of being that it is a continual self-creation *ex nihilo* at each successive instant of time; nothing sustains it in being, and, like the God of the Scholastics, it sustains meaning and value in being, and if it ceases to think of them they disappear. In his analysis Sartre takes up the most compulsive, "determined" behaviors to describe what he means. He takes, for instance, the case of the gambler who has freely and sincerely decided not to gamble any more and who suddenly sees all his resolutions melt away as soon as he gets near a gaming table. To explain this by some hypothesis of "psychological determinism" would be a comfortable "attitude of excuse,"[26] but Sartre sees something else. There is, he says, no inner "struggle of reason with the passions," no inner debate, but rather, on the one hand, *the apprehension* of "not wishing to play any more," and, on the other, of "the total inefficacy of the past resolution."

> The resolution is still *me* to the extent that I realize constantly my identity with myself across the temporal flux, but it is no longer *me*—due to the fact that it has become an object *for* my consciousness. I am not subject to it, it fails in the mission which I had given it. The resolution is there still, I *am* it in the mode of not-being. What the gambler apprehends at this

24. *The Transcendence of the Ego, op. cit.,* p. 95.
25. *Ibid.,* p. 93.
26. *Being and Nothingness, op. cit.,* p. 40.

instant is again the permanent rupture with determinism: it is nothingness which separates him from himself; I should have liked so much not to gamble any more; yesterday I even had a synthetic apprehension of the situation (threatening ruin, disappointment of my relatives) as *forbidding me* to play. It seemed to me that I had established a *real barrier* . . . and now I suddenly perceive that . . . it is no more than a memory of an idea. . . . In order for it to come to my aid once more, I must remake it *ex nihilo* and freely. Not-gambling is only one of my possibilities, as the fact of gambling is another one of them, neither more or less. *I must rediscover* the fear of financial ruin. . . . It depends on me alone to lend it my flesh. . . . I perceive with anguish that *nothing* prevents me from gambling.[27]

Man is, therefore, a nothingness within being ("at the heart of being," says Sartre) and this freedom from being anything determined distinguishes him both from God (who would be a consciousness in-itself) and from pure being. Man alone is autonomous, i. e., the reality who is responsible for history and for morality.[28] This "nothingness" is at once the source of his only dignity and also of his profound anguish. Man is the "unhappy consciousness" because he is never what he is and is always what he is not.

b. THE MODALITIES OF NOTHINGNESS.

Up to now we have examined the sense of the first member of Sartre's definition of consciousness and have seen, at least roughly, what he means by saying that consciousness is not what it is (i. e., its objects, the ego, its states and affects). There remains the second part of the definition: namely, *consciousness is what*

27. *Ibid.*, p. 33.

28. In *Existentialism Is a Humanism* Sartre lays down the ethical maxims that govern both his philosophy and his literature, such as: "Thus, the first effect of existentialism is that it puts every man in possession of himself as he is, and places the entire responsibility for his existence squarely upon his own shoulders. And, when we say that man is responsible for himself, we do not mean that he is responsible only for his own individuality, but that he is responsible for all men." And later: "Those who hide from this total freedom, in a guise of solemnity or with deterministic excuses, I shall call cowards. Others, who try to show that their existence is necessary, when it is merely an accident of the appearance of the human race on earth—I shall call scum." (As given in Walter Kaufmann's edition, *Existentialism from Dostoevsky to Sartre* [New York: 1957], pp. 291, 308.)

it is not. Is it possible to characterize this negativity in a positive way? Sartre himself asks at the beginning of Part I of *Being and Nothingness*: But does this consciousness *exist*?[29] His answer is that, to be sure, consciousness *ek-sists*, not in the manner of being-in-itself but through its nihilating behaviors, through its negations that distinguish it from being and, in so doing, create the "world" as the world of human consciousness. It is in his descriptions of such nihilating activities as questioning, negating, imagining, abstracting, doubting, etc., that Sartre establishes the evidence on which his definition of consciousness is based and presents us with his phenomenology of consciousness. We cannot do more here than to recall some of these analyses briefly.

Sartre begins with *questioning* or *contesting* as the distinguishing characteristic through which consciousness becomes "unstuck" from being and experiences itself as (1) a "lack" or a *nihilation* of being and (2) as the source of *negativities (négatités)* which it "secretes" through a continual activity of nihilating. Being does not question itself; it *is* what it is. But consciousness is precisely "*a being such that in its being, its being is in question in so far as this being implies a being other than itself.*"[30] Questioning is thus the fundamental attitude of consciousness towards being. It is a *negative* attitude, opposed to the positivity of being.

> [Consciousness] must arise in the world as a *No:* it is as a No that the slave first apprehends the master, or that the prisoner who is trying to escape sees the guard who is watching him. There are even men (e. g. caretakers, overseers, jailers), whose social reality is entirely that of a No upon the earth. Others so

29. *Being and Nothingness, op. cit.,* p. 29.
30. *Ibid.,* p. lxii. Contrary to popular belief the number of neologisms invented by Sartre is not great; his philosophical writings are, on the contrary, singularly free of jargon. The two most important neologisms he employs to explain his theory of consciousness are: *néantiser* ("to nihilate") and *négatité* ("negativity" understood as the noematic correlate of an act of nihilation). It is unfortunate that some English translators have not seen fit to follow Hazel Barnes's judicious decision to translate *néantiser* as "nihilate" (*op. cit.,* p. 17, note) and have, instead, used the erroneous and misleading "annihilate" and other unfortunate circumlocutions.

as to make the No a part of their very subjectivity, establish
their human personality as a perpetual negation. This is the
meaning and function of what Scheler calls "the man of resentment"—the man who is a No.[31]

But there are subtler behaviors, he continues, which reveal
that consciousness is the being whose nature "is to be conscious of
the nothingness of its being." These are noetic attitudes of in-
terrogation such as abstracting, isolating, imagining, doubting,
denying, which have as their objects *négatités*. In a sense, yet to
be refined, Sartre thus posits a number of negativities as the
objective correlates of certain noetic acts of consciousness which
he terms "acts of nihilation." *The negative* thus has a much
wider noematic and noetic status in Sartre's philosophy than in
classical philosophies, and it includes the experience of absence,
of otherness, of possibilities and potentialities, of the unreal and
the imaginary, of the "ideal" reality of the objects of inference
and demonstration, even of moral and physical evil, of psychophysical limitations and contingency. The noetic attitude operative in all such experiences—though they are of an extremely
complex and polymorphous variety—is that of *nihilation*.

What does this mean? Perhaps we can best approach this
fundamental structure of consciousness, as Sartre himself does, by
generalizing the conclusions of his phenomenology of the imagination.[32] He shows in these studies that "imagining" is typical
of *all* acts of consciousness; it is the concrete activity of producing *the unreal* on the background of the real.

The imaginary appears "on the foundation of the world," but
reciprocally all apprehension of the real as world implies a

31. *Ibid.*, p. 47.
32. Sartre's two books on the phenomenology of the imagination (*L'
Imagination*, 1936, and *L'Imaginaire*, 1940) constitute his greatest single
contribution to phenomenology and represent his most original philosophical work. There is a good English translation of *Imagination* by Forrest
Williams (University of Michigan Press: 1962), marred only by a very
occasional lapse, but the English translation of *L'Imaginaire* under the
title *Psychology of Imagination* (New York: Philosophical Books, 1948) is
probably the most misleading and incompetent translation of Sartre which
has ever been done. Given the extreme importance and value of this work
for understanding Sartre's philosophy, this translation is most unfortunate.

hidden surpassing towards the imaginary. All imaginative consciousness uses the world as the nihilated foundation of the
imaginary and reciprocally all consciousness of the world calls
forth and motivates an imaginative consciousness as grasped from
the particular *meaning* of the situation.[33]

To be sure, all consciousness is consciousness *of something*,
but in order to be conscious of something in particular, in the
concrete, I must *nihilate* all the rest. Sartre likes to repeat the
dictum of Spinoza: *Omnis determinatio est negatio*. This nihilating determination of consciousness is operative, he says, not only
on the level of abstract thought (in which I must always isolate
some property or quality that does not "exist apart" in the concrete) but also on the level of actual perception in which all
perceived objects are organized as figures that emerge from and
are "detached from" their ground. When I arrive at the Café
Bonaparte expecting to find my friend Pierre and do not find
him, *I experience an absence*. I look around the bar, at the
bartender, at the customers, at the tables, and say to myself: "He
is not here." But my intuition of his absence is prior to any
explicit judgment, and this experience motivates my judgment.
It is not that I discover his absence in some precise spot in the
bar; Pierre is absent from the *whole* café. In itself the café with
its fixtures, its odors, its clients, is wholly positive; but in my
particular experience of the absence of Pierre, the whole of the
café as I experience it is *nihilated*, i.e., becomes the ground from
which Pierre emerges in the mode of being absent. This is not an
activity of "categorial" or creative imagination by which I con-
jure up some image or "species" of Pierre numerically distinct
from Pierre himself. Pierre indeed exists somewhere and I intend
him as existing in that place (wherever it is), but I experience
this existence as not being *here*. It is because Pierre is absent
that I can intuit his absence as a possible presence—and this is,
for Sartre, due to the fundamental, *operating* intentionality of a
prejudgmental imagining consciousness. Thanks to my imagination Pierre can be experienced as an absence that can become the
focal point of my consciousness on the background of the really

33. *Psychology of Imagination, op. cit.*, p. 273. Translation corrected.

perceived café. Imagination is, therefore, the faculty of the unreal, of nihilation par excellence, by which I "perceive" something under the mode of its not being present. Or, to turn to
actual perception, when I perceive something as a determinate
object on the background of the world as a synthetic totality, I
must nihilate the world as a totality, i. e., I must treat it as
ground, in order to perceive this object as distinct from it. Our
world, as the correlate of perceiving, imagining, thinking consciousness, is, says Sartre, constructed in such a way that we always pose the unreal on the ground of the real and the real on
the ground of the unreal owing to a nihilating activity of consciousness. What consciousness adds to being is, thus, "the
unreal."

Sartre calls his realm of "the unreal" *nothingness,* as opposed
to being-in-itself (which is utterly independent of consciousness). But it is important to note that, though Sarte likes to play
on the word "nothingness," this "nothingness" is not an "absolute
nothingness" (the *nihilum absolutum* of Parmenides and the
Scholastics) but rather *the objective correlate of nihilating consciousness.* It is, he says, the "infra-structure" of the real, which
does not exist *in-itself* but is produced and "held in being" by
consciousness. This is why we must distinguish being-in-itself
from the "world." *In itself* being is wholly positive, without gaps
or holes, without possibilities, without any negativity. But
being, as the object of consciousness, i. e., as the world, is structured by consciousness and, as such, is composed of both being
and nothingness (*négatités*). In order to perceive any particular
object in the world, I must de-realize the rest of my perceptual
field, and, conversely, the possibility of the de-realization of particular objects enables me to perceive such objects on the background of the real *even in their absence.* This is not to say that
there is for Sartre such a thing as an intuition of nothingness;
intuition is always *of something.* The unreal is always grasped
on the background of the real, and the real is always grasped on
the background of the unreal. The nihilating "detachment" of
objects from a ground, which is operative in both perception and
in imagination, is strictly correlative in each case: "the imaginary"

is always given *in and with* the real. The experience of nothingness, i. e., the unreal, the absent, the potential, etc., is always given *in and with* the experience of being—as the particular contribution of consciousness. Moreover, consciousness can never nihilate being-in-itself, or being as a totality. An act of nihilation is the "negating" or the "isolating" (or the "questioning") of a particular being on the basis of the totality of being; it in no way affects being-in-itself. It is *an experiential structure* of being which has its sole foundation in consciousness.

In the history of philosophy, from the time of the Scholastics to Bergson, it has been customary to take the "is not" in negative judgments as a pure operation of judging consciousness, a production of the mind with a foundation in reality but devoid of any objective correlate *(non-ens superadditur enti)*. Sartre proposes a more "realistic" account of nothingness. In asking a question, he writes, *there exists* for the questioner the permanent *objective possibility* of a negative reply. This "objective possibility" is not, however, *being;* it is a *négatité,* being *as experienced,* being *as nihilated.*

> In relation to this possibility the questioner by the very fact that he is questioning, posits himself as in a state of indetermination; he *does not know* whether the reply will be affirmative or negative. Thus the question is a bridge set up between two non-beings: the non-being of knowing in man, the possibility of non-being of being in transcendent being.[34]

Rather than take the negative judgment (which is a derived and "subsequent" act of consciousness) as the foundation of nothingness, Sartre attempts to show that there is a prepredicative experience of nothingness which precedes and is prior to any judgment of fully reflexive consciousness. Non-being is always experienced with reference to some human expectation that is neither primarily cognitive nor judgmental. The question is formulated in an interrogative judgment, but questioning itself is prejudgmental and even precognitive. I can question by a look, by a gesture.

34. *Being and Nothingness, op. cit.,* p. 5.

If my car breaks down, it is the *carburetor,* the *spark plugs,* etc., that I question. If my watch stops, I can question the watchmaker about the cause of the stopping, but it is the various mechanisms of the watch that the watchmaker will in turn question. What I expect from the carburetor, what the watchmaker expects from the works of the watch, is not a judgment; it is a disclosure of being on the basis of which we can make a judgment. And if I expect a disclosure of being, I am prepared at the same time for the eventuality of a disclosure of non-being. If I question the carburetor, it is because I consider it possible that "there is nothing there". . . .[35]

For Sartre, the very intentionality of consciousness is founded on the presence of nothingness in experience, on the pervasive possibility of the expectations and "empty intentions" of consciousness being disappointed. To perceive a city as *destructible* is to perceive it as it *is not,* but as it *could be.* In itself the city is neither destructible nor indestructible; it is consciousness which discovers such potentialities in things and, in so doing, confers on beings a meaning and a value for consciousness. Even for the city that is in fact destroyed, for example, by a tornado, *in itself* the storm has only brought about a rearrangement and a redistribution of matter; there is *no less* being after the storm than before, there is only *something else.* But this *something else* has a meaning only for a witness who can retain the past and compare it to the present in the form of the *no longer,*[36] i. e., through a nihilating act of consciousness.[37]

35. *Ibid.,* p. 7.
36. *Ibid.,* p. 8.
37. It would be interesting to go through the history of philosophy to examine the various "positive" senses that philosophers have given to nothingness and compare them with the noematic status Sartre gives to the wide range of "negativities" that he uncovers. Clearly he is very much indebted to Heidegger's conception of *Nichtung,* though unlike Heidegger Sartre does not posit any origin for nothingness other than consciousness (or "human reality") itself. He is also clearly under the influence of Hegel's *Logic* and the Hegelian interpretation of Plato's *Parmenides,* according to which the movement of negation is shown to be the very definition of intellectual thought. But we could go back to Democritus, to Plato, and to Aristotle as well. In the *Sophist* Plato shows that the *idea of non-being* is a necessary condition for any multiplicity among the ideas: every idea is itself and *is not* all the others. Like Sartre, Plato seems

We are now in a position to understand more exactly the sense of Sartre's paradoxical definition of consciousness (as the being that is not what it is and is what it is not), and the meaning of his continual play on the words *being* and *nothingness*. That there is a deliberate, but neverthless an instructive, ambiguity in his use of these words is evident. On the one hand *Consciousness* (the *cogito*) can be used to designate either (1) the prepersonal, operating intentionality that *is there* prior to the emergence of the ego or (2) my empirically experiencing self at the moment of reflexive awareness when this consciousness emerges as "mine" in the world. At the same time, *Being* as it is used to designate me the experiencer (the "I am") can designate either (1) the "I am" in the state of facticity, as immersed in being, as a bodily nature, or (2) the being that I am in the mode of not-being what I am. Finally, *Nothingness* is used to designate either (1) the impersonal consciousness that *is wholly* its activity of nihilation or (2) the objective correlates of this consciousness which it "sustains in being" and which are the objects of a whole range of cognitive, affective, and moral experiences.

However, if we interpret the ambiguous and paradoxical passages in the light of the passages in which Sartre expresses himself clearly, we can establish the *results* of his phenomenology of consciousness without difficulty. Consciousness is the being that is wholly intentional, whose unique property is to be *conscious-*

---

to take this relationship of the participation of all ideas in being (conceived as "self-identity") and nothingness (conceived as "otherness") in an "objective" sense. Aristotle introduced an even more positive notion of nothingness into philosophy with his doctrine of potency and act as constitutive principles of physical substances. "Pure potency," in the language of Aristotle, can be translated into good English as "nothingness." Potency is an aptitude to exist, to become what it *is not;* it is the "positive nothingness" that defines the given potentialities of this concrete physical substance. To say that this block of marble is "potentially" a statue is to say that it *is not* a statue but that it has in its very nature the structural possibility of being made into a statue. It certainly seems no more scandalous to speak of "nothingness" in the way Sartre does than to speak of "pure potentiality" as Aristotle did. In fact, Sartre uses the term "nothingness" to designate just such future possibilities, potentialities, principles of explanation, etc., through which consciousness confers meaning on being.

ness of being. This intentional structure is not a positive property (since consciousness is not a substance and cannot have accidental properties or qualities "inherent" in it) but an activity of
nihilating which produces negativities. These negativities are
maintained by consciousness in the only reality or "being" they
can have, namely, as the noematic correlates of consciousness.
It is thus through consciousness that "nothingness" comes to
things.[38] The reason why such a consciousness and all its works
are designated by the deliberately paradoxical term "nothingness"
is that the ontological reality of such a nihilating consciousness
is necessarily *freedom.* By *freedom* Sartre means "the permanent
possibility of dissociating oneself from the causal series which
constitutes being and which can produce only being."[39] Since
being (*Dinglichkeit*), in the *strong* sense, is wholly on the side of
being-in-itself, the being of consciousness must be a non-thinglike
existence. We could, using a more rigorous terminology, designate being-in-itself as *being* and consciousness as *existence,* but
Sartre for his part prefers to maintain the ambiguity and to play
on the *two senses of existence,* i. e., as designating both *being*
and *consciousness* at one and the same time. He shows in his
"ontological proof"[40] that both the *esse* of consciousness and the
esse of being are *transphenomenal,* though this single term
designates two regions of being which are utterly distinct from
and opposed to each other. The one, being-for-itself, is freedom,
spontaneity, indeterminacy, intentionality, *consciousness of being.*
The other is inert, thinglike, determined and positive, pure
being-in-itself. The "existential dialectic" that is instituted between being and consciousness *in fact* because of the immersion
of consciousness in nature through a body is the story of the
nihilating activity of consciousness, i. e., the eternally unsuccessful attempt to "reconcile" being-for-itself and being-in-itself.
Since consciousness, as freedom, is necessarily separated from ever
being or becoming a determined thing, by "the infinite distance
of nothing," any attempt to reduce the one to the other, to de-

38. *Being and Nothingness, op. cit.,* p. 22.
39. *Ibid.,* p. 23.
40. *Ibid.,* pp. lxff.

rive the one from the other, to show that they are realities in the same sense or of the same order, is doomed to failure. Thus the ultimate intention and the guiding aim of Sartre's phenomenology of consciousness is to "de-substantialize" consciousness completely, to show that it has none of the characteristics and is subject to none of the laws of "things," and, secondly, to show that for this very reason it cannot be *this or that* quality but can only be approached through an examination of the polymorphous diversity of its nihilating behaviors. The unifying structure of these acts of consciousness can be expressed, negatively, as the experience of being no-thing, or, positively, as the experience of being free (i. e., indeterminate).[41] The evidence that Sartre presents in both cases seems to be strictly experiential or "phenomenological."

II

Sartre as Existential Psychoanalyst

In his phenomenology of consciousness Sartre establishes a notion of freedom which can be called "cognitive freedom," since it is wholly developed and achieved on the most funda-

41. I cannot in this paper go into the ethical aspects of Sartre's general theory of consciousness. He prefers to express the ethical consequences of his theory in hyperbolic and imaginative terms, as when he states that man is "condemned to be free" and when, at the end of *Being and Nothingness,* he declares: "Man is a useless passion." This last phrase has misled at least one of his critics to interpret his entire philosophy as one of despair (Wilfrid Desan, *The Tragic Finale* [Cambridge, Mass.: 1954]). However, if we try to understand Sartre's meaning, and compare this passage with those in which he speaks of love as "a useless passion," of beauty as "useless," of artistic creativity as "useless," and of the career of writing itself as "a useless activity" (compare, for example, *What Is Literature?*, trans. Bernard Frechtman [New York: 1965], pp. 75, 122), we will see that what he is saying is not so scandalous. Man is, for Sartre, the being who does not have a predetermined and fixed nature; he does not produce moral acts like a peartree produces pears; the evolution of his moral life does not follow the pattern of the automatic and "natural" actualization of his potentialities. He is a being who does not have a *use* (and consequently may not be "used"); pens are used for writing; stallions are used for breeding; man is not "for" anything other than himself and, in this sense, as opposed both to God and to nature, he is "useless."

mental level of reflection and awareness, as opposed to the level
of deliberate volition. On the most fundamental level, therefore,
freedom for Sartre is not a question of the "freedom of the will"
but of cognitive distance and awareness. However, when he turns
to the immersion of consciousness in being, its relationships with
its own body, with matter, and with other persons, he discovers
and describes the element of *facticity* or *situation* within which
consciousness is necessarily imprisoned. Within such *facticity*
consciousness still possesses the freedom of a "non-substantial
absolute," but a new dimension of this freedom appears as that
of the *free project* of the whole human composite. Thus Sartre
begins with a philosophy which is not "personalist," which is not
a philosophy of the "ego" or of the "self" but of *pure consciousness*—and this distinguishes him from the school of reflexive
analysis. But to his description of this first, most fundamental,
level of consciousness he adds a description of the "embodied"
consciousness and moves from the level of a purely cognitive
freedom to the willed freedom of concretely human and "personal" projects. The examination of such "projects of being" is
the task of what he calls "existential psychoanalysis."

Existential psychoanalysis for Sartre is not some new therapeutic technique or an attempt to establish the theoretical
foundations of psychiatry. It is rather the attempt to discover
and describe the structures of the radical decisions or choices, the
"projects of being," which give unity to a particular life and
enable us to understand it in the concrete. "That unity—for
which substance was only a caricature—must be a unity of responsibility, a unity agreeable or hateful, blameable or praiseworthy,
in short *personal*. This unity, which is the being of the man
under consideration, is a *free* unification, and this unification can
not come *after* a diversity which it unifies."[42]

Thus existential psychoanalysis reintroduces the category of
the "person" as the concrete result of the free projects of a consciousness within and as related to its factual situation, as "determined" by all the laws of heredity, physiology, sociology, eco-

42. *Being and Nothingness, op. cit.,* p. 561.

nomics, psychology, etc., which operate on it from without and make it appear (even to itself) as a "substance" or a thing among things. But within this factual situation consciousness remains "free," and its most fundamental project, the project that defines its uniqueness and distinguishes it from every other thing and every other person, is not to be found in the analysis of the determinisms that simply describe its concrete facticity. Sartre's existential psychoanalysis is, as he says, based on a "refusal to consider man as capable of being analyzed and reduced to original givens, to determined desires (or 'drives'), supported by the subject as properties by an object."[43] Sartre entitled his novels, collectively, "paths of freedom" and, so to speak, told the story of a number of individual quests. His existential psychoanalysis is the *concrete science* of freedom, i. e., of the free creation of consciousness by itself *within* the facticity of its "situation," its "past," its "environment," its "own body," and in the face of its "death" and "other persons."

In his phenomenology of pure consciousness Sartre had shown that freedom was the behavior of nihilation. "The only being which can be called free is the being which nihilates its being."[44] But, in the realm of concrete action, "nihilation is defined as the project toward the in-itself."[45]

> The for-itself is a being such that in its being, its being is in question in the form of a project of being. To the for-itself being means to make known to oneself what one is by means of a possibility appearing as a value. Possibility and value belong to the being of the for-itself. The for-itself is defined ontologically as a *lack of being,* and possibility belongs to the for-itself as that which it lacks, in the same way that value haunts the for-itself as the totality of being which is lacking. . . . Freedom is the concrete mode of being of the lack of being.[46]

Sartre is fully convinced that all meaning and value come from consciousness, that even the meaning of "nature" and of the many factual determinisms that limit and define the realm of particular, concrete choices comes from the consciousness that

43. *Ibid.,* p. 561. 44. *Ibid.,* p. 567.
45. *Ibid.,* p. 565. 46. *Ibid.,* p. 565.

thus discovers itself "in situation." Thus whatever has a meaning, has a meaning only for and to the consciousness that confers
this meaning upon it. A stone is light or heavy only with reference to the human project that finds it an obstacle and attempts
to remove it; a mountain is difficult or easy to climb only for the
consciousness that has decided to "possess" it by climbing it. The
very determinisms by which we define our place in the world and
which we recognize as our own "obstacles" are determinisms only
to and for consciousness. Thus the description of the affective
qualities of objects—of which Sartre gives an extended example
in his description of the "slimy" or "viscous"—is a description of
the concrete structures of consciousness rather than of being-in-
itself. He offers, in fact, a "psychoanalysis of matter" inspired by
Bachelard as one of the foundations of his method. It seems
that he believes such an analysis, more promised than delivered
in *Being and Nothingness*, will reveal general structures of the
human world. But the chief aim of Sartre's existential psychoanalysis is to discover those free, individual choices of being
which are unique in each life, that pattern of action which will
reveal the meaning of an individual life in its total, complex,
existential density. Such a "fundamental project," as he calls it,
is—at least in the normal adult—a *perfectly conscious* though not
necessarily deliberate choice of a style of life.[47] We must remember
that "conscious" for Sartre includes and *is* primarily the prereflexive, nonpositional consciousness that *can* take itself as an
object but that is always "ahead of itself." Its choices, even those
that it discovers only little by little and that it attemps to understand, are the work of consciousness—not of inert "being." Thus,
"The choice is not *less* conscious or *less* explicit than a deliberation but rather . . . it is the foundation of all deliberation and . . .
as we have seen, a deliberation requires an interpretation in
terms of an original choice."[48]

Sartre's examination of such "fundamental projects" is based
on a theory of human reality which flows from his phenomenology of consciousness and which requires the rejection of the
"mythology" of Freud and other naturalistic systems of psycho-

47. *Ibid.*, p. 461.   48. *Ibid.*, pp. 461–62.

analysis. First of all, consciousness-in-situation (the concretely existing person) is a unified whole, a "totality," and not a haphazard "collection" of discrete forces, drives, or other hypothetical subliminal entities. Existential psychoanalysis does not attempt to reduce the complex psychic phenomena to their molecular and atomic physiological or physical sources but attempts to study the fundamental unity of the concrete experiencing subject as he is in his own subjective and conscious experience. It considers man-and-his-world as a unitary, structured whole. "The *principle* of this psychoanalysis is that man is a totality and not a collection. Consequently he expresses himself as a whole in even his most insignificant and his most superficial behavior."[49]

The job of existential psychoanalysis is to "decipher," to "determine," and to "conceptualize" the total meaning of a given life through the discovery of its "original choice"—not original in the sense of being temporally the first but in the sense of being the most deep-seated and most profoundly unifying choice, in terms of which all other choices can be related to one another and understood. Since such an original choice must be *conscious*, Sartre rejects the Freudian "hypothesis of the unconscious." His criticism of the "materialistic mythology of psychoanalysis" is well known and need not be repeated here.[50] But this does not mean that Sartre rules out *any* conception of the unconscious. He is well aware that human behaviors must be "interpreted," that they have "symbolic" meanings hidden even to the behaver himself; Sartre himself insists on the large realm of the "prelogical" and the "prereflexive" in experience. What he rejects is the notion of a conscious ego as a weak and derived plaything for drives that manipulate it from beneath. There may be such drives in the sense of purely psychophysiological mechanisms, but these are then "objects" of consciousness, a part of the "facticity" of a given human situation, not the projects or choices of consciousness itself. Thus in searching for the unifying choice that reveals the peculiar quality of an individual life, Sartre believes that—if and to the extent that we are able to push our

49. *Ibid.*, p. 568.   50. *Ibid.*, pp. 50–54.

investigations far enough—we will find this original choice to be conscious.

In making such investigations we will not be past-oriented, as is Freudian psychoanalysis, but will concentrate on the future-directed intentions, aims, goals, projects, and desires by which an individual defines himself in the world. This methodological principle is also a consequence of Sartre's general theory of consciousness. The person as a totality is not a "fixed character" (in the Greek sense of the word "character") but a future-directed center of striving, a dynamic unity whose present acts "secrete its past." Repeating Hegel's phrase *Unser Wesen ist was gewesen ist,* Sartre defines a person's past as the "essence" or "whatness" (the "being") of his consciousness. It has *no operative force* in the present—in which consciousness always remains an "absolute" spontaneity. But we can investigate the past as the "history" of the particular concretization of this concrete life-project. Unlike the Freudians, however, we will not find there causal forces that operate on present consciousness. The past defines what I *have been* up to now, but, precisely because I am conscious of it *as past,* I can accept it, reject it, interpret it, like any object in the world. Once I am dead I will be identical with what I have been, my essence and my existence will coincide, my consciousness as a for-itself will disappear and I will lie in being as an object, an essence. While I am alive, however, my past is an object like any other (which I am not necessarily in a privileged position to interpret, though it is the sedimentation of my own acts). We see here the meaning of Sartre's cryptic dictum that "existence precedes essence."[51] My essence, i. e., the being I am,

51. *Existentialism Is a Humanism, op. cit.,* pp. 289ff. There is a double sense of this "essence" that a man creates for himself. It is on the one hand a man's project, the goal that he projects for himself into the future and by which he defines himself to himself, and on the other hand it is his "past" as the sedimentation of this project in his acts. To say that existence precedes essence is to say that man is *what he does,* and since he is *free* his essence cannot be given to him beforehand, prefabricated, like a "substantial form" which, if left to itself, will realize the potentialities of its nature. Thus Sartre's notion of "essence" differs radically from both the ancient Scholastic notion and the modern Husserlian notion (i. e., as the a priori meaning-structures given in experience).

"what" I am, is something that results from my free choices in the present and is in no way predetermined; I *am* my acts of choice and thus I gradually "create" my own essence, the sense of my life. The only "being" I will ever have is that which I freely choose and create, which is "in suspense" at each instant prior to my death, because in the operating present, i. e., as existing, consciousness is a "nothingness." We see here also that the "nothingness" of consciousness is not restricted to the purely cognitive freedom of reflection but is also the "being" of the volitional choices by which I define myself. In the present moment of free choice I am my choices in the *mode of not-being*; once the choice has been made, even if I should later make a choice that nullifies it for the future, this particular choice is beyond my power, is a part of my being which will remain forever fixed in the past, is what I am in the *mode of being*.

Consciousness is thus a *project of being*. In "bad faith" consciousness takes itself for a substance, for a thing, for a role, for an ego, etc. But, more fundamentally, the life of this consciousness is the acts and choices by which it defines itself and gradually gives itself an "essence." It is therefore useful to examine a given person's past in the greatest detail possible if one is to understand his fundamental project and thus grasp him in his essentiality. Unlike Freud, however, Sartre does not conceive this to have any therapeutic value, nor can he admit that certain privileged traumatic experiences in the past can *causally* affect present consciousness.

The greatest difficulty with Sartre's existential psychoanalysis does not lie in its theoretical presuppositions, which flow from his general theory, but in the unfinished character of his exposition of its method. In the final sections of *Being and Nothingness* he sketched out some of the guiding considerations for such a method, but he recognizes these to be extremely abstract and incomplete. We might get a better idea of this method by examining some of the applications he has made of it up to now,[52]

52. Up to now Sartre has produced four major attempts at existential psychoanalysis, all of which exist in English translation: (1) *Baudelaire,* trans. Martin Turnell (New York: 1950); (2) *Anti-Semite and Jew,* trans.

but the "applications" themselves present most baffling problems of interpretation and hermeneutics.[53] The length of this paper does not permit a full-scale analysis of these works, one of which, *Saint Genet*, is itself a wide-ranging tome of over six hundred pages. I will, therefore, summarize Sartre's most general principles and then show with a brief example taken from his work how they could be applied in a concrete case to "illuminate" or "reveal" the meaning of an actual life-project.

The "three big categories of concrete human existence," writes Sartre,[54] are *to be, to have, to do*. And he shows that the only "being" (i.e., essence) a consciousness can have its own past, the sedimentation of its own acts in a personal history. As an existing, experiencing subject I choose and create this essence by projects of appropriation (and destruction) and by my actions. There is thus a profound truth hidden in the ancient alimentary epistemologies, which describe knowing as a kind of appropriation (absorption, digestion, assimilation) of being by consciousness. Any number of human behaviors (emotive, affective, cognitive) can be described as attempts to conquer and

---

George J. Becker (New York: 1960); (3) *Saint Genet, Actor and Martyr*, trans. Bernard Frechtman (New York: 1963); and (4) "The Venetian Pariah," trans. Wade Baskin, in Jean-Paul Sartre, *Essays in Aesthetics* (New York: 1963). The last, which is an existential psychoanalysis of Tintoretto, has been abandoned in an unfinished state. It seems that Sartre, in writing it, intended to give his ideas on aesthetics under the guise of a concrete existential analysis just as he gave a good deal of his "ethics" in the analysis of Jean Genet. Critics have generally found the book on Baudelaire to be singularly unsuccessful, whereas the work devoted to Genet has received much greater acclaim. Sartre's volume on anti-Semitism, though marred by certain omissions and a very "rapid" treatment, has been widely accepted as a sound study in existential psychoanalysis, even though it deals with an intersubjective and historical attitude rather than with an individual life-project.

53. With his characteristic lack of restraint in these matters, Philip Thody writes: "Sartre's critical method involves an identification of himself with the author he is studying—or, rather, an explanation of the author's problems in terms of Sartre's own experience and ideas . . . which at one and the same time both gives the essay its originality and invalidates its conclusions." *Op. cit.*, p. 145.

54. *Being and Nothingness, op. cit.*, p. 576.

possess being and to make it not only "mine" but "me." We must try to understand, in the concrete, how the climbing of a mountain gives me the right of possession, the right to affix my flag to it; how the conquest of a woman makes her mine and the motive of my jealousy; how the assimilation of the thought of an author gives me the right to interpret him.[55]

There are two phenomena in particular which are involved in such projects of being through appropriation, and to which Sartre gives special attention. (1) On the one hand "to possess is to wish to possess the world across a particular object,"[56] and this is necessarily—in the concrete—a delimitation of one's being. The concretization of one's being in a particular mode of the appropriation of being involves the "surreptitious appropriation of the possessor by the possessed."[57] If I am what *I have*, I cannot be—to that extent—anything else. To the extent that this appropriation gives me "being," I become "solidified" and am constricted to a way of being which excludes other modes of appropriation which could—prior to this choice—equally well have become mine. If I decide to take *this* woman, if I wish to climb *this* mountain, if I think like a Spinozist rather than a Husserlian, I am choosing my being through taking on the qualities of others and to that extent am no longer myself, i. e., free. (2) At the same time this appropriation can never be "innocent." There is a violation and a "destruction" essential to the very project of appropriation: in appropriating I necessarily alter and transform ("digest") what I possess. Knowledge like exploration is a "rape of the world." Sartre believes that the examination of

55. Sartre says in one place that "man is what he prefers," and he shows that artistic creation, scientific exploration, and just playing are all ways of possessing the world. He believes that one can, in principle, follow a man's preferences *usque ad minima* to discover the unified pattern of his life. On "eating" he writes for example: 'To eat is to appropriate by destruction; it is at the same time to be filled up with a certain being. . . . It is not a matter of indifference whether we like oysters or clams, snails or shrimp, if only we know how to unravel the existential significance of these foods." *Ibid.*, pp. 614–15.

56. *Ibid.*, p. 597.

57. *Ibid.*, p. 609.

the modes and symbols of "sexual possession" (the Acteon complex) as well as those of possession by "eating" (the Jonah complex) will reveal this. If I conquer *this* mountain or *this* woman, explore all their possibilities, rob them of their secrets, I cannot then leave them *as they are*. If I assimilate the thought of Plato to the point of becoming a "Platonist," my interpretation will nevertheless do violence to Plato, because I cannot ever *be* what I possess, and must always manipulate it as an object for myself.

Of all the general categories of analysis, however, Sartre places most emphasis on the *to do*.[58] Sartre is primarily a moralist, a "pragmatist," a philosopher of action. In repeating the triple Kantian question (What can I know? What should I do? What can I hope for?), his strongest accent is placed on the *What should I do*? In short, he is the *anthropologian* of twentieth-century philosophy. In his volume *What Is Literature?*, which he wrote just after World War II, he places himself on the side of those who reject the morality of those "who wish to possess the world" in favor of "those who want to change it." He finds in the Marxist plan to change the world not any eternal, unchanging, "metaphysical" meaning, but rather a contemporary value and possibility, a project to which he allies himself in order to give meaning to being and to create a truth. Both in himself and in others he is most sensitive to these political and ethical actions and choices.

It seems that in the lives of all men, projects "to have" and projects "to do" are intermingled; indeed, Sartre shows in *Being and Nothingness* that projects which appear at first to fall under the category of "doing" (sport, play, sexuality) frequently have the sense of "appropriation" and "possession" and can be reduced to them. But there is a distinction, and this radical distinction lies at the basis of his existential psychoanalysis of Jean Genet. We will therefore do best to turn briefly to that work, which is at once Sartre's most successful attempt at employing and justify-

58. In the French there is a play on the double meaning of *faire* as "to make" as well as "to do."

ing his method and the only place up to now where he has given us any extended treatment of his existentialist ethics.[59]

Sartre takes delight in criticizing the morality of the "possessors" (the bourgeoisie, the Christians) and poses the question of what the moral structure of a society would be which would not be dominated by the economic facts of scarcity and want and in which a man could not be defined by what he possesses or owns. He tries to show that the Christian virtues are all the virtues of property-owners. In order to practice the saintly potlatch of divesting oneself of everything, of total abnegation, of selling all that one has and giving to the poor, one must first possess something. The medieval definition of private ownership as the right to "use and abuse" the fruits of the earth is a symbol of God's feudal power and rights over the world and men as their Lord and Master; through property men insert themselves in this hierarchical structure of ownership and define themselves through their possessions—they participate in the dominion of God. But what if it should turn out that the Christian God is not the landlord of the earth? A new morality would be required. Sartre has never done more than assert the possibility and necessity of such a new morality. He has not claimed to have discerned it with any clarity. In any event, we are concerned here only with one illustrative case: the bastard Jean Genet. Sartre explains his purpose in this study as follows:

> I have tried to do the following: to indicate the limit of psychoanalytical interpretation and Marxist explanation and to demonstrate that freedom alone can account for a person in his totality; to show this freedom at grips with destiny, crushed at first by its mischances, then turning upon them and digesting them little

59. At the close of *Being and Nothingness* Sartre had promised to devote a future work to existentialist ethics. He has not done so. It may be that the work of Francis Jeanson (*Le problème moral et la pensée de Sartre* [Paris: 1947]), which Sartre explicitly approved as giving his own ideas on ethics, seemed to him to have filled this need. It is more likely, however, that he considers the elaboration of his existential psychoanalysis a necessary precondition to the writing of a systematic moral philosophy. The structure and content of *Saint Genet* seem to bear this out and may very well contain most of the reflections Sartre intended to put into his promised sequel to *Being and Nothingness*.

by little; to prove that genius is not a gift but the way that one invents in desperate cases; to learn the choice that a writer makes of himself, of his life and of the meaning of the universe, including even the formal characteristics of his style and composition, even the structure of his images and of the particularity of his tastes; to review in detail the history of his liberation.[60]

When, at the age of about ten, Genet was discovered and named a "thief" by his foster parents and the "good people" of the country district of Marvan, he accepted his destiny as a way of being, and he *wanted to be what he was.* To the "capitalist" and "bourgeois" morality in which he was raised, *to be is to belong* to someone, and *to possess* property of one's own is the measure of one's reality. Sartre gives a lengthy and probing description of "the plot of the liturgical drama" through which Genet *became aware of what he was* (and which he ritually repeats throughout his life). Without parents, without a name, without possessions, he was, as an infant, farmed out by the government to a family of small land-owners which was paid to take him in. Though treated with kindness, he was made to feel from the beginning that everything he received *was given* to him out of Christian charity; he did not have a "natural right" to anything and was deprived by the strictest laws of heredity from coming into the possession of this land. In a situation in which a man's being is determined by what he has, how does one who has nothing assert his right to be? By stealing. If he had instead been brought up in a proletarian environment, living in the suburbs of a large city, says Sartre, and if he had been weaned by parents who believed that property was theft, he would perhaps have learned earlier that a man is also what he *does.* But, in this case, Genet, as a child of ten, is the accomplice of the grownups whom he believes, trusts, and admires.

He who was not yet anyone suddenly becomes Jean Genet. . . . It is revealed to him that he *is* a thief and he pleads guilty, crushed by a fallacy which he is unable to refute; he stole, he is therefore a thief. . . . What he *wanted* was to steal; what he *did,* a theft; what he *was,* a thief. . . . What happened? Actually, almost nothing; an action undertaken without reflec-

60. *Saint Genet, op. cit.,* p. 584.

tion, conceived and carried out in the secret, silent inwardness in which he often takes refuge, has just *become objective*. Genet learns what he *is objectively*. He is a thief by birth, he will remain one until his death. . . . And if he *is* a thief, he must therefore always be one, everywhere, not only when he steals, but when he eats, when he sleeps, when he kisses his foster mother.[61]

In Sartre's analysis Genet becomes the very embodiment of "bad faith," the person who takes himself for what he is, now as a thief, later as a homosexual and a traitor, like a substance. But what is different in the case of Genet is that he assumes this "essence," which he at first accepted from others, so completely that he "sanctifies" it and even endows it with subjectivity. He moves from the level of possessing his character to that of *doing* it, and this is why Sartre describes his project as one of being a "saint," of becoming one who completely assumes his destiny, who is not to be judged by men, who holds up to humanity the example of the complete embodiment of its moral ideals and possibilities.

Sartre's argument is tortuous and difficult, but the essence of his method is stated in the early part of the book when he lists and contrasts the "categories of being" and "categories of doing"[62] of which the rest of his book is the development. "The hero," for instance, is a category of being; "the saint" is a category of doing. The two are opposed (like the other categories) chiefly by the degree and kind of subjectivity they designate. Categories of being are particular "objective essences" or "labels" with which

61. *Ibid.*, pp. 17–18.
62. *Ibid.*, p. 62. The list of the categories is as follows:

1. Categories of *Being*	2. Categories of *Doing*
Object	Subject, consciousness
Oneself as Other	Self as oneself
Essential which proves inessential	Inessential which proves essential
Fatality	Freedom, will
Tragedy	Comedy
Death, disappearance	Life, will to live
Hero	Saint
Criminal	Traitor
Beloved one	Lover
Male principle	Female principle

we endow the activities of consciousness after the fact. They are always "particular" characteristics. Categories of doing are the acts of consciousness themselves, the preverbal and even pre-cognitive choices in which the experiencing subject chooses his essence. They are not particular concretizations of consciousness but its very project of nihilating being as a whole.

The story of Genet is not one of "conversion" to the right side of morality but of "salvation" within the morality which he ac-cepts from his foster parents, as its "other side." He does not contest it. He accepts it; he makes himself to be the "evil" crim-inal which this morality judges him to be. He is, of course, in bad faith. No more than anyone else can Genet *be* what he is called. But this prospect of ultimate failure is no more serious in his life than in any other. The project of "conversion," i. e., to *be* honest, heterosexual, and faithful, would be no more success-ful. In any case, one's ultimate lack of success in achieving an "essence," of endowing oneself with being, is irrelevant because it is the project itself, the striving, which alone gives structure, unity, and meaning to a life.

Hence the profoundly disturbing character both of Genet's writings and of his life—which is the reason Sartre chose him as an instructive example. He is not a moralist. He does not, like Gide,[63] propose the new morality that is needed; he accepts the one that condemns him; he is a saint in reverse. Society, says Sartre, is not disturbed because of the *content* of Genet's writings; we are long familiar with such aberrations and we welcome them to literature so long as they are recognized as such and described *as objects.* "We 'normal' people know delinquents only from the outside, and if we are ever 'in situation' with respect to them, it is as judges or entomologists."[64]

---

63. It is a well-known and frequently commented upon fact that Sartre's one point of admiration for Gide—a person whose work he does not other-wise admire and whose proclivities he does not share—is Gide's refusal to accept the morality in the name of which he was condemned by others, his insistence that it was *he* who was in the right, and his consequent attempt to elaborate his own morality.

64. *Saint Genet,* p. 586.

One is willing to allow a repentant culprit to confess his sins, but on condition that he rise above them; the *good* homosexual is weaned away from his vice by remorse and disgust; it is no longer part of him. He was a criminal but no longer is. He speaks of what he was as if he were *another,* and when we read his confession we feel ourselves *absolutely other* than the poor wretch he is speaking about.[65]

The difference with Genet is that "he never speaks to us *about* the homosexual, *about* the thief, but always *as* a thief and *as* a homosexual. His voice is one of those that we wanted never to hear . . . he invents the homosexual *subject*."[66] We are willing enough to arrogate to ourselves and all of mankind the exploits of the few inventors, geniuses, creators, among us. When our astronauts reach the moon, when our aviators exceed the speed of sound, when our scientists penetrate the floor of the ocean, we are all ready to contemplate our virtues and utter, "What a glorious creature is man." But, says Sartre, if there is a "reversibility of merits" according to which *we all* deserve the accolades given to our aviators, there is also a "reversibility of crime," and the existential psychoanalysis of Jean Genet is not just another case history but the description of our own "human possibility."

What is noteworthy in all this is the vacillation of the self that occurs in us when certain minds open before our eyes like yawning chasms: what we considered to be our innermost being suddenly seems to us to be a fabricated appearance; it seems to us that we have escaped only by an incredible stroke of luck from the vices that repel us most in others; we recognize, with horror, a *subject*. He is our truth as we are his; our virtue and his crimes are interchangeable.[67]

This brief sample of Sartre's analysis must suffice here. His purpose in this work is to describe Genet's project of "sanctity" and martyrdom to the morality of the possessors, as a "free" and "conscious" project and therefore as an authentic accomplishment of man. It is because it is a work of "freedom" and not of

65. *Ibid.,* p. 587.
66. *Ibid.*
67. *Ibid.,* p. 589.

"nature" that it deserves our study and that it falls under a general phenomenology of consciousness. Ultimately, the purpose of Sartre's essays in existential psychoanalysis seems to be ethical: "Genet holds the mirror up to us: we must look at it and see ourselves."[68] I do not mean to assert that the *only* value of these analyses is to establish the basis for a Sartrean ethics, but this seems to be his own chief passion and preoccupation. "I have," he has said, "a passion to understand men." The method of existential psychoanalysis is one of the instruments he has developed to enable him to pursue this aim.

In the first part of this paper I have limited myself to a faithful and sympathetic exposition of the broad lines of Sartre's general theory of consciousness and in the second to an illustrative example of its more concrete applications. I have, therefore, prescinded from a discussion of the various criticisms that his position calls forth both on the level of the general theory and on the level of its embodiment in the method of existential psychoanalysis. These criticisms must be left for a later study.

68. *Ibid.*, p. 599.

Essay Seven

A Central Theme of
Merleau-Ponty's
Philosophy

FREDERICK A. OLAFSON*

The untimely death of Maurice Merleau-Ponty in 1961 was a tragic loss both for philosophy and the wider world of letters. It was all the more to be deplored since it occurred at a time when he had fairly begun what was evidently to be a fundamental restatement of his philosophy. While the chapters of that incomplete work, which have recently been published under the title *Le visible et l'invisible*,[1] give hints of the new and clearly very important ideas which Merleau-Ponty intended to elaborate, it is not possible on the basis of such fragmentary indications to assess how significant these new departures might have proved to be. For us Merleau-Ponty must therefore remain the philosopher we had come to know through his earlier books and essays. Nevertheless, for this very reason this posthumous work has a special value, for it contains a number of luminous and penetrating treatments of themes to which Merleau-Ponty had returned again and again in the course of his philosophical career; and it thus underlines once again the essential unity of his thought. In this paper I will try to show that an understanding of one of these themes and of Merleau-Ponty's characteristic mode of dealing with it can clarify the underlying philosophical concerns that are reflected in works like his *Phenomenology of*

* Graduate School of Education, Harvard University, Cambridge, Massachusetts.

1. Ed. Claude Lefort (Paris: 1964).

179

Perception.[2] In this way I hope it will be possible both to bring out a number of significant affinities between Merleau-Ponty and certain philosophical movements in the English-speaking world and at the same time to do justice to the highly original character of his thought.

I

Merleau-Ponty is often—and rightly—described as an existentialist and yet even a slight acquaintance with his work makes it quite plain that in a number of important respects he by no means conformed to either the popular or the academic stereotype of the existentialist philosopher. To be sure, that stereotype itself, through its dominating preoccupation with matters of ethos and mood, reflects serious misconceptions; but the fact remains that Merleau-Ponty's mind was marked by a certain coolness and fastidiousness that are in notable contrast to Sartre's passionate *entrain,* not to speak of Heidegger's somewhat troglodytic intellectual style. No doubt these differences were due, in part at least, to the fact that in spite of all his political radicalism and his impatience with reigning philosophical orthodoxies, Merleau-Ponty was an academic philosopher and as such was more inclined to be critical and cautious in his affirmations than are those in whom philosophical inspiration assumes the character of a natural force. Nowhere, by the way, does this critical skill and somewhat detached dialectical virtuosity appear to better advantage than in his dissection of Sartre's Marxism in *Les aventures de la dialectique.*[3]

These distinctive features of Merleau-Ponty's intellectual style reflect deeper differences of substance. Thus Merleau-Ponty does not appear ever to have been influenced in any very important way by the "dark" philosophers of the nineteenth century—whether Kierkegaard or Nietzsche—whose intransigent vision of

2. Trans. Colin Smith (London and New York: 1962); originally published in Paris, 1945. Merleau-Ponty's other major work is *The Structure of Behavior,* trans. A. L. Fisher (Boston: 1963).

3. "Sartre et l'ultramarxisme," *Les aventures de la dialectique* (Paris: 1955).

the human condition was to become such an important element in the thought of Heidegger. The significance of this fact may not be readily evident. While it is widely agreed at the present time that what we call existentialism represents a confluence of a number of distinct lines of thought and that among these the most important are Husserlian phenomenology and the critiques of rationalism carried out by Nietzsche and Kierkegaard, the relationship to one another of these very diverse ingredients is not always well understood. More specifically, it needs to be recalled that the internal dialectic of Husserl's own philosophy had generated difficulties which some of his followers—such as Heidegger—felt to be so serious that they could be resolved only by a quite radical reorientation for which the voluntarism of Nietzsche and Kierkegaard provided the principal models. So different, however, did the philosophical idiom and ethos of the new "existential" phenomenology inspired by these sources prove to be from those of Husserl that its origin as a response to questions that can be understood only within the context of Husserl's philosophy was often obscured. In Merleau-Ponty's writings by contrast, the line of development out of and beyond Husserl'is much more easily visible, precisely because his disagreements with Husserl took the form of detailed counteranalyses and counterarguments addressed to some of the latter's major theses and not, as was the case with Heidegger, the form of a massive replacement of one philosophical idiom by another.[4] The fact that Merleau-Ponty maintained a continuing contact with Husserl's philosophical position even while departing from it on important points, is in turn at least partly due, I suggest, to the absence of strong competing intellectual allegiances of the kind I have noted in the case of Heidegger. It is surely significant that in place of the latter's reflections on Nietzsche, Merleau-Ponty has given us essays on such figures as Machiavelli and Montaigne.[5] These writers had their own comments to make on the power and scope

4. Merleau-Ponty's own estimate of Husserl is to be found in his essay "The Philosopher and His Shadow," *Signs*, trans. R. C. McCleary (Evanston: 1964).

5. Also in *Signs*.

of human reason but their scepticism was of an older and more
detached kind that certainly seeks to moderate the overweening
pretentions of reason but remains quite alien in spirit to the type
of superheated counterassertion that was later to become the
characteristic mode for attacks on established forms of rationalism.

In two other respects, Merleau-Ponty differs significantly from
other major figures in the existentialist movement. First, he was
deeply versed in and indebted to the behavioral sciences, notably
psychology. No doubt the antiscientific bias of existentialism
has been exaggerated in popular accounts, but the fact remains
that Heidegger and Sartre have not been prepared to jeopardize
the independence and self-sufficiency of their own systems of
thought by resting any part of their argument on results achieved
through scientific investigations as Merleau-Ponty did by drawing
so heavily on the work of the Gestalt psychologists in his theory
of perception. In general, he was not at all disposed to accept
any hard and fast principle of the division of labor between
philosophy and the natural sciences of the kind postulated by
Husserl; and he repeatedly challenged the cognate distinction
between "essential truths" and "matters of fact" on the ground
that, in the absolute form in which it is usually advanced, it
conspicuously fails to do justice to the complex and reciprocally
fructifying relationship of interdependence in which philosophical analysis and scientific inquiry stand to one another.[6]

The other feature of Merleau-Ponty's thought which sets him
apart from other existentialists is perhaps the most important of
all. I have in mind his strong insistence on the philosophical
centrality of social considerations, whether in the context of an
effort to understand scientific inquiry or morality or to elaborate
a general theory of mind. After Merleau-Ponty's death, Sartre
was to recall that even in the earliest days of their association,
when Sartre himself was caught up in what he later came to re-

6. A good statement of Merleau-Ponty's views on the relation of philosophy and the special sciences is contained in his essay "Phenomenology and
the Sciences of Man," reprinted in *The Primacy of Perception*, ed. James
Edie (Evanston: 1964), especially pp. 64–78.

gard as a very misleading form of moral individualism and was resolutely uninterested in the social and political context of philosophical reflection, Merleau-Ponty was already a political realist and tended to discount all purely individualistic forms of moral idealism.[7] In his later philosophical work, he laid great stress on the postive and essential contribution that is made to the individual's effort to encompass and understand his world by the shared meanings that society places at his disposal; and he appears never to have been inclined to treat all forms of collective or cooperative action as so many derogations from the pristine authenticity of the purely individual project.[8] As a result he was spared the necessity of sharply correcting in mid-career his theory of society and of history as Sartre has felt obliged to do by reason of the exaggerated and one-sided individualism which he now imputes to his earlier thought.

These differences which I have been noting and which might be interpreted by some as placing Merleau-Ponty outside the mainstream of existentialism seem to me to have a quite opposite effect. I would argue that by virtue of being relatively untouched by a number of the intellectual influences that were to contribute to the forming of present-day existentialism Merleau-Ponty's writings afford us a much clearer insight into some of the under-lying and, in a narrower and more technical sense, philosophical issues which were of crucial importance in the emergence of existential phenomenology but which have been obscured by a somewhat meretricious "existentialist" rhetoric. The prominence of epistemological and conceptual issues within his philosophy undoubtedly has much to do with its close contact with Husserlian phenomenology, which I have already noted. Indeed, it could be argued that this contact was too close since it often led Merleau-Ponty to interpret some of Husserl's doctrines, particularly the theory of the *Lebenswelt* of his later years, in a way

7. In his "Merleau-Ponty Vivant," *Les Temps Modernes* (October, 1961). This essay has been translated by Benita Eisler under the title "Merleau-Ponty" in a recent collection of Sartre's essays, *Situations* (New York: 1966).
8. See, for example, his *Humanisme et Terreur* (Paris: 1947), in which he went so far as to present a defense of the Moscow trials of the thirties.

that forces the points of similarity with the views Merleau-Ponty himself was developing at the expense of the manifest and important differences between them.[9] In any case, while Husserl's phenomenology undoubtedly provided the major themes to which Merleau-Ponty was to devote such an immense labor of reinterpretation and revision, it did so not so much because it was the most considerable contemporary re-statement of an essentially Cartesian philosophy of mind, but rather because Husserl, for all his acknowledgement of a debt to Descartes as the discoverer of "transcendental subjectivity," had also, in Merleau-Ponty's view, indicated how the deep-seated vices of the Cartesian philosophy might be overcome. Merleau-Ponty was himself a life-long student of Descartes and had been reared in an academic tradition in which the root assumptions of both philosophy and psychology still reflected a Cartesian conception of mind. In France, during the years up to the World War II—or so it seemed to Merleau-Ponty and to Sartre—an uncritical and often unwitting Cartesianism with heavy infusions of Kantian idealism still dominated academic philosophy. This pervasive neo-Cartesian style of thought is often referred to in Merleau-Ponty's writing—sometimes as what he calls "la pensée réflexive," sometimes as "intellectualism"—and it is always the object of very severe criticism. Perhaps "critical idealism" would be the best general description for this type of philosophy, which found its most distinguished French representative in Léon Brunschvicg—a thinker almost unknown outside of France but of considerable importance if one wishes to understand the kind of philosophy against which both Merleau-Ponty and Sartre were to react so strongly.

For some reason very little if any attention is paid in most accounts of existentialism to this immediate philosophical background; and yet it has a special importance for philosophers in the English-speaking world. For while closely parallel figures in Anglo-American philosophy are not easy to identify, "critical

9. This is not to deny that Merleau-Ponty was aware of these differences, as, for example, the footnote at the end of Part II of *Phenomenology of Perception* makes very clear.

idealism" is by no means an exclusively French or continental doctrine, and when allowance is made for differences in philosophical idiom, many of its central tenets to which Merleau-Ponty's critique addresses itself can be seen to have a clear affinity with certain forms of phenomenalism that are familiar to us from our own recent philosophical past. There are of course very important differences between Anglo-American phenomenalism and critical idealism. Nevertheless, it is impossible to read Merleau-Ponty without being struck again and again by the similarity of his arguments to many of those that have been directed against the sense-datum theory as argued by such philosphers as C. I. Lewis and H. H. Price. When one recalls how important a role radical and systematic criticism of such views has played in the current phase of philosophical development in the English-speaking world, it becomes plausible to suggest that two movements of reaction against what is in many respects a single philosophical position may have something more in common. I will return to a consideration of this possibility later in this paper.

One more general observation is appropriate before turning to a more detailed characterization of the philosophical position to which I have been alluding. While it has often been noted that existentialism is in large part a revolt against philosophical idealism, the idealism in question is usually supposed to be Hegel's; and the form and motives of the criticism to which it is subjected by existentialists are most frequently identified with those of Kierkegaard. Seen in this light, the objectionable features of idealism are its cosmic complacency and its refusal to recognize the discreteness and contingency of individual lives, which it takes into account only as so many interrelated and ultimately harmonious ramifications of the world spirit in its self-constituting activity. An interpretation of existentialism as a protest against a world view of this kind understandably enjoys wide acceptance and appeal, since an analogy between the world-spirit with its totalitarian pretensions and certain political systems can easily be drawn; and the existentialist is thereby made to appear as the critic not just of a system of philosophy but of tendencies in the modern world which are still very much with us and are by no means confined to the social systems that we normally called totalitarian.

The fact is that Hegel's is not the only possible form of idealism, nor are the faults of idealism as a moral or social philosophy the only targets of existentialist criticism. Specifically, the kind of critical idealism to which I have proposed Merleau-Ponty's philosophy should be seen as a reaction is motivated primarily by epistemological and logical considerations rather than by moral or social or theological prepossessions; and the same holds true for existentialism insofar as it takes the form of a critique of such a doctrine. There may well be affinities between a certain position on epistemological issues and some of the characteristic theses of idealism as a general worldview; and a case can be made for the view that the Cartesian method eventually leads to a position like Hegel's. However that may be, the fact remains that the epistemological and logical inspiration of the existentialist movement has long since been lost from sight through an almost exclusive preoccupation with some of the larger and (at least superficially) more comprehensible theses which it is thought of as defending. A study of Merleau-Ponty's philosophy, by contrast, has the advantage of permitting us to reverse this rather dubious order of priority and to consider these root issues without being reminded at every turn of the vast ideological commitments which, one way or another, we are incurring.

II

The main features of the philosophy of critical idealism can be exhibited by recapitulating a certain dialectic between sense experience and conceptual thought that figures prominently in the writings of its leading representatives.[10] The starting point for

10. In this section I have sought to reproduce a typical movement of thought such as can be found, for example, in Brunschvicg's *La vie de l'esprit*, but I have also drawn heavily on Husserl's *Ideas*, particularly in my characterization of the transcendental ego that emerges from the process of reflection.

this dialectic is typically the notion of a sense datum, i. e., of the presence to consciousness of some quality that is usually held to be internally simple and the apprehension of which is necessarily veridical—if only because of its rigidly delimited scope. This sense datum does not have to be thought of as the sensory core of our actual experiences and can simply be postulated as the ideal residue of a process of reductive analysis in the course of which all references to what is not presently given are somehow pared away or discounted. While the classical empiricists argued that all objects of empirical knowledge must be constructed out of these units of pure sensation by means of just a few simple relationships such as contiguity and resemblance, the next step in the critical idealist's argument is to point out how far such an incorrigible apprehension of a sense datum or indeed of any momentary collection of such sense-data falls short of what we ordinarily mean by the perception of objects. Since no criteria of transtemporal identity apply to the sense datum, an apprehension of it cannot give us any objective or "public" quality, much less the object to which such a property belongs or any part of that object. How then is this gap between the sense datum and the perception of objects to be spanned? Clearly, by an act of judgment which interprets the datum as a quality of a certain kind of object which is in turn situated in an objective milieu of some kind. The making of this judgment is a distinctive form of mental activity and the content of the judgment consists of the concepts whose function it is to transform the apprehension of sense data into a perception of stable public objects. In our ordinary experience this distinction between passivity and activity—between the presence of a sense datum and the interpretation that is added by the application of a concept—is not at all clearly recognized. Precisely for this reason, the first objective of critical idealism must be to establish that distinction securely and thereby to make it impossible for common sense to persevere in its conviction that "things" are simply there and that all their characteristics, from the sensuous to the categorial, can simply be read off by means of the familiar procedures of empirical observation.

At this stage in the critical idealist's analysis, the concepts we use in judgment and indeed those judgments themselves are still understood as referring beyond the sense datum and beyond all our mental activities to an object that exists by itself and against which the content of such judgments must be tested. It is clear, however, that once we have committed ourselves to an interpretation of perception as the application of a concept to a sense datum, the possibility of such a test or comparison as this implies is called into question. In such a comparison, the terminal apprehension of the object itself would have to be analyzed as itself involving the application of a concept to a sense content, and in this way the object itself would be fatally drawn into the ambit of our activity of conceptual interpretation instead of serving as an independent touchstone by which the latter might be tested. In other words, it becomes clear that *all* reference to objects is conceptually mediated and that there is no set of privileged comparison objects the apprehension of which would not require such mediation. Stated somewhat less cautiously, this conclusion amounts to saying that the only objects with which we have any commerce and of which we can have any knowledge are intentional objects—objects which, as Husserl says, we constitute by means of concepts or meanings—and that the world itself is simply the total intentional object. As Merleau-Ponty puts it, the world becomes the concept "world."

This reversal of perspective by virtue of which all objects become no more than so many points of intersection in the network of our conceptual activity in fact represents the outcome of the phenomenological reduction as Husserl describes it.[11] In the course of that reduction the perceptual acceptance of the world that is characteristic of what Husserl calls the "natural attitude" is progressively modified through a growing awareness of the part we play in the constitution of objects, and finally the world is reduced to the status of the intentional correlate of that

11. See Husserl's statement in *Ideen, I* (Husserliana, III sec. 135 [The Hague: 1950], 329) that "all the real and ideal realities which fall under the reduction are represented in the phenomenological sphere by the total manifolds of meanings and propositions that correspond to them."

meaning-conferring activity. If I may be permitted to describe that process in a manner that is at once too Hegelian and too oriented toward language to be entirely faithful to Husserl's meaning, I would say that the movement from the natural to the transcendental attitude is one through which I gradually come to appreciate the fact that I am, so to speak, the owner and operator of a total conceptual system. This requires, as the late John Austin said, "a prising of language off the world," i. e., a break with the naive conceptual realism that submerges conceptual and meaning-conferring activity in the flux of experience; and it leads through an appreciation of the unity of the systems of meaning which we have, as it were, been unconsciously applying to an understanding of the thoroughgoing parallelism between the various forms of objectivity and the intentional acts by which they are constituted. In the course of this reinterpretation of our relationship to the world, our conception of ourselves necessarily undergoes a profound modification since we are forced to distinguish between ourselves as particular existents *in* the world with a definite spatiotemporal location and a limited range of knowledge and perception and our "transcendental" selves for which the empirical self is just one object among the objects that fall within the purview of the total system of reference over which the transcendental self presides. This "new" self is of course derived from the old empirical self through a process of redescription and reconceptualization in the light of all the distinctions that are implicit in our total conceptual scheme; and from this process it emerges as the transcendental agent that operates and applies the total conceptual system. In the final apotheosis of transcendental subjectivity, I even overcome the condition of finite selfhood by constituting a milieu of transcendental intersubjectivity in which the perspectives of different individual human beings are harmoniously related to one another to form a single public world that is the true correlate of the system of meanings we employ.

In many respects the outcome of the process of radical reflection which I have been describing is similar to forms of phenomenalism which are familiar in the English-speaking philosophical world. In both cases the underlying motive of the analysis is to avoid all forms of representationalism and dualism and to exhibit the object of knowledge as ideally arrayed through the whole series of its perspectival variations before a pure consciousness. In both cases there is a determination to explicate every feature of our original perceptual relationship to the world and every mode of objectivity with which we are confronted in terms of immanence, i. e., in terms of relationships that can be traced out among the intentional or conceptually delineated objects of our mental acts. Thus reality comes to be defined in terms of a certain convergence or coherence among our ideas, and, as Merleau-Ponty says, perception becomes simply a "pensée de percevoir"—a special case of that "inspection d'esprit" before which all forms of objectivity must present their credentials. When a reference to something that transcends or remains opaque to consciousness seems to be involved in the uncriticized experience of everyday life, it is shown by reflective analysis to be merely an anticipation of a later term in the series of my possible experiences; and the apparent opening of consciousness on something distinct from itself or its immanent object turns out to be no more than a special configuration within the sphere of phenomenal immanence itself.[12] One important difference must, however, be noted. In a phenomenalism of the Husserlian type, there is no tincture of any disposition to reduce or to eliminate ideal and abstract terms of thought in favor of constellations of sense data. Essences or, as I would prefer to call them, concepts are not all formed by abstraction from sense particulars, and they are just as capable of being objects of consciousness as are sense contents.[13] Indeed in Husserl's view

12. An especially dramatic statement of this conclusion occurs in Husserl's *Tranzendentale u. Formale Logik* (Jahrbuch für Philosophie und *Phänomenologische Forschung* [Halle: 1929], X, 208), where it is laid down that "there is no conceivable point at which the life of consciousness could be penetrated and we would come upon a transcendence which would have a meaning other than that of an intentional unity appearing within the subjectivity of consciousness itself."

13. For a brilliant analysis of Husserl's view that meanings can be given, see H. Asemissen's *Strukturanalytische Probleme der Wahrnehmung in der Phänomenologie Husserls*, Kant-Studien (Ergänzungsheft), 1957, especially pp. 70–77.

the latter arrange themselves into meaningful forms of objectivity only to the degree that we dispose of such abstract concepts as those of "material object," "quality," "relationship," etc.

This then is the final version that critical idealism gives of our relationship to the world. In Merleau-Ponty's words,

> Mettant en face de l'esprit, foyer de toute clarté, le monde réduit à son schema intelligible, une réflexion conséquente fait évanouir toute question touchant leur rapport, qui est désormais de corrélation pure: l'esprit est ce qui pense, le monde est ce qui est pensé. . . . Ainsi avec la corrélation de principe de la pensée et de l'objet de pensée s'établit une philosophie qui ne connait ni difficultés, ni paradoxes, ni renversements: une fois pour toutes j'ai saisi en moi avec la pure corrélation de celui qui pense et de ce qu'il pense la vérité de ma vie, qui est aussi celle du monde et celle des autres vies.[14]

In short, the world has been assimilated to the status of an object of knowledge and while we are of course unable to overcome in practice all the latencies and lacunae that characterize the actual state of our knowledge, we at least know what conditions that fully constituted and displayed object would have to satisfy. Because we can thus anticipate the movement of our knowledge toward its ideal goal, we thereby constitute ourselves in advance as the κοσμοθεωρος for whom the world is in fact no more than an intentional object. For such a being no question can arise respecting his relation to the world or his presence in it, because all the familiar modes of attachment to a place and a time, to a body and a situation, by virtue of which we are incarnate

---

14. "By setting over against one another the world which has been reduced to its intelligible schema and mind which is the locus of all clarity, a consistent philosophical deliberation in effect suppresses all questions about their relationship to one another—a relationship which must henceforth be treated as one of pure correlation. Mind is what thinks, the world is what is thought. . . . In this way by virtue of a correlation in principle of thought and the object of thought a philosophy is established which recognizes no difficulties or paradoxes or reversals. In this pure correlation of that which thinks and of that which is thought I have grasped once and for all the truth of my life which is also the truth of the world and of other lives" (*Le visible et l'invisible*, p. 71). Such passages as this inevitably recall the sections of Wittgenstein's *Tractatus* in which the "I" of solipsism is described. See especially para. 5.6.

beings, will have been "objectified" and thus transformed into objects of knowledge which can no longer bind or restrict a cosmic spectator whose relationship of belonging to the world has been replaced by a "survol du monde."

III

Merleau-Ponty was not of course the first French philosopher in this century to express radical dissatisfaction with "intellectualism," and the criticism to which he was to subject it has a superficial similarity to that of Bergson. It is not surprising, therefore, that just as Bergson was attacked as an irrationalist, so Merleau-Ponty's critique of the pretentions of critical idealism has been misunderstood as a repudiation of reason in favor of some ill-defined "life" or "experience."[15] In fact, any such animus against theoretical reason by reason of its movement away from our primary perceptual contact with the world is wholly lacking in Merleau-Ponty's case, as I have already indicated; and in contrast to Bergson the point of his critique is not to show that conceptual thought necessarily involves a distortion of a reality to which we have access only in pure intuition. Instead, his primary philosophical concern is to show that, through the medium of critical idealism, theoretical reason can give no satisfactory account of its own genesis and development and that it falls into very serious errors when, at the prompting of that philosophy, it describes our primary perceptual experience of the world, out of which all scientific activity develops, as simply a confused and indistinct form of the rapport of consciousness to reality which is clearly explicated at the level of reflective analysis.

L'illusion des illusions est de croire à ce moment qu'en vérité nous n'avons jamais été certain que de nos actes, que depuis toujours la perception a été une inspection de l'esprit, et que

15. See, for example, the comments that followed the presentation of Merleau-Ponty's paper "The Primacy of Perception" to the Société Française de Philosophie which are reprinted in *The Primacy of Perception,* trans. James Edie (Evanston: 1964), pp. 27–42.

la réflexion est seulement la perception revenant à elle-même, la conversion du savoir de la chose à un savoir de soi, dont la chose était faite, l'émergence d'un liant qui était la liaison même.[16]

When perception and our precritical experience of the world are thus assumed to be simply somewhat confused or blurred equivalents of the relationship of a fully constituted subject to a fully constituted object, there can be no serious philosophical motive for an inquiry into any structures of perceptual experience that may be distinctive and peculiar to it. And yet just such an inquiry is needed—a kind of second-level reflection or "surréflexion" in which the movement of conceptual thought away from the original perceptual matrix is examined without assuming that the former somehow gives us the truth of the latter. When Merleau-Ponty spoke of the primacy of perception, he was expressing his deeply rooted belief that the ultimate bearer of the vast conceptual apparatus we call science is the human animal that is situated at a definite point in space and time and perceives the world *with* its body. If so, the task of philosophical reflection must be to help us to understand human reason, in its full range of diverse and sophisticated forms, as so many modes of orientation within a fundamental relationship to the world which we cannot understand by a retroactive application to it of the methods and concepts of the sciences that grow out of it. The characteristic vice of most philosophical theories of perception—what Merleau-Ponty calls "le préjugé du monde"— is that they set out from certain unquestioned assumptions with respect to the nature of the object of perception as we have come to know it through subsequent scientific investigation and then

16. "The supreme illusion is to believe on reaching this level of reflection that in truth we have never been certain of anything but our own (mental) acts and that perception has always been a mental intuition; and that reflection is simply perception coming back to itself—a conversion of a knowledge of things into a knowledge of self that was implicit in it, the emergence of a synthesizing agent that was the synthesis itself" (*Le visible et l' invisible,* p. 59). There is an obvious similarity between this "illusion" and Leibniz's assimilation of perception to thought for which he was so severely censured by Kant.

seek to understand human consciousness on the model of the fully explicit intellectual activity that is the mental counterpart of such fully constituted objects. As a result, the characteristic features of our perceptual experience are explained as a mélange of sense impressions and conceptually mediated "inferences" along the lines described above through a generalized application to the whole of our perceptual experience of the contrast between observation and inference with which we are familiar at the level of explicit intellectual activity. The animating intention of Merleau-Ponty's whole philosophy is quite simply to challenge the propriety of this retroactive application to perception of models drawn from the domain of judgment and conceptual thought; and by breaking the compulsive hold this model has established over philosophical treatments of perception Merleau-Ponty seeks to free us for the task of describing anew the distinctive structures of the perceptual milieu.

The philosophical position from which Merleau-Ponty hopes to work out a more satisfactory account of perception is in an important sense intermediate between the critical idealism he wishes to correct and the straightforward physicalism which he was far too much of a Cartesian ever to consider seriously. Thus on the one hand he argues, with Husserl, that the world of science is not fully intelligible unless its relationship to human subjectivity has been exhibited; and he certainly holds, against the physicalist, that mental acts are distinct from brain function and that they in fact occur. At the same time, however, he insists that the perceptual experience to which the world of science is to be related is in no sense the pure consciousness of the detached Cartesian spectator, but rather the perspective on the world of a creature that is *in* the world in a sense that cannot be rendered by any phenomenalistic analysis of the knowledge relationship. Thus at one and the same time, Merleau-Ponty accepts the Cartesian and Husserlian gambit and requires that all our knowledge of the world authenticate itself within an autonomous milieu of consciousness and then proceeds to describe that milieu itself in terms that often seem to identify it with a certain relationship of the human body to its natural environment. Clearly, if a contradiction is to be avoided, Merleau-Ponty must find a way of distinguishing between the body and its natural environment as these are described and explained in the scientific account of the world—which must not, he argues, be assumed in our theory of perception—and the body and the world as these appear in the context of his own account of perception. Whether this distinction can be satisfactorily worked out is, I suggest, one of the most critical questions that arise for any final appraisal of Merleau-Ponty's philosophy, but it is also one that lies outside the scope of this paper.[17]

Since Merleau-Ponty's theory of perception is to such a large extent a corrective for mistaken approaches to the subject, it will be useful to review briefly the criticisms he makes of intellectualistic theories of perception and the alternative views he proposes. These criticisms deal with the perception of natural objects as well as with our perception of our own bodies and of other persons; and in each case Merleau-Ponty argues that the errors of critical idealism spring from an effort to interpret perception in such a way that it progressively absorbs into itself the context *within* which it would ordinarily be thought of as taking place. To begin with the perception of objects, it is a fact, as the critical idealist so often points out, that even when I am most confident that I am actually perceiving a material object, I see only one or two sides of it and the rest remain hidden. If I am led to reflect upon perception, I may well be persuaded by arguments that turn on the similarity of illusory and veridical perceptions, to modify my initial confidence that the object itself is what I see and to declare instead that I directly apprehend only one of its perspectival aspects. Moving farther along this track of reasoning, I may then argue that the residual "unseen" sides of the object I am looking at are no more than the series of perspectival "views" of it that I could obtain. Even if my analysis of the original perception of the object recognizes a certain nonsensuous directedness or intentionality—a pointing beyond what

17. It is clear from the working notes that this is one of the major problems to which Merleau-Ponty intended to address himself in *Le visible et l'invisible.*

is given to what is not given—this referential component of my perception can itself be taken "neat," i. e., just as a phenomenon, disjoined from that to which it is a reference.[18] The result of this sequence of reductions is that the object will no longer be thought of as present now as the real terminus of my "seeing." It has been broken up into the "visual thing" and the "tactile thing," and as such it is distributed through the temporal series of my experiences. From being an element in the environment within which my perception occurs, it has become a certain set of relationships among units of experience which are defined in terms of what an illusory and a veridical perception have in common, and the apprehension of which is therefore logically prior to and independent of the distinction between veridical and nonveridical apprehensions of an objective state of affairs.

Merleau-Ponty's arguments against a phenomenalistic analysis of perception are too detailed and too variegated to be adequately summarized here. Many of them are psychological in character and challenge the propriety of treating sense data, which are evidently the end result of an elaborate series of reductive operations upon ordinary perceptual experience, as though they represented our primary mode of apprehension of material objects. Other arguments are intended to show that the very analyses by which the phenomenalistic case is made covertly employ the prereflective distinction between veridical and nonveridical perception and cannot therefore claim to replace it. But perhaps the most significant challenge that Merleau-Ponty offers to the phenomenalists is his argument that the phenomenological reduction can be complete only if it makes use of assumptions that no pure description of our experience can yield by itself. As I have already noted, an exhaustive reduction would require that the referential and self-transcending movement of natural perception be taken just as it is given phenomenally, i. e., as a referring but without its referent. But to de-

18. This point is well made in Hubert Dreyfus, "Husserl's Phenomenology of Perception" (unpublished Harvard doctoral thesis, 1964); there the whole relationship between Husserl's and Merleau-Ponty's theories of perception is explored.

scribe it in isolation from that to which it is a reference is surely to alter it in a crucially important respect insofar as such a description is possible at all. If that alteration and the shift away from the natural attitude of perceptual acceptance that it entails are then justified by arguing that the referent *could* only be some future sequence of experiences of the object in question, then the credentials of the theory on which this assumption is based need to be presented, and it must be shown on what grounds this theory can claim to override and correct the deliverance of pre-critical experience. If no such grounds can be presented—as Merleau-Ponty plainly believes—then perception will have to be described as a much more radical form of self-transcendence than any series of possible experiences could possibly yield; and the nonequivalence of existential judgments and statements about such series will have been established. This nonequivalence is in fact the point of the existentialists' distinction between being and essence which has been widely misunderstood, perhaps because critics have taken too literally some of the highly figurative language that the existentialists have used in expounding the irreducibility of things to the phenomenal qualities by which we know them.[19]

If, in spite of important differences of philosophical idiom, Merleau-Ponty's treatment of the perception of objects moves along lines parallel to Anglo-American discussions of the same themes, some of his most original ideas have to do with the role of the body in perception. Since Descartes, it has been a crucial step in the isolation of the transcendental ego to argue that my body, in spite of its apparently unique position, is no more than one object among other objects and that as such it is just as susceptible of reductive phenomenalistic analysis as any other body. It has also been generally agreed that standard methods of causal explanation are in principle perfectly applicable to "my"

19. It should be noted that the existentialists distinguish between "being" and "existence" and also between both these terms and "essence." "Being" is the term they most frequently use in speaking of things to convey what might be called their "extraphenomenal" ontological status. "Existence" tends to be reserved for "conscious human existence," and "essence" applies to both phenomenal qualities and concepts.

body; and in this way my relationship to my body is definitively assimilated to my relationship to other objects of knowledge. Even when Husserl points out that it is an essential feature of all my perceptions of the world that my body is always "co-present," he shows no disposition to distinguish between the way in which my body is apprehended and the way other objects are.[20] As Merleau-Ponty points out, however, the result of this traditional Cartesian treatment of the body as an object among objects is to generate grave problems concerning the role of the sense organs in perception. It becomes just an empirical fact that I cannot see unless I have eyes; and since the relationship of physiological functions to acts of consciousness is entirely external and contingent, true "seeing" must always remain an act performed by the "eye of the mind" which in itself bears no mark of an essential relationship to the organs of sense.

Merleau-Ponty's criticism of this conception of the body, like his criticisms of phenomenalism generally, are often psychological in character and draw extensively on the studies that have been made of the body image in both normal and pathological cases. His intention is of course to show how very far our ordinary experience of our bodies is from conforming to this phenomenalistic and intellectualistic model. In this connection he repeatedly lays great emphasis on the fact that objects are normally perceived in the context of an activity of the body; and he insists that this feature of perception, which has been so solidly established by empirical psychological investigations, cannot be adequately translated into the Cartesian language of mental acts of association and interpretation. Important as these psychological discussions are to Merleau-Ponty's argument, he also has a number of distinctively philosophical points to make against the phenomenalistic treatment of the body as simply one object of a single, standard kind of knowledge. Thus he raises the question

20. I am not unmindful of the fact that in *Ideen II* Husserl presented detailed analyses of the experience of one's own body and of the bodies of others and of the differences between the two, but I could also argue that at no point does he depart from a basically phenomenalistic treatment of both types of experience.

of how the kind of limitation implied by our inescapably perspectival knowledge of objects could ever be imposed on a consciousness as completely independent of its body as the phenomenalists suppose it to be. At a deeper level Merleau-Ponty is arguing that references to the body and its various possible dispositions remain logically primitive; and he is making much the same kind of point against phenomenalism that has been made by those philosophers who point out that the presently nongiven terms in the series of my representations can be actualized only by carrying out certain bodily movements. We can of course attempt to close the circle by translating these references to the body into phenomenalistic language, but we can never absorb entirely all references to some state of the body that is in fact a condition for the sequence of experiences that is being projected. As I read him, Merleau-Ponty is making a case not just for what I have called the logical primitiveness of these references to the body, but also for the epistemological distinctiveness of the type of knowledge they represent. Again a parallel to recent Anglo-American discussions suggests itself—in this case to the attempts that have been made to gain recognition for what is called our "non-observational knowledge" of what we are doing at any given time.[21] For Merleau-Ponty the kind of assurance with which we can declare our intentions, and which is evidently not the result of observations such as we institute in the case of external objects, reflects an apprehension of our bodies in terms of a schema of action which is also a mode of orientation within our natural environment.

The problem of our perception of other conscious beings has always been the most serious obstacle in the way of a thoroughgoing application of the phenomenalistic thesis to all objects of knowledge. It is a problem that was not recognized in its full seriousness by the classical writers in the Cartesian tradition; and while Hume was prepared to accept a theory of the self as a

21. See S. Hampshire and H. L. A. Hart, "Decision, Intention, and Certainty," *Mind* (1958), 1–12. Hampshire's book *Thought and Action* (London: 1959) at many points seems to enunciate theses very similar to Merleau-Ponty's on this and other points.

construction out of bits of mental content, he proposed no comparable theory of other selves as compounded out of *my* possible impressions and ideas. The difficulty of the problem and the radical discontinuity it introduces into our system of the world are appreciated fully only when I bear in mind that the alien consciousness I postulate as somehow existing beyond "its" body is not only in principle unincorporable into any smooth sequence of experiences that *I* might have, but also has to be defined as a consciousness of the same objects and the same world which I progressively explicate in phenomenalistic terms.[22] To be sure, the body of the other presents no difficulties and can be treated in exactly the same way as I treat my own, i. e., as a natural object governed by natural laws and comprehensible in terms of the same sort of causal regularities as any other object. But the very facility with which we can deal with the body of the other only aggravates the difficulty of somehow fitting the other, as a consciousness that is radically distinct from its body, into *our* world. As Merleau-Ponty reminds us, the only solution for the hopeless problems generated in this way is to assert that human beings "meet" only in the sense and only to the extent that an ideal coincidence of their "theories of the world" can be assumed; and in both the Leibnizian and the Hegelian form, doctrines of this kind have proved notably fertile in paradoxes. In any case, they uniformly require that we give up all ideas of a concrete perceptual encounter with another sentient being and indeed the notion itself of "seeing" another person.

It is precisely this character of a direct encounter with other conscious beings that Merleau-Ponty wished to restore to an important place in the philosophical theory of perception. As in the case of our perception of material objects, so in the case of our perception of other persons, we meet something that is not exhausted by the mental act through which it is apprehended; but

22. Husserl was, I think, the first philosopher to give prominence to the role of intentionality in our concept of other conscious beings and to stress the fact that an alien consciousness is not just a collection of mental contents but also a referential relationship to the *same* objects which I experience. See *Cartesian Meditations,* trans. Cairns (The Hague: 1960), pp. 120–28; and *Ideen,* II, Husserliana (The Hague: 1952), 168–69.

the two cases involve quite different types of transcendence. When I recognize the reality of another point of view on the same world that I have already perceived and construed in a certain way, what I recognize is not just another transcendental spectator whose "cosmological eye" reflects the same fully constituted object or world that I have already in view, but rather a quite concrete—because incarnate—system of actions and intentions that may run athwart or reinforce my own. In any case I am made inescapably aware that I and *my* world form the objects of an independent appreciation and one that is made not by an absolute and disengaged spectator but by an agent that is situated in the same world as I and comprehends it, as I do, through schemata of action. As Merleau-Ponty points out, the failure of philosophers to deal adequately with "other minds" is simply the reverse side of their inability to give a satisfactory account of our relationship to our own bodies and of the behavioral intentionality that is at the heart of that relationship. If the confusions that dog our understanding of the body were dispelled, we might be in a position to extend the same form of analysis to the perception of the body of other persons, i. e., to a perception of them not as machines but as systems of comportment and modes of orientation within the same world in which I find myself. When my concepts of the body and of consciousness are not impoverished by being blown up to the point at which the one confronts the other statically in a relation of perfect correspondence and when both are understood in terms of a kind of incarnate intentionality, other persons need no longer represent a remote and forever inaccessible "inspection d'esprit" operating from beyond the barrier of the body. They can instead be recognized as presences within my perceptual world that are none the less real because they do not yield themselves up exhaustively in the way that a consistent phenomenalism would require.

These, then, are some of the main lines of Merleau-Ponty's critique of the intellectualistic and reductionistic tendencies that he imputes to "la pensée réflexive." His effort in each case is to show that the attempt to exhaust these different elements in our perceptual world through an analysis in terms of their being for consciousness must fail. At the same time he is trying to do something more. By means of the often highly figurative language that he employs, he seeks to convey to us the mute presence of the things that are reached by our perceptions but never absorbed by them. In the working notes that accompany *Le visible et l'invisible* there is a brief passage in which Merleau-Ponty seems to suggest that this presence of things is something of which we need to be reminded. Perhaps, he says, it is not just certain mis-conceived philosophies of perception but human perception itself that tends to become oblivious to itself as what he calls "perception sauvage" and "tends to see itself as an act and to forget its latent intentionality." He further notes as a kind of paradox the fact that while "philosophy is language through and through it nevertheless consists in rediscovering silence."[23] Clearly any attempt to achieve by means of language a new and deeper sensitivity to a dimension of the perceptual world that is opaque to conceptualization has its dangers, and Merleau-Ponty often seems to associate language so closely with conceptual thought as to make it quite unclear how it could possibly be a vehicle for the philosophical insights he wishes to make it con-vey. In any case, it is clear that his own philosophical practice logically commits him to the view that language *can* be so used; and the passages I have just quoted indicate that in that wider use it would serve a significant quasi-moral purpose by counter-acting a tendency of human consciousness to close in upon itself.

IV

I now wish to take note very briefly of a similarity between Merleau-Ponty's position as it emerges from the account I have given and certain views that are widely shared within the "ordi-nary language" wing of the analytical movement in philosophy. Both existential phenomenology as developed by Merleau-Ponty and ordinary language philosophy are concerned to vindicate the integrity of the familiar everyday world of what may be called

23. *Le visible et l'invisible,* pp. 266–67.

"middle-sized" objects as well as of the systems of reference by which the latter are delineated.[24] This defense is intended as a rebuttal to both scientific and philosophical doctrines that cast doubt on the logical and ontological credentials of the entities that pass current in the world of perception and of precritical common sense. On the scientific side, a case has often been made, though with varying degrees of sophistication, for the view that nothing but atoms and molecules "really" exists and that perceptual objects and the statements we make about them must all be regarded as deriving in principle from the truths of microphysics. Against claims of this type Merleau-Ponty, like the neo-Wittgensteinians, defends the logical autonomy of the distinctions that block out our perceptual world; and he argues that the relation of dependence runs the other way, since the entities of theoretical physics would make no sense to a being who did not have the concept of a material object. This defense of the middle-ground constitutes at the same time a rejoinder to those philosophical doctrines, whether of logical atomism or absolute idealism, which seek to show that the objects of perception are either constructions out of ultimately simple units, whose existence has to be postulated for reasons that are completely independent of perception, or that such objects suffer from internal incoherencies that can be resolved only at the level of a monistically conceived absolute. While these quite different metaphysical positions may be more visible in the immediate intellectual background of ordinary language philosophy, their counterparts are also discernible among the predecessor philosophies to which the existentialists were to develop such a sharp allergy.

This affinity between Merleau-Ponty and the ordinary language analysts seems to me to be important and to deserve much more attention than it has so far received. But lest I should be thought to be proclaiming a new principle of philosophical oecumenism, I wish to conclude by drawing attention to two closely related

24. John Wild was one of the first to draw attention to this affinity in his article "Is there a World of Ordinary Language?", *Philosophical Review*, LVII, No. 4 (1958).

respects in which Merleau-Ponty's position is noticeably at variance with the views of the analytical school. First, Merleau-
Ponty never conceived of his own inquiries as having a purely
logical or—even in a very broad sense of the term—"linguistic"
import.[25] It is true that he had substantial reservations about the
Husserlian doctrine of categorial intuition; and his later essays in
particular tend more and more toward a rather pragmatic-sound-
ing account of the essential or structural features of consciousness
as being those around which a more coherent and perspicuous
conception of human subjectivity can be organized. It is also
true that he recognized the importance of language as a medium
in which some of our most fundamental modes of comportment
toward the world are deployed. Nevertheless, it has to be made
quite clear that Merleau-Ponty on several occasions explicitly
rejected the view that the task of philosophy is simply to trace
out the internal logic of established *Wortbedeutungen*. However
important language and linguistic behavior might be as data
for philosophical reflection, the portrait of the philosopher as a
kind of glorified lexicographer, enjoying no freedom in the de-
vising of more adequate linguistic instruments for the expression
of the insights that philosophy seeks to gain, was obviously and
deeply repellent to Merleau-Ponty.

The reasons for this attitude are not hard to divine, and they
go to the heart of Merleau-Ponty's very marked differences with
even those strains in analytical philosophy which might otherwise seem most congenial to his point of view. In spite of all his
vindication of common sense and his defense of the integrity of
the perceptual milieu, Merleau-Ponty's whole philosophical effort
is quite clearly inspired by a sense of the profoundly mysterious
and paradoxical character of human subjectivity. Nothing could
be more alien to the spirit of his philosophy than the self-
stultifying smugness of some contemporary masters of ordinary
language in whom any residual tendency to philosophical puzzlement is checked by frequently consulting the O.E.D. Merleau-

25. Perhaps his clearest statement of his views on this point is his brief
contribution to the discussions held at Royaumont in 1957 which have
been published in *La philosophie analytique* (Paris: 1962), pp. 93–96.

Ponty quite certainly had a good deal more in common with St. Augustine, who was similarly struck with wonder at the mysteries of human consciousness, than with those who wonder only at the puzzlement of others. Nor was he satisfied simply to describe the different systems of reference to the world and to let them subsist side by side in a kind of irenic pluralism. As his last work clearly shows, he felt that he must at least attempt to press further in the hope of gaining a deeper understanding of the nature of a world that can be approached and talked about in so many different ways. We cannot judge how successful that further inquiry would have proved to be. We must, however, feel a deep regret that it was not completed.

Essay Eight

Husserl and Wittgenstein
on Language

PAUL RICOEUR*

The kind of confrontation that I propose here is not intended to generate a hybrid offshoot. Each philosophy is an organism which has its internal rules of development. What we may best do is to understand each better by means of the other and, perhaps, formulate new problems that proceed from this encounter.

Husserl and Wittgenstein allow a certain amount of comparison, thanks to the parallelism of their development—that is, from a position in which ordinary language is measured on a model of ideal language to a description of language as it functions, as everyday language or as language of the *Lebenswelt.* (These are provisory terms that have to be qualified by the analysis itself.)

Therefore I propose to consider two cross sections: one at the level of the *Logical Investigations* on the one hand and of the *Tractatus* on the other; the second at the level of the last works of Husserl and of the *Investigations.*

I

At the first level the comparison may be focused on the function played by the theory of meaning and by the theory of picture respectively. Why this choice?

In the first *Logical Investigation* the theory of meaning is put in an intermediary position. Before that, in the *Prolegomena,*

* Faculté des Lettres, Université de Paris à la Sorbonne, Paris, France.

Husserl had elaborated a pure logical theory, conceived as the axiomatics of all possible theories, i.e., of all necessary closed systems of principles. This was a pure logic in the sense that a logical proposition is free from contamination by anything psychological; it is a "truth in itself." It is the task of a phenomenology of meaning to locate the logical contents within the wider circle of "signs" (*Zeichen*) ; among "signs" they belong to the class of "signifying signs." Logical contents are thus considered as the meanings of certain expressions (hence the title: *Ausdruck und Bedeutung*). As such they are only kinds of signifying expressions—but not mere cases. They display a specific function: they represent the *telos* of every language or level of language. And because logical structure is the *telos,* meaningful expressions cover a wider field than logical contents, and phenomenology must precede logic. Two examples may be useful: the description of *Erlebnisse* may be rigorous, without being *exact* in the logico-mathematical sense: we may speak rigorously of inexact essences. Furthermore, ordinary language is full of expressions that are equivocal not by chance but by nature; these "circumstantial" or "occasional" expressions—such as personal pronouns, demonstratives, adverbial locutions ("here" and "now")—achieve their meaning in relation to a situation and an audience with which speaker and listener are acquainted. As to the analysis of the meaningful act, I shall not repeat it here (meaning as an "aiming" that animates and permeates the signifying layer and provides it with the power of representing something, of having something as its object). It is the position of this analysis in the course of the *Logical Investigations* which interests me. I said that this analysis occupies an intermediate position. What is beyond and why have we to go further?

We were brought back from logic to phenomenology. We are now brought back from a phenomenology of "expressions" (of signifying signs) to a phenomenology of *Erlebnisse* in general. It is the task of the fifth logical investigation to elaborate a concept of "consciousness"—not only of consciousness as a whole, as monad, but of consciousness as the transcending process implied in each *Erlebnis,* of consciousness as *intentional*. Signifying expressions were still facts of language; intentionality covers the field of all transcending acts: perception, imagination, desire, will, perception of, desire of, will of.

After having founded logical contents on linguistic expressions, phenomenology founds the latter on the power of intentionality, which is more primitive than language and is linked to "consciousness" as such.

Language is therefore an intermediary between two levels. The first one, as we said, constitutes its *ideal* of logicity, its *telos*: all meanings must be able to be converted into the logos of rationality; the second one no longer constitutes an ideal, but a ground, a soil, an origin, an *Ursprung*. Language may be reached "from above," from its logical limit, or "from below," from its limit in mute and elemental experience. In itself it is a medium, a mediation, an exchange between *Telos* and *Ursprung*.

Can we now compare the picture theory of the *Tractatus* with this theory of meaning? No, if we consider the context; yes, if we consider the position and the function of this specific theory.

Like Husserl, Wittgenstein intends to build "a discourse in the kind of philosophy that uses logic as a basis." The central part of the *Tractatus*, concerning propositions (*Sätze*), propositional signs, logical form, truth functions, and truth operations, agrees with this requirement. The "proposition" is the pivot: "An expression has meaning only in a proposition" (3.314). But the *Tractatus* as a whole overflows this structure and does not use logic as a basis. Why? Because logic is concerned with "possibilities of truth" (4.3; 4.4; 4.41). But tautology and contradiction are the two extreme cases among the possible groups of truth conditions (4.46). The *Tractatus* must also take into account a nontautological concept of truth, truth as concordance between propositions and facts. The picture theory comes in here: "the totality of true thoughts is a picture of the world" (3.01). But "tautologies and contradictions are not pictures of reality" (4.462). We have therefore to elaborate a picture theory distinct from that of truth conditions, as Husserl had to elaborate a theory of meaning distinct from that of logical propositions.

The context is different, but the position and the function are comparable.

The context is different. First, because Husserl intended to overcome the absoluteness of logical truth, while Wittgenstein has to overcome the senselessness of tautology; second, because the *Tractatus* has to start with propositions concerning the world (1; 1.1; 1.11, etc.)—facts, states of affairs, objects (things). Whatever the status of these propositions (and everybody knows how controversial it is), they precede the analysis of the "picture" and must precede it, since the picture is itself a fact—"a picture is a fact" (2.141)—therefore something in the world. But it is an odd fact, since it is a fact that represents other facts (*vertreten*).

This context seems to exclude any kind of comparison. For a phenomenologist the starting point of the *Tractatus* would appear to be the ultimate expression of the "naturalistic" attitude (unless we reinterpret these first propositions in the terms of the later Husserl, as a description of *Lebenswelt*, or in those of *Sein und Zeit*, as an analysis of being-in-the-world; but this would be rather hazardous).

In spite of this difference concerning the course and the development of both works, the picture theory, once introduced, displays a range of implications that exceed not only the logical framework of that philosophy but also the realistic requirements of the starting point; an implicit—and perhaps abortive—phenomenology of the "meaning" grows out of the ontology of facts, states of affairs, and world.

The picture—like the meaning for Husserl—is the essence of all language; it covers the field of spoken and written languages and of all articulated signs: photographs, diagrams, plans, maps, musical scores, records—i.e., all kinds of representations through which the disposition of elements or of parts in the "fact" is expressed by a corresponding disposition in the picture.

The picture is a correspondence between structure and structure (2.12). But as soon as we have introduced this concept of correspondence we must find *within* the picture the principle of it. Wittgenstein calls it the "pictorial form" (2.15; 2.151), which is the condition of the "pictorial relationship" (2.1513; 2.1514). In the case of factual truth there is no trouble; we may speak of an *identity* between the picture and what it depicts (2.16; 2.161); the pictorial form may even be conceived as what a picture has in common with reality (2.17). But a less realistic interpretation of the pictorial form appears with the representation of possibility, of nonexistence,[1] and above all with false representations. Here the "sense" is no more something in common, but an inner feature: there may be representation (*Darstellung*) without depiction (*Abbildung*). This concept of *Darstellung* as distinct from that of *Abbildung* is the closest to phenomenology (2.22; 2.221–2.224) ; it culminates in this assertion: "What a picture represents [*darstellt*] is its sense" (2.221). As in Plato, the idea is an idea of something but not necessarily of something which *is*. Here phenomenology occurs.

But this phenomenology tends to abort: the absence of reflectivity in the picture precludes all explicit phenomenology: "A picture can depict any reality whose form it has" (2.171); "A picture cannot, however, depict its pictorial form: it displays it" (2.172). Why? We don't know. Henceforth the picture theory has to be absorbed into the theory of logical forms (2.18) ; a picture, the pictorial form of which is a logical form, will be called a logical picture. The *Tractatus* will be mainly a theory of the logical picture.

Husserl helped us to discover within the *Tractatus* tensions, paradoxes, and above all an aborted phenomenology of meaning, crushed between the initial realistic propositions of the *Tractatus* about world and facts and the logical kernel of the *Tractatus*.

But at the same time, we may perhaps understand why Wittgenstein had to elaborate a new frame-work for the meanings of ordinary language and to substitute his conception of language-games and of language as usage for the picture-theory. But we shall better understand this new stand after having considered the corresponding development in Husserl.

1. Wittgenstein seems to admit possibilities and negations in his concept of reality (2.06; 2.201).

II

The predominant problem in the late philosophy of Husserl proceeds directly from the early one. As we said, language is an intermediary between logical structures that constitute its *telos* and the lived experience that gives it an origin. It is mainly this second side of the problem which the late philosophy takes into account, without losing sight of the other side, as the *Logic* of 1929 proves.

But this relation between language and prelinguistic experience is not a simple one. It implies in its turn a new polarity between two trends: the first one, symbolized by the "reduction," implies a suspension, which does not necessarily mean a retreat within an ego secluded from reality but the kind of break with natural surroundings which is implied in the birth of language as such; there is no symbolic function without the sort of mutation that affects my relation to reality by substituting a *signifying* relation for a natural involvement. Reduction, we might say, means the birth of a speaking subject. This reduction has its reflection in the structure of the sign itself; the sign is "empty" in the sense that it is not the thing, but indicates the thing, and is not itself, since it exists only to indicate.

Now this distanciation, this suspension, this reduction, which constitutes the sign as sign, opens a new and complementary possibility, that of *fulfilling* or *not fulfilling* the sign. There is a problem concerning fulfillment because of the emptiness of the sign as sign.

The problem of fulfillment is in a sense as old as phenomenology; we find it in the sixth logical investigation. But as long as the reduction had not been explicated, as it was in the *Ideas* and the *Cartesian Meditations*, it was not a problem but only a solution. It becomes a problem as soon as a first naïveté is broken, the naïveté of vision as a given—as though vision were a ray of light filling the cavity of the sign. This naïveté, too, must be lost. The return to the things themselves is the name of a problem before being an answer. We have to discover that the idea of complete or ultimate fulfillment is itself an ideal, the ideal of adequation; more than that, this ideal cannot be fulfilled in principle; the perception is by nature perspectival and inadequate; syntactic and categorical factors are always implied in the least judgment of perception; and the thing itself, as a unity of all its profiles or perspectives, is presumed, not given. Therefore, what we call "intuition" is itself the result of "synthesis," of passive syntheses that already have their syntax, that are articulated in a prereflective and prejudicative (or prepredicative) sense.

This is why Husserl was led to raise in new terms the problem of fulfillment. The prepredicative and prelinguistic structures are not given; we cannot start from them. We have rather to be *brought back* to them by the means of a process that Husserl calls *Rückfragen* ("back-questioning"). This *Rückfrage* definitely excludes any recourse to something like an "impression" in the Humean sense. It is from within the world of signs and on the basis of the *doxa* in the sense of the *Theaetetus*—i.e., of judgments of perception—that we "inquire" regressively towards a primordial lived experience; but this so-called lived experience, for men who were born among words, will never be the naked presence of an absolute, but will remain that toward which this regressive questioning points.

We have elaborated in this way a model of analysis which can be called a *genesis,* but not a genesis in the chronological sense; it is a genesis of the meaning, sense genesis, which consists in unfolding the layers of constitution deposited as sediments on a presupposed raw, mute experience.

The dynamics of genesis has thus been substituted for the status of fulfillment: this genesis allows us to introduce, in the framework of "transcendental logic," the notion of individuals, of world as horizon, beyond the something in general required by "formal logic." But individuals and world are the correlates of the *Rückfrage*.

As we have seen, the latest philosophy of Husserl has developed one of the directions implied in his first analysis of meaning; it has only been dramatized by the episode of reduction, which made of fulfillment a problem for itself. But the position of language as the intermediary between logic and experience, between *telos* and origin, has been reinforced by this new function of mediation between the absence constitutive of the sign and the articulated world that always precedes it.

When we jump from Husserl to the *Philosophical Investigations* of Wittgenstein, we have the impression that the author does not even consider the possibility of coming back from a logical language to ordinary language by way of a regressive inquiry. On the contrary, he confronts language directly and notices how it functions in ordinary, everyday situations. We are told not to think but to look. Language is immediately removed from the field of philosophical perplexities to that of its successful functioning. This field is that of *use*, in which language produces certain effects, reactions, adapted responses, in the realm of human and social action. We may compare this field of use to that of *doxa* in Husserl, with the difference that Wittgenstein examines its actual functioning, not its transcendental conditions.

The first advantage of Wittgenstein's approach is to relax the hold of a unitary theory of the functioning of language; we start without a model. What does one find? Innumerable uses, a few of which Wittgenstein supplies in paragraph 23.

In order to do justice to this countless multiplicity, Wittgenstein introduces his famous *games*; the point of the comparison lies in the fact that the diversity of these games is not subsumed under what might be regarded as essential to a language and that each is appropriate to a particular situation. Each game delimits a field in which certain procedures are valid as long as one plays that game and not another. Each is like a condensed model of behavioral patterns in which several players occupy different roles.

The second advantage of this reduction of language to a bundle of particular games concerns denomination (naming). According to Wittgenstein, a good part of our philosophy of meaning proceeds from an overestimation of the role of denomination, which has been regarded since Augustine as the paradigm case of the speech act; but naming is a special game played under certain circumstances (for example, when I am asked, What is that called? Or when I resort to "ostensive definitions" that remain dependent upon the game of learning and assigning names).

This critique of denomination is liberating, inasmuch as it gets rid of any atomistic theory of language for which the simple constituents of reality would correspond to logically simple names, to true proper names. The critique of the picture theory is itself implied in that critique of denomination, if it is true that the picture relation is a privileged form of the relation "name-thing."

In this way the critique of denomination (para. 50) opens the horizon to a resolutely pluralist conception of the uses of language; these uses form families, without there being an essence to the language games and therefore to language itself (paras. 65, 77).

But has Wittgenstein succeeded in avoiding a general theory of language? There is at least one idea that looks like a general idea concerning language, that of usage: "for a *large* class of cases—though not for all—in which we employ the word 'meaning' it can be defined thus: the meaning of a word is its use in the language" (para. 43). It is worth dwelling on this notion of use which can initiate a discussion with Husserl.

Indeed the notion of use is primarily a way of resuming the old battle against entities. It is this critique that is at stake in the discussion of denomination: entities are sublimated names; language becomes a contemplative activity, a vision of the meaning of words. The notion of use is thus directed against any theory that would make meaning something occult, either in the sense of a Platonic reality or in the sense of a mental entity. As a result of its public character use conceals no mystery. In the practice of language everything is exposed; it is even a matter of indifference whether this use is or is not accompanied by a mental process, by images or feelings. "What we do is to bring words back from their metaphysical to their everyday use" (para. 116).

It is at this very point that Husserl and Wittgenstein dissent.

The flexibility of language as mediating between several levels, as pointing toward logicity but also towards life, has been eliminated by this closed definition of language as *use*. What is lacking here is the dialectic between the reduction, which creates distance, and the return to reality, which creates presence. The concept of use is undialectical in this sense. Language games, according to Wittgenstein, are directly incorporated into successful human activities; they represent forms of life: "hence the term language-game is meant to bring into prominence the fact that the speaking of language is part of an activity, or a form of life" (para. 23). But do we coincide with life? In Husserl the life world is not viewed directly but posited indirectly, as that to which the logic of truth refers back. Wittgenstein on the contrary seems to situate himself immediately in this world of everyday experience, in which language is a form of activity like eating, drinking, and sleeping.

I propose that a theory of meaning requires two dimensions, not one. According to the first, meaning is not use nor is language a "part of an activity or a form of life"; the meaning is a term within a system of inner dependences, as Hjelmslev used to say. This constitution of the sign as sign presupposes the break with life, activity, and nature which Husserl has symbolized in the reduction and which is represented in each sign by its emptiness, or its negative relation to reality. This constitution of the sign as sign, at the level of a system of signs, distinct from natural things, is the presupposition of the other dimension of the sign, i.e., the use of meanings, by combination in sentences in a given situation. The first side is the semiotic side; the second is the semantic one, that of the speech act—what Wittgenstein calls in an appropriate way "the speaking of our language." With this distinction it is possible to retain Wittgenstein's notion of use and even to draw from it all the advantages of its application to life in an indefinite variety of uses, exceeding its logical functions. The concept of language as *use* concerns only the speech act; it is true that it is a form of life, but this is no longer true of language as a system of signs; the symbolic function, which constitutes the sign as such, originates in the distance between thought and life.

It is because it does not belong to life, because it is, according to the Stoics, an "incorporeal" entity, a "lecton," that it can transform all our human activities, all our forms of life, into meaningful activity. But if the first trend in language is a centrifugal movement in relation to life and the activities of living, the *use* of language becomes itself problematic. It is no longer enough to look; one has to think. We are forever separated from life by the very function of the sign; we no longer live life but simply designate it. We signify life and are thus indefinitely withdrawn from it, in the process of *interpreting* it in a multitude of ways.

And, above all, if language is only a mediation, an intermediary between several levels, between *Logos* and *Bios*, a critique of ordinary language is itself possible; the philosopher is playing a game that is no longer a form of life.

We are no longer engaged in a practical activity but in a theoretical inquiry. It is for this attitude of reflection and of speculation that the life world figures simply as an origination of sense, to which a regressive inquiry refers back endlessly. But philosophy itself is made possible by the act of reduction, which is also the birth of language.

Essay Nine

The Relevance of
Phenomenological Philosophy
for Psychology

HERBERT SPIEGELBERG[*]

I

THE ISSUE AND ITS BACKGROUND

I would like to begin with a brief exposition of the background for my choice of topic.

As far as psychology is concerned, one might well maintain that phenomenology has arrived in the American world, much more than it has in American philosophy, where it is still largely considered an exotic plant. Thus, in a recent symposium on behaviorism and phenomenology at Rice University, sponsored by the American Psychological Association,[1] phenomenology was given equal ranking with behaviorism, apparently as one of the two major alternatives in psychology today. Among the participants, all native Americans, were such leading psychologists as Sigmund Koch and B. F. Skinner. And not only Robert B. MacLeod, long a spokesman for a phenomenology of "disciplined naïveté," pleaded the case for phenomenology. Carl Rogers, the founder of client-centered therapy, invoked phenomenology as the most important new ingredient of his "science of the person." On the other hand, none of the philosophers invited, neither Norman Malcolm nor Michael Scriven, had any known ties with philosophical phenomenology. Even MacLeod, the most un-

[*] Department of Philosophy, Washington University, St. Louis, Missouri.

1. T. W. Wann (ed.), *Behaviorism and Phenomenology* (Chicago: 1963).

equivocal proponent of phenomenology stated, "emphatically," that in his view, "what we call psychological phenomenology is not to be confused with Husserl's philosophy." (p. 51.)[2] Thus the phenomenology considered at the symposium was one without any live ties with phenomenological philosophy. Does this mean that phenomenological psychology has declared its final independence? If so, is this total emancipation a good thing for psychology as well as for philosophy? Was their indisputable connection in the past merely a historical accident without lasting significance? It is these questions which I would like to discuss by proposing the topic of the relevance of phenomenological philosophy for psychology.

One way of doing this would be to show the historical connections between the two in a way which would make it plain that they have essential and understandable links, even though they are now often forgotten. While this can be done and seems to me eminently worth doing, my own experience has shown me that this can grow into a formidable enterprise. Such an attempt would have to consider more than just the lifework of Husserl, central though his position in the phenomenological movement was and remains, even after he moved more and more to left of center. For, as I would like to re-emphasize here, phenomenological philosophy is not synonymous with Husserl's work. A comprehensive appraisal of the contributions of phenomenological philosophy to psychology would have to include the work of Alexander Pfänder, Moritz Geiger, and Max Scheler, Heidegger's hermeneutic phenomenology, and the existential phenomenologies of Gabriel Marcel, Sartre, and Merleau-Ponty.[3] All

2. In a similar vein Alfred Kuenzli, in prefacing his anthology of articles on *The Phenomenological Problem* (New York: 1959), referred to Husserl as "not especially pertinent to the concerns of contemporary psychologists" (p. IX).

3. I am preparing such an account with the aid of the National Institute of Mental Health under the title "Phenomenology in Psychology and Psychiatry." A volume of translations from the writings of Alexander Pfänder, dealing mostly with his phenomenological psychology, entitled "Phenomenology of Willing and Motivation," will appear presently with the Northwestern University Press.

I can do now is to present some of the evidence in the case of Edmund Husserl, too often looked upon as the antipsychologist par excellence.

Another and ultimately more valid way of tackling the issue would be to consider, without regard to the historical connections, the essential relationships between phenomenological philosophy and psychology. I shall try this to the extent of discussing at least some respects in which psychology presupposes phenomenology in a more than psychological sense. But I chiefly want to demonstrate it concretely by introducing an exemplary case where philosophical phenomenology and psychological phenomenology seem to me to converge without being sufficiently aware of it, and where they may actually be interdependent. For I would like to make this clear: I am not thinking of a one-way street from philosophy to psychology but of a two-way exchange. It is philosophical phenomenology as well as psychology which stands to benefit from such a relationship.

But before I proceed with the task, I had better state in what sense I am distinguishing between phenomenological philosophy and phenomenological psychology. In so doing I do not want to suppress the fact that in the early days of phenomenology, i.e., around 1900, Husserl himself defined phenomenology as a descriptive psychology, much to his later regret. In trying to undo the damage, with only partial success, he stressed the point that phenomenology was not concerned with empirical facts, as is genuine descriptive psychology, but with the essences and essential relations of the psychic phenomena, regardless of whether there are any instances of such essences in existence. But there are other differences. Phenomenology, conceived by Husserl as the science of the essential structure of consciousness, comprised not only the acts of consciousness, which he later called the noetic acts, corresponding to what a phenomenological psychologist like Carl Stumpf had called psychic functions: consciousness points essentially to referents beyond itself, to "intentional objects," to which Husserl later also attached the name of "noematic objects." These, too, belong to the rightful domain of phenomenology—for instance, by way of a phenomenology of the body or of works of art, which deal with their essential structures and their ways of appearing. These intentional or noematic objects lie clearly beyond the field of a psychology that is concerned merely with what are strictly psychic phenomena.

On this occasion I shall not raise the question of whether phenomenology, conceived as the descriptive science of the phenomena of consciousness, is itself essentially philosophical or rather a study that precedes all philosophy and science. All I want to consider is the relation between the phenomenology undertaken by such nonpsychologist philosophers as Edmund Husserl in contradistinction to the one launched by such non-philosopher-psychologists as Donald Snygg, the first representative of what I would like to call an American phenomenology from the grassroots. My question is then: Is what Husserl did under the name of phenomenology relevant for psychologists, particularly those who now do the sort of things which these grass-roots phenomenologists advocate?

I also feel a need to state what I understand here by the term "relevance," a term whose vagueness may easily seem evasive. Unfortunately I am not familiar with any explicit discussion of this crucial term and shall have to draw some distinctions especially for this occasion.[4]

1. The strongest case of relevance is the one where something is both the necessary and sufficient condition of something else; this, according to Bertrand Russell, is the relevance of logic to mathematics.

2. The relevance is slightly reduced when the condition is necessary, but not sufficient; the relevance of mathematics to physics is of this nature.

3. A further weakening of relevance occurs when the condition is no longer necessary, though sufficient; thus formulation

4. For confirmation and substantiation of my impression see Wayne A. R. Leys, "Irrelevance as a Philosophcial Problem of Our Time," *Memorias del XIII Congreso Internacional de Filosofia,* IV (1963), 173–85.

of a science in any modern language may be sufficient for its completion, but not necessary.

4. Finally, something may be relevant to something else even when it is neither its necessary nor sufficient condition. Nevertheless, its presence may make an important difference in the total situation, changing its entire configuration. It may be neither necessary nor sufficient for predicting a person's behavior to know about his phenomenal perspective and feelings. But it certainly adds substantially to a full understanding of his conduct, and is in this sense relevant.

Now in speaking about the relevance of phenomenological philosophy to psychology I do not mean to decide immediately what type of relevance is at stake. Clearly no one would claim that philosophy is the necessary and sufficient condition for a scientific psychology, nor even that it could ever be its sufficient condition. However, it may be that it is its necessary though insufficient foundation. This stronger thesis would be definitely in line with Husserl's views. But even a weaker thesis, according to which philosophy would merely "make a difference" without being indispensable, would be enough to establish its relevance for psychology.

II

On Husserl's Contributions to Psychology

But before discussing the systematic question, I would like to supply a minimum of historical facts about the actual relationship between phenomenological philosophy and psychology.

The belief is still widespread that Husserl was a sworn enemy of psychology. The fire behind this smoke is that at one crucial stage of his career Husserl had mounted his celebrated attack on psychologism. But this attack has to be seen and understood in its proper context: Husserl's attempt to prevent psychology from overextending itself by the kind of imperialism that would put it in complete control of the intellectual globe. But at the same time he was concerned to help psychology in the pursuit of its legitimate tasks.

A full understanding of this seeming ambivalence in Husserl's attitude toward psychology would demand a close study of his spiral-like course of development. It would have to consider the philosophical inspiration of the mathematician "E. G." Husserl by the new descriptive psychology of Franz Brentano and the hope, expressed particularly in the "psychological and logical studies" of Husserl's *Philosophy of Arithmetic* (1891), never completed, of supplying the missing foundation of mathematics by such a psychology. It would have to take account of his seeming about-face in the first volume of his *Logical Investigations* (1900), with its classic critique of psychologism, and his further shift in the second volume to a new correlative method that accorded both the psychic act and the transpsychic content equal rights. For this latter approach Husserl adopted the name of "phenomenology," defined as the study of the essential nature of consciousness in its intentional structure. But soon the scales tipped back toward the subjective pole of the relationship: under the title of "transcendental phenomenology" Husserl undertook with growing insistence to locate the origin of all phenomena in a constituting subjectivity, a subjectivity that he always wanted to keep strictly separate from the merely factual subjectivity of empirical psychology, as he interpreted it, but which still implied the primacy of the subjective pole of the relation over its "objective" correlates.

However, this is not the place for plotting the curve of Husserl's progress or even of the variations in his proximity to actual psychology—of which, in any case, he did not keep abreast. Rather, the important thing in the present context is to give as clear a picture as possible of Husserl's basic attitude toward psychology. It is important not to misinterpret his opposition to psychologism, first merely in logic and then along the entire front of philosophy, as hostility to psychology as such. His campaign involved only the freeing of philosophy from the abortive attempts of psychologists after the manner of J. S. Mill to convert logic into a branch of psychology and to make the factual laws of thinking the foundation of the logical laws and their claims to validity. In order to understand Husserl's antipsychologism it is necessary also to realize that what he understood by psychology was the kind of psychophysics and psychophysiology which considered the psyche merely as part of a biological organism, to be explored by the experimental methods of the Wundtian laboratories.[5]

Phenomenology, as Husserl finally conceived of it, was anything but opposed to psychology as a science. As he saw it, the two are essentially related.[6] A true phenomenological psychology, once developed, would "stand in close, even closest relation to philosophy."[7] Even with regard to the psychology of his time with its "immense experimental work and its abundance of empirical facts and in part very interesting regularities," Husserl expressed genuine admiration, particularly when it was in the hands of such experimentalists as Carl Stumpf and Theodor Lipps, who had seen the importance of descriptive clarifications before rushing off to the laboratories.[8] But his final verdict was damning and blunt enough: Husserl denied the typical psychology of the time the right to call itself a rigorous science.[9] For this so-called science, in its eagerness to collect factual and experimental material, had failed to make sure of its basic concepts and operated instead with the crude and uncritical terms of everyday language. Incidental discussions of terminological questions were insufficient to provide better foundations. Hence Husserl argued that only a full-fledged phenomenology that had investigated the essential structures of the phenomena in their variety could make sense of the experimental findings. Empirical psychology, then, presupposes phenomenological psychology, a psychology

5. For this point I may refer to the pertinent section in *The Phenomenological Movement*, pp. 149–52.

6. "Phenomenology and psychology are closely related, inasmuch as both are concerned with consciousness, though in a different manner and in a different attitude." (*Logos*, I [1911], 302.) *Philosophie als strenge Wissenschaft*, ed. Wilhelm Szilasi (Frankfurt-am-Main: 1965). Also in *Phenomenology and the Crisis of Philosophy*, trans. Quentin Lauer (New York: 1965), adequate, but not free from defects.

7. *Ibid.*, p. 321.

8. *Ibid.*, p. 304.

9. *Ibid.*, p. 320.

that works out the fundamental distinctions of the psychological phenomena on the basis of the celebrated, if not notorious, essential insights (*Wesenseinsichten*).

What did Husserl himself contribute to the laying of such a phenomenological foundation for psychology?[10]

He did not write a systematic work on phenomenological psychology. What was published under this title were his notes for lectures that he delivered in 1925 and again in 1928.[11] There does not seem to be any basis for the belief that he ever meant to publish them as an independent book. Nevertheless the text now before us provides, at least in its second half (pp. 130ff.), the best picture of what kind of topics a phenomenological psychology in Husserl's sense would have to include and how he wanted it to treat them. Typical items are: the stratification of the psychic phenomena (Section 21), their unity (Section 24), perception (Sections 28–39), temporality (Section 40), the ego (Sections 41f.), and the subject as monad (Section 43). But this is clearly not a complete system of phenomenological psychology.

However, we can also refer to extended chapters and sections in other works published or authorized by Husserl himself which take up the kind of psychological topics envisaged in "Philosophy as a Rigorous Science." Thus the analyses of perception in *Ideen*, those of the inner consciousness of time in the lectures edited by Martin Heidegger, and those of experience in *Erfahrung und Urteil*, as elaborated by Ludwig Landgrebe, contain a wealth of basic descriptions and distinctions which are of considerable significance for psychology.

But, especially in the present context, it would make little sense to insert here a complete catalog of Husserl's treatment of various psychological topics. The only meaningful thing would be to show concretely how he dealt with an exemplary phenomenon.

10. For a very helpful attempt to bring together Husserl's main psychological findings systematically see Hermann Drüe, *Edmund Husserls System der phänomenologischen Psychologie*. But it hardly justifies the use of the term "system" in the usual sense, a term which Husserl himself usually rejected.

11. Phänomenologische Psychologie, ed. Walter Biemel (*Husserliana*, IX [The Hague: 1962]).

The most obvious candidate would be his account of the intentional structure of consciousness. This would involve showing how each conscious act, e.g., our consciousness of the building in which we are assembled, is essentially a consciousness *of*, namely, of the (intentional) object to which consciousness refers. In addition to this basic pattern, introduced by Franz Brentano's descriptive psychology, Husserl pointed out that in intentional consciousness the immediate data of our awareness, such as our sense impressions of colors or textures, are ascribed to objects and in this sense objectified. Even more important, the referents of the many acts in which this building is experienced are ascribed to one identical object into which the different appearances or perspectives are integrated or synthesized.

But to give a full and meaningful picture of these investigations into the structure of consciousness would clearly exceed the frame of this lecture. Besides, I can refer the more interested reader to the preceding contributions of my colleagues Roderick M. Chisholm and Aron Gurwitsch. Instead let me try to say something about the more general question of the role of phenomenological psychology in the total setting of Husserl's philosophy.

Quite apart from his early purpose in utilizing Brentano's psychology as a foundation for the philosophy of arithmetic, Husserl thought of psychology as an important if not as the only avenue to the new fundamental science of phenomenology, and particularly to its fully developed form: pure or transcendental phenomenology. This phenomenology was to be the study of the essential structures of consciousness purified from all "transcendent" existential beliefs. The purification was to be achieved by means of the celebrated phenomenological reduction, which was to "bracket," or, better, suspend all such beliefs and find the ultimate foundation for all philosophy and science in immanent subjectivity. One of the difficulties for this new radical conception of phenomenology was this: While in his *Ideen* (Section 31) Husserl had pointed out the theoretical feasibility of such a reduction on the basis of a free decision, he had not shown to his own and others' satisfaction why such a drastic step was neces-

sary. Most of his later efforts consisted in mustering arguments
for the rational necessity of this step. And one of his major reasons was the "crisis in psychology," a crisis which, as he saw it,
could be overcome only by giving psychology a new foundation
in transcendental phenomenology.

Husserl developed this line of reasoning in several places:

1. In his lectures on "Phenomenological Psychology" of 1925
and 1928, he tried to show how psychology is transformed, once
it is based on phenomenological philosophy.

2. In his ill-fated[12] article on "Phenomenology" for the *Encyclopaedia Britannica,* Husserl began with a section on pure psychology, i.e., a psychology free from physical and physiological
ingredients, along the lines of Brentano's descriptive psychology
(or psychognosia), and one that focused on "intentionality" and
was based both on a limited phenomenological reduction to "inner experience" and on an "eidetic" reduction to essences. In
a second section Husserl tried to show how such a phenomenological psychology could serve as the foundation for transcendental phenomenology. For as Husserl saw it, there is a fundamental ambiguity in the way in which the world appears in our
consciousness: in what sense is it real? This ambiguity calls for
radical elucidation. Even phenomenological psychology shares
the naïveté of all science in its simple belief in the reality of the
natural world. But at least in focusing on the phenomena of
"inner" experience such a psychology is already on the road to
the subjective matrix. Carried through to the end it would lead
to the complete transcendental reduction of all existential beliefs, as characteristic of transcendental phenomenology.

3. Finally, in the *Crisis of the European Sciences and Transcendental Phenomenology* of 1935ff., Husserl returned to psychology
as an approach to phenomenology—now, however, second to the
new and more publicized approach, that via the study of the life
world. He saw the reasons for the crisis in psychology in the in-

---

12. "Ill-fated": After having gone through four German versions, now
published in *Husserliana,* IX, the German version of this article was truncated by the inadequate "translator."

compatibility between an objectivistic approach in the style of Galilean science and the merely subjective approach from inner experience. Transcendental phenomenology would provide a new foundation for both in the constituting function of transcendental consciousness.

But the ultimate proof for the historical relevance of Husserl's phenomenological psychology could be supplied only by showing its traces in the work of the psychologists of the time. This is what I am trying to do on a larger scale in some of my historical studies. Here I shall merely give a few examples.

1. Husserl exerted considerable influence on the work of the younger psychologists associated with Georg Elias Müller, especially on David Katz, in Göttingen. Apart from the general credit Katz extends to Husserl, there is evidence that such distinctions as that between surface color and film color had some connection with Husserl's theory of the intentional structure of perception, surface colors being perceived as aspects of the intentional object or noema.

2. Husserl's phenomenology of thinking left extensive traces in the work of the Würzburg school of Oswald Külpe, particularly in the writings of August Messer and Karl Bühler, whose theory of language was also indebted to Husserl.

3. Apart from a growing general appreciation of Husserl's intentions among the founders of Gestalt psychology, one of its younger members, Karl Duncker, took a particular interest in Husserl's research.

4. Even more conspicuous is the corroborative influence of Husserl's early phenomenology on psychiatrists like Jaspers in his *General Psychopathology*. Ludwig Binswanger also put to use some of Husserl's later transcendental phenomenology.

It would take considerable time and care, however, to trace these influences in detail. It should also be pointed out that these influences were often not "total" but "partial," i.e., either merely stimulating or reinforcing or confirming. Such partial influences may actually be more valuable than the total ones.

III

THE POTENTIAL RELEVANCE OF HUSSERL'S PHENOMENOLOGY
FOR PSYCHOLOGY

It is not from the historical effects that the full relevance of Husserl's phenomenology for psychology can be demonstrated. Anyhow, these influences have issued almost exclusively from the incipient phenomenology of his early *Logical Investigations*. The full-fledged pure or transcendental phenomenology of the *Ideas* and of his subsequent work has remained relatively ineffective. The most important question is therefore whether this phenomenology is essentially capable of and destined to make significant contributions.

In the present context, I can offer merely the following general considerations.

1. A full empirical psychology worthy of its name must include a pure psychology of the phenomena of consciousness. This consciousness is essentially intentional. But in order to give an adequate account of intentionality we need the kind of phenomenological investigation which the traditional psychophysical psychology, at any rate, fails to provide. In other words, a psychology that does not abandon consciousness after the manner of strict behaviorism presupposes a description of the intentional structures as given in immediate experience, regardless of whether they are matched by physical counterparts. As Husserl sees it in the *Britannica* article, this description presupposes a kind of bracketing reduction after the manner of phenomenology.

2. Empirical psychology presupposes a framework of fundamental concepts or essential structures. Perhaps a more direct way of demonstrating this prerequisite would be to point out that the usual texts in empirical psychology simply presuppose a set of concepts such as function, act, content, perception, conation, etc. Rarely, if ever, are they accompanied by explicit definitions. In fact, these concepts often seem to be not much more than stipulations vaguely based on ordinary usage. What phenomenology aims at is to put foundations under these seemingly arbitrary stipulations. It wants to derive psychological

definitions from what is called, perhaps a little pretentiously, an essential insight (*Wesensschau*), or a little more concretely, from grasping the essential types that can be intuited on the basis of a systematic variation of the observed phenomena. Seeing and describing such essential structures might put an end to the appearance, if not the reality, of definitional anarchy.

3. Phenomenology can provide a genetic understanding of the way in which the contents of our consciousness are constituted in our experience. Such constitution occurs either passively—when contents crystallize, as it were, without our participation, as in ordinary experience—or actively when we construct such contents, as in acts of judgment or in the imagination. Constitutive phenomenology, by paying special attention to these processes and describing them, leads to a much better understanding of the historic development of consciousness and its correlates than does a merely static description in the style of Husserl's earlier phenomenology.

Husserl claims that these steps—description of pure subjective experience, identification of essential types, and constitutive phenomenology—are indispensable to making psychology an exact science. In this case phenomenology would of course be relevant in the strong sense. It would certainly be a serious challenge to all existing psychology that is still innocent of such a phenomenology. Personally I doubt that the plight of present-day psychology is that precarious. Thus in the field of description of subjective consciousness a lot of conscientious work has been done not only by psychology of perception and descriptive psychopathology but also by our psychological novelists. As for the reflection on the basic concepts of psychology, the reexamination of basic definitions is by no means absent from the theory and philosophy of psychology.[13] Even the field of constitution is not

13. I am thinking here particularly of the recent development of a philosophy-based "philosophical psychology" (see, e.g., Donald Gustavson [ed.], *Essays in Philosophical Psychology* [New York: 1964]). But apart from the question of the effect of these painstaking studies on the psychologists, the emphasis of analytic philosophizing on ordinary usage rather than on the structure of the phenomena raises the question of whether it can avoid dependency on the accidents of historical language and reach essential types.

uncultivated; thus the recent development in Continental psychology of what goes by the name of *Aktualgenese* in the second Leipzig School of Fritz Sander is a careful attempt to study the genetic constitutions of *Gestalts*. Moreover, some of Piaget's genetic psychology attempts at least something parallel to, if not identical with, constitutive phenomenology.

My conclusion is that at least implicitly some of the tasks outlined by Husserl are being tackled, however inadequately, in current research in psychology. Their explicit treatment might indeed be of considerable help to the cause of a truly scientific psychology. But it would be strange if these tasks, urgent as they are, had not been discovered and attacked in ongoing research. What I submit, therefore, is that while an explicit phenomenology can be relevant to psychology in its actual work, it is not indispensable as long as psychology implicitly attends to its phenomenological foundations. But this does not mean that a more explicit attack could not be of considerable value. Of this potential aid I would like to give an example.

IV

PHENOMENOLOGY AND FIELD THEORY: A CHANCE FOR CO-OPERATION

Let me now turn away from merely theoretical considerations of what may be called "metaphenomenology." Instead I would like to show in a specific instance how philosophical phenomenology could become relevant in an area of recent growth in psychology in a manner that would at the same time stimulate philosophical growth. I have in mind the conception of the phenomenal field as developed in recent psychology and as paralleled by Husserl's much dramatized, and perhaps at times overdramatized, conception of the life world.

Psychological field theory as such owes its major development to the work of Kurt Lewin. Long before Husserl's conception of the life world had become generally known, Lewin formulated his conception of a life space as the frame of reference for a person's actions and movements.[14] He even devised an elaborate system for plotting these movements by utilizing the patterns of mathematical topology.

What must not be overlooked in taking account of and paying tribute to these pioneering studies is that Lewin is exclusively concerned with problems of action. His life space is consequently defined in terms of "the totality of facts which determine the behavior of an individual at a certain moment" (p. 12). Also, the life space or "hodological space" is organized according to the chances of personal access, which is often blocked by obstructive barriers. Questions of merely theoretical perception or emotional relationship are not considered as such. Moreover, while Lewin stressed the difference between the physical field and the psychological field, he defined life space facts dynamically as *real* in the sense that they have real effects on behavior, even though these effects need not be physical. What is even more striking is the absence of any references to phenomenology, striking particularly in view of Lewin's German background and at a time when Wolfgang Köhler, to whom the *Principles* were dedicated, along with other gestaltists put increasing emphasis on phenomenology. As a matter of fact, in 1917 Lewin himself had published a brilliant descriptive study of the phenomenal transformations of the landscape in stationary war, which he himself called a piece of "phenomenology."[15] I suspect that his later avoidance of the term is indicative of his wish to keep aloof from all such philosophical entanglements, not only with Husserl's phenomenology but also with the "New Positivism" and its physicalism (*op. cit.*, p. 19). His chief concern was clearly to stay close to phenomenally observable behavior.

The "phenomenal field" as the basic concept in phenomenological psychology makes its explicit appearance in the first American text in the field by Donald Snygg in co-operation with

14. *Principles of Topological Psychology* (New York: 1935).
15. "Über die Kriegslandschaft," *Zeitschrift fur angewandte Psychologie,* XII (1917), 440–47, reported in Heider, Fritz, *On Perception and Event Structures, and the Psychological Environment* (Psychological Issues, 1, 3 [1959], 112ff.).

Arthur W. Combs.[16] It is defined as "the entire universe, including himself, as it is experienced by the individual at the instant of action" (p. 15). As such it is contrasted with the "objective physical field." More specifically, the field is identified with "the universe of naïve experience in which the individual lives, the everyday situation of self and surroundings which each person takes to be reality." Snygg and Combs describe the phenomenal field as more or less fluid, as "organized and meaningful," for instance on the basis of the figure-ground relation. The phenomenal self forms a special sector within the total phenomenal field as its "most permanent part" (p. 76). It "includes all those aspects of the phenomenal field which the individual experiences as part or characteristic of himself" (p. 78).

This concept of the phenomenal world has been taken over by Carl Rogers, who also uses such terms as "world of experience" or "experiential world."[17] With the individual as its center, "it includes all that is experienced by the organism, whether or not these experiences are consciously perceived." The introduction of the term "organism" may seem to imply a rejection of consciousness. However, at a later stage,[18] when Rogers emphasizes the noun "experience" for the phenomenal field, he makes it plain that "it does not include such events as neuron discharges or changes in blood sugar, because they are not directly available to awareness." Thus the term "organism" has clearly to be understood in a purely psychological sense.

Finally, I would like to mention a potentially even more sophisticated conception of the phenomenal world developed by Saul Rosenzweig in his theory of personality, also called "idiodynamics," an orientation that "adopts the dynamics of the individual as the fundamental ground of systematization in psychology."[19] A fundamental feature of this idiodynamics is the

16. *Individual Behavior: A New Frame of Reference for Psychology* (New York: 1949).

17. *Client-centered Therapy* (Boston: 1951), p. 483.

18. "Therapy, Personality and Inter-personal Relationships," *Psychology: A Study of a Science,* ed. Sigmund Koch, III (New York: 1959), 197.

19. See especially "The Place of the Individual and of Idiodynamics in Psychology: A Dialogue," *Journal of Individual Psychology,* XVI (1958), 3–21.

dominance of the "idioverse" (lately also called "idiocosm"), "the name given to the individual's universe of events." These events constitute "the population of the idioverse," which is to be explored by several methods, phenomenology among them. What seems to me significant about this conception is that here the idea of the phenomenal field is enlarged to that of the one encompassing world of the individual. True, thus far there is no further development of the idea, and no concrete idiocosms of specific individuals are described. But it should not be difficult to supply them as each case history in idiodynamics is bound to do.

It would be easy to show that similar conceptions occur among sociologists and anthropologists. What is so often called "culture" in all its ambiguities seems mostly an attempt to describe that part of man's social field which is not only shared by men but is man-made.[20]

The rise of such concepts in different schools of psychology and social science is symptomatic of the need for a systematic study of the phenomenal world. Such a study would require a clear conception of the structural organization of this world, of its dimensions, and of the proper categories for describing it. How far has the new grassroots phenomenology been able to supply it? If it has, I confess that I have not yet come across any such attempt. Lewin's model of life spaces for action is a promising beginning. But apparently little has been done on the basis of this foundation in more recent phenomenological psychologies of the phenomenal field in its entirety.

How far is philosophical phenomenology able to fill this need? At this point I would like to introduce Husserl's conception of the life world, which, while foreshadowed already in texts from the twenties, made its full-fledged appearance only in his mostly posthumous work on the *Crisis of the European Sciences and Transcendental Phenomenology*.

20. To my knowledge the only person who has noticed and stressed the parallel between cultural anthropology and phenomenology is Grace de Laguna in her article on "The Lebenswelt and the Cultural World" in the *Journal of Philosophy*, LX (1960), 777–91.

In order to do justice to this conception, one must be aware of the context in which it occurs. This context is the attempt to show the need for a transcendental phenomenology. Husserl wanted to demonstrate this need by a variety of approaches, all leading to the realization that the foundations for enterprises such as psychology or science in general can be supplied only by tracing their foundations in the subjective sphere, which Husserl called transcendental subjectivity. In his *Crisis* book Husserl takes a new approach to this goal by starting out from the everyday life world of the ordinary person, which is so different from the objectivized world of science. However, one must not expect of Husserl any sustained study of the life world for its own sake. All he needed for his purposes was the identification of those features in it that lead back to the fundamental layer in subjectivity in which they are constituted. Yet Husserl was increasingly aware of the fact that in order to show these origins he had to explore the life world to a much greater extent than he had done in his earlier work, where he had included the life world within the "natural world" explored by objective science.

Nevertheless, what can be found in the pertinent section of Husserl's last work proved highly suggestive to those who consider the independent exploration of the life world one of the most important contributions made by Husserl's phenomenology. It contains at least the rudiments of a structural theory of the life world. One of its basic features is that it has a center in the experiencing subject (in contrast to the uncentered objective world of science), designated by the personal pronoun singular in the case of the private world of the individual and by the plural in the case of social group worlds. The life world is polarized around these centers and displays such spatial characteristics as closeness or farness, being above or below, left or right—all characteristics that as such have no place in the scientific world with its objective co-ordinates. It also shows such emotional characteristics as "home" (*Heimat*) and "foreign" (*Fremde*), familiar and strange, old and novel. Husserl points to the cultural anthropology of Lucien Lévy-Bruhl as supplying striking illustrations of what a life world contains. But otherwise the published part of the Husserl papers does not show concrete developments of the conception. Yet it would require little imaginative variation and extension of this pattern to supply it.

How much toward a systematic phenomenology or, as Husserl also calls it, an "ontology" of the life world has then been achieved thus far? What we have is certainly nothing like a "rigorous science" in Husserl's sense. Beyond the outlines of the basic structure of the life world and some of the categories, spatial and emotive, which would be distinctive to it, no general framework with basic propositions, definitions, and laws is in sight. What constitutes a "world" in this sense? Is there only one life world per person? Or can a person live "in several different worlds," as we often say? How far are these life worlds articulated, subdivided, etc.? This is not a mere matter of pigeonholing. Eventually any comprehensive account of a person's life world needs a framework that would allow us to plot its characteristic profile.

What has such a phenomenology of the life world to offer to the psychologist in his need for a fuller understanding of the phenomenal world? Clearly not a ready-made model or framework. But even in its rudimentary form Husserl's phenomenology of the life world may contain some new tools, some new dimensions, some suggestions toward what a full-fledged phenomenological psychology of the phenomenal world requires.

Let me go even a little further than Husserl and suggest some structural dimensions for the charting of life worlds. For instance, life worlds are articulated according to zones and regions. By "zones" I understand the concentric shells around the focal center of each life world arranged according to its closeness to or significance for the focal subject; by "regions" I mean the areas within the life world organized according to the content of these zones, i.e., the material fields of his interests. Obviously, zones and regions will intersect.

The articulation of the life world according to zones is foreshadowed in Aron Gurwitsch's important work on *The Field of Consciousness*, with its distinction between the thematic object, the thematic field, and the marginal field. True, his distinctions

apply primarily to single perceptions. Yet they can easily be
transposed to the perceived life world in its entirety. We can
then distinguish between a central area, relatively well lit up, a
penumbral belt around it, and a surrounding zone fading off
from full shade into twilight and final darkness. Such zones
may be based on degrees of acquaintance, according to familiarity
or novelty of content—obviously a transitory division, since
novelty will change to familiarity. But zoning may also be based
on emotional closeness, which may be much more persistent;
criteria for such emotional closeness may be preferences, real or
imaginary—the latter in case we stop to think what contents we
would rather like to have or to do without.

The articulation of the life world according to *regions* would
have to be based on an inventory of the variety of objects and
concerns with which we are in living contact. Here any attempt
to be complete would be doomed to defeat. Typical regions
would be one's own body, spatial environment, family, friends,
and economic, political, cultural, and religious concerns. By way
of an example, I shall merely try to indicate relevant features of
the lived spatial environment. For the average adult upper-class
Westerner this will usually be centered in his private room, surrounded by his house or apartment, oriented toward the street,
placed within the town or city in which he happens to be permanently or temporarily settled. This immediate life environment usually stands in very loose connection and sometimes, in
cases of disorientation, in no connection at all with geographical
space, which is, chiefly, imagined space (though flying may
do something for a better fusion of the two). Even this geo-
graphic space appears in all sorts of profiles, represented, for instance, on maps of the United States as mirrored in the typical
perspectives of the inhabitants of some of our "hub" cities.

Each person also lives in a special time world in which different parts of present, past, and future appear in different perspectives, are very differently articulated, are empty or full, have
very different meanings, etc. The importance of these time profiles has been shown especially by phenomenological psychopathology.

Man's social world is a most important area in his life world. What persons are included in it, by name or anonymously? How "close" or how "distant" do we feel to each of them? How do we rank them? How far are we aware of others' inner life worlds?

Then, what place do cultural products occupy in a man's life world? What does sport or art mean to him?

How does he see the entire cosmos in relation to himself? How much of his life is permeated by a sense of religious meaning?

In the present context there would be little point in developing a blueprint for a systematic study of life worlds. It is enough if this sketch can convey a sense of the vastness of the task and the need and chance to develop schemes and the proper categories for the description of life worlds, schemes that are indispensable for a fuller understanding of other individuals, sexes, generations, races, and ages. It is simply not enough to project ourselves into their places. We also need the directives for the proper exploration of the worlds for which these "places" are the centers.

Beyond such clarifications of the basic conceptions, philosophical phenomenology can offer the services of its intentional analysis to a study of the phenomenal world. Not only specific intentional objects but the encompassing field and world are given in characteristic acts and appear in different modes. Hence a study of the content of the phenomenal world invites the parallel study of the various acts, as well as of the modes, perspectives, degrees of intuitive concreteness or emptiness, clarity and vagueness, etc., in which they are given.

Finally, the genesis of a life world, its transformations, and, in short, its history present new tasks for any kind of phenomenology. There is, of course, the merely factual or empirical task of tracing the growth and transformations of the phenomenal world in each individual life, its widening and narrowing, its revolutions and realignments. But in addition to preparing the ground by outlining such possibilities, phenomenology may again show certain essential and typical structures and laws pertaining to such "genesis." Thus one might well hypothesize that any enlargement of the life world affects the relative importance of the central areas, or that modifications of the phenomenal world presuppose the loosening of the rigidity of one's native world—in short, an open attitude.

V

CONCLUDING REMARKS

I hope I have made this clear: I do not claim that phenomenological philosophy contains all the answers to the questions, asked and unasked, of empirical psychology. Such extravagant claims would only be too apt to backfire—and it is no secret that they have backfired in the past. What I do want to suggest, however, is that certain developments in both fields have converged far enough to make the comparing of notes and the exchange of questions and answers meaningful. American phenomenological psychology from the grassroots and imported phenomenological philosophy are not as far apart as is often believed. The precedent of William James, itself an influence on Husserl's phenomenology, is sufficient proof of that. Undeniably there are obstacles to communications. There is the disregard of aprioristically minded phenomenologists for empirical psychology. And there is the esoteric style of much of their writing, of which the workers in the scientific vineyard are understandably afraid. But none of these obstacles are essential. Both parties stand to gain from increased dialogue. Neither one has the right to pose as the authoritative teacher. Both have their unresolved problems—and their skeletons in their respective closets. And both have common foundations: the phenomena in their unexhausted and inexhaustible richness and wonder, and their common objective, the attempt to understand them as far as is humanly possible.

Let us suppose this lecture to have shown that phenomenological philosophy is not altogether irrelevant to the enterprise of the psychologist: then I could still imagine that someone will ask, Why pick just on psychology? Is phenomenology not just as relevant to any other science or human enterprise? I will not deny that my case has important implications for all these fields, from mathematics to religion. And I am not particularly interested in drawing any comparisons, invidious or complimentary. But this much I think can be said in pleading a special significance of phenomenology for psychology: It was hardly accidental that phenomenology came into being as a result of a cell division within descriptive psychology. For when this psychology had lapsed into psychologism in the abortive attempt to solve the universal tasks of philosophy, phenomenology as a new kind of a study of consciousness took over this task.

But there may be even stronger reasons for the special claims of psychology on phenomenology than the historical ones. There is a special fascination about psychological phenomena in their closeness to everyone's existence. Also, in their irreducible richness and depth of qualitative variety they present a special challenge and opportunity for phenomenological pioneering.

Long before the beginning of psychology as a science, Heraclitus proclaimed: "You would not find out the boundaries of the soul, even by travelling along every path: so deep a logos does it have."[21] Let me, in concluding, slightly modernize the translation of this venerable fragment: "There is no end to psychology, no matter what method it uses; for in its essence the depth of the psyche is unfathomable." Perhaps the ultimate relevance of phenomenological philosophy for psychology is its clear sense for this depth dimension in the phenomena of the psyche.

21. G. S. Kirk and J. E. Raven, *The Presocratic Philosophers* (Cambridge, England: 1957), Heraclitus, 235 fr. 45, p. 205.

Existentialism and the Alienation of Man

ALBERT WILLIAM LEVI[*]

Of books and articles about, to say nothing of references and allusions to, the concept of "alienation" there is literally no end. But, tempted as we may be to be impatient with what we find has become a cliché, or annoyed with the abuses that have characterized the uses of so ambiguous and slippery a term, we are nonetheless forced, I think, to take it seriously. For if it is ubiquitous in the vocabulary of present-day philosophy, psychology, and social science, this testifies to more than a linguistic fad, and if we find it difficult in any particular case to pin down its meaning, this is because like the term "good" its import is comprehensive and its many usages analogical.

The fact is that almost every historical period has some basic value universal, some global evaluative concept that it employs as a criterion of personal orientation and social criticism. What the concept "well-being" (eudaemonia) was for the classical Greeks, what the term "sinful" meant for the early Middle Ages, what the notion of the "unnatural" or the "contrary to nature" meant for the seventeenth and eighteenth centuries, the idea of "alienation" signifies for modern culture. And if we are puzzled and distressed to find it applied at once to the attitude of the beatnik disaffiliate, to the political apathy of the urban voter, to the theater of Beckett, Brecht, and Ionesco, to the disaffected industrial worker, to the philosophy of Sartre, to the curious painting and invertebrate sculpture of Claes Oldenburg and Jim Dine,

[*] Department of Philosophy, Washington University, St. Louis, Missouri.

and to the indignant critic of American foreign policy in Santo
Domingo or Viet Nam, this should not prevent us from appre-
ciating its broad cultural relevance and attempting to perceive
the core meanings that lie beneath a veritable promiscuity of
applications.

In what follows I want to do three things: I want first very
briefly to canvass its philological antecedents. I want secondly
(and at the risk of stating dogmatically what is in fact an inference from a series of investigations that I cannot detail) to
present what seem to me the core meanings that lie behind its
multiple uses. And I want finally to show how these core meanings cast considerable light upon the way in which the existential
philosophers proceed in their psychological analyses, their metaphysical examination of the self, their implicit appeal to moral
values, and their social criticism.

The Latin term *alienatio* has a long and distinguished history.
Cognate with the verb *alieno* (to alienate, to sell, to estrange, to
become apostate, to become insane) and with the adjective
alienus,-a,-um (foreign, contrary, hostile, averse, distracted), it
appears characteristically in the works of Caesar, Cicero, and
Seneca. Its French derivative *aliénation* appears as early as Cal-
vin's *Institutes* ("We excuse his confession through the alienation
of his spirit, caused by wine.") and during the reign of Louis
XIV in the *Memoires* of St. Simon, and throughout the eighteenth century in the three analogical meanings, which are also
to be distinguished in its Latin ancestor: (1) the transfer or
conveyance of property to another; (2) estrangement or loss; and
(3) madness, lunacy, mental derangement. Of these three it is
clearly the second that constitutes its philosophic relevance, and
to this norm of usage the English is most constantly allied.
Wycliff in 1388 says that "alienation from God is to man wicked-
ness." Burton in 1621 speaking of Macedon says: "Alexander
saw an alienation in his subjects' hearts." Burke in 1770 speaking of the American colonies says: "They grow every day into
alienation from this country." The German equivalent, the verb
Entfremden, with a similar meaning appears also in the writings
of Luther, of Goethe, and of Wieland, and indeed it is the Ger-

man ambience of the first half of the nineteenth century, particularly the practice of Hegel and the early Marx, which have fixed once and for all the resonance the term "alienation" now bears in the vocabulary of the existentialists and in the social criticism of the twentieth century. To this fateful resurgence I should now like briefly to turn.

It is at once apparent from the basic text—Hegel's *Phenomenology*—that the reference to alienation is metaphysical, that time and history are here fundamentally irrelevant and that what we are dealing with is a structural character of the universe mirrored in its characteristic substance—consciousness. Two sections of ˌthe *Phenomenology*[1] bear the burden of Hegel's account of metaphysical alienation: that on "das unglückliche Bewusstsein" (the unhappy consciousness) and the later treatment of "Der sich entfremdete Geist: die Bildung" (the self-estranged spirit: culture). The first examines what it means to be a self. The second explores the phenomenology of the self as a developmental entity. The self is free insofar as it maintains its identity, keeps simply and solely in touch with itself, maintains the undivided unity of its self-existence.[2] But this purity is compromised internally, for consciousness itself is a thoroughgoing dialectical restlessness ("das Bewusstsein selbst ist die absolute dialektische Unruhe"), a fortuitous imbroglio, the giddy whirl of a perpetually self-creating disorder ("der Schwindel einer sich immer erzeugenden Unordnung"). For the Cartesian doubt is inseparable from the Cartesian "cogito," and skepticism, whether reflexive or outward-directed, creates an object and thus an other which becomes a problem for a consciousness integral and undivided. The absolute subject directs itself to an object and in so doing doubles itself and becomes a duality. Thus we have here "that dualizing of self-consciousness within itself, which lies essen-

1. G. W. F. Hegel, *Phänomenologie des Geistes* (Berlin: 1964), pp. 151–71 and 347–83. In the English translation of J. B. Baillie (New York: 1949), the equivalent pages are 241–67, 507–58.

2. *Phänomenologie*, p. 152: "Im Denken bin Ich frei weil ich nicht in einem Andern bin, sondern schlechthin bei mir selbst bleibe und der Gegenstand der mir das Wesen ist, in ungetrennter Einheit mein Fürmichsein ist. und meine Bewegung in Begriffen ist eine Bewegung in mir selbst."

tially in the notion of mind; but the unity of the two elements is not yet present. Hence the *Unhappy Consciousness*, the alienated soul which is the consciousness of self as a divided nature, a doubled and merely contradictory being."[3] It is this idealist passion for unity, this obsession for integral experience which sees every atomism as a fall from grace, every pluralism as a compromised integrity, that has provided the first paradigm for the contemporary experience of alienation. What in Hegel appears as the natural tragedy of spirit becomes the pathos of pluralism when removed from the metaphysical universe of discourse and given the romantic twist appropriate to an age of cultural self-pity.

Hegel's later treatment of spirit in self-alienation only canvasses the consequences of its primordial dialectical restlessness. For spirit discovers its content in a reality that is just as impenetrable as itself—a world external and negative to self-consciousness. Hegel's insight here is only that which Sartre later plagiarized without acknowledgement and made the basis of the metaphysics of *L'Etre et le Néant*—that the immediate self is without substantial content and that in Hegel's terms only the alienation of personality ("die Entfremdung der Persönlichkeit") permits its contact with those realities that are the generating sources of its content. My language is perhaps faulty, for it is the idiom of metaphysical realism, and Hegel never permits the existence of an objective reality not created by the activity of spirit itself. Therefore from the first construction by spirit of a twofold world, divided and self-opposed—the world of the self and its object and the kingdom of pure self-consciousness (both of which are kingdoms of self-alienated spirit)—springs a second division in which enlightenment (*Aufklärung*) completes the self-estrangement of the spirit and in its restlessness turns for new safety and the peace of a precarious equilibrium to the sphere of human culture.

3. *Ibid.*, p. 158: "Die Verdoppelung des Selbst-bewusstseins in sich selbst, welche im Begriffe des Geistes wesentlich ist, ist hiemit vorhanden, aber noch nicht ihre Einheit, und das unglückliche Bewusstsein ist das Bewusstsein seiner als das gedoppelten nur widersprechenden Wesens."

"The world of spirit now separates into a duality. The first is the world of reality—its self-alienation. The other is the one which, raising itself above the first, spirit constructs for itself in the empyrean of pure consciousness. This second world as opposition to the first alienation is for this very reason not free of it; on the contrary, it is only the other form of alienation which consists precisely in having a conscious existence in and embracing both worlds."[4] The Hegelian language is, as usual, awkward, but its meaning is clear. Self-consciousness only becomes definite, only achieves real existence as it alienates itself from itself. This alienation is dual. It creates on the one hand the world of nature and on the other the world of art—of human culture. Each is a form of objectification not only in its "otherness" but literally in that it divides into a universe of nature and of cultural objects, and it is only conceptually that this alienation in turn alienates itself and becomes again the final unification of the whole.

The tradition of Parmenides and Spinoza dies hard. Totality and integral wholeness remain a persuasive value for the metaphysical mentality. In Hegel this value is explicated in terms of the pervasiveness of its opposite, and alienation becomes that inevitable process through which otherness makes its persistent claim. "Fragmentation" and "division" are the key meanings that the term alienation has now acquired, and it is a tribute to the inherent persuasiveness of the Hegelian point of view that this core of meaning has lingered on long after the metaphysics that gave it cogency has become philosophically obsolete.

The second "moment" in the fixing of the meaning of the term "alienation" comes in the writings of the early Marx. Beginning in the ambience of Hegelian thought, and never able to break completely with the influence of its conceptual scheme, Marx nonetheless reinterprets the sphere of alienation as proposed by

4. *Ibid.*, p. 350: "Die Welt dieses Geistes zerfällt in die gedoppelte; die erste ist die Welt der Wirklichkeit oder seiner Entfremdung selbst; die andre aber die, welche er, über die erste sich erhebend, im Aether des reinen Bewusstseins sich erbaut. Diese, jener Entfremdung *entgegengesetzt*, ist eben darum nicht frei davon, sondern vielmehr nur die andre Form der Entfremdung welche eben darin besteht, in zweierlei Welten das Bewusstsein zu haben, und beide umfasst."

Hegel, and he adds to it a further dimension of meaning. It is in the dialectical opposition between the Marxian and the Hegelian interpretations of this concept that some of the deepest schisms of existentialist thought have arisen, and it is therefore of some importance to distinguish the two usages and to consider what is at stake in their opposition. What is primarily at stake is the role of time and history—the ingression of meaning into the stream of social events. Put in the briefest possible way, Hegel is the phenomenologist of alienation, Marx is its social historian. It was Hegel's insight that division, separation, and estrangement are at the heart of every form of reality. It is the purpose of Marx's early writings (and particularly of the "Economic and Philosophic Manuscripts" of 1844) to show that the history of man's alienation is the history of capitalism in the Western world. It is the issue of whether alienation is a permanent phenomenological structure or a contingent historical occurrence, whether it inheres in "the human condition" or qualifies "the condition of man under capitalism," and its consequence for social criticism lies either in a deepening of the tragic sense of life or in an optimistic commitment to the principles of social meliorism. It is in this form that the problem has arisen to haunt later existentialist thinkers.

The enormous role that the concept of alienation plays in the work of the early Marx is based upon a sentiment of profound indignation. It is as if one woke out of a deep sleep to discover that the comfortable and familiar world in which one had been living had altered overnight, had become strange and ugly, had indeed turned into something monstrous. The Marxian treatment of alienation is but an explication of the monstrousness of the capitalistic world. If the human ideal is a community of men living in harmony and freely developing the qualities appropriate to their natures in intercourse with one another through creative activity, then there is indeed something perverse about the actual condition of man in industrial society. His economic relations promote not sympathy but exploitation. His orientation is no longer "creation" but "acquisition." His interpersonal relations as exhibited in the class struggle are dictated not by mutuality but by that competitive hatred which reduces the human essence to the status of a mere means to ends intrinsically ignoble.

Marx's treatment of alienation begins in the atmosphere of Hegel, for at first he sees it in the light of Hegel's "separation" and "division." In his meditation of 1843 on Bruno Bauer and "The Jewish Question," he notes that religion is an expression proving that man has been *separated* from the community and from other men; he calls attention to the fateful *division* of man into the public and the private person, and he points out the universal secular *contradiction* between the political state and civil society.[5] But as the analysis continues throughout the *Economic and Philosophic Manuscripts,* the emphasis subtly changes. "Division" and "separation" are used less frequently, the emphasis upon social stratification succumbs to a more concrete analysis of the effects of mechanical productivity and commercialism, and indeed the very centrality of the term "estrangement" (*Entfremdung*) is supplanted by the term *Verdinglichung* (thingification).[6] This is the new and crucial dimension of meaning that Marx has added to the concept of alienation.

Marx's treatment of alienation is based upon the perception that the conditions of capitalist production ultimately constitute a violation of the worker's human nature precisely because they bring about an alteration of his status from that of "person" to that of "natural object." It is the insight never abandoned and appearing many years later in *Das Kapital* that under the commodity orientation there is a pervasive tendency for "definite social relations between men" to assume "the fantastic form of a relation between things."[7] In the *Economic and Philosophic*

5. *Karl Marx: Early Writings,* trans. T. B. Bottomore (London: 1963), pp. 15, 21.

6. I apologize for the barbarous neologism "thingification" as my translation of *Verdinglichung,* but in my opinion it is the only accurate rendering. "Objectification" too often means the transforming of a subjective idea or fantasy into a reality, while "reification" has traditionally been used (as in the criticism of the Platonic theory of ideas) for the making substantial of a mere abstract noun or universal. Marx's meaning is precise—it is the *transformation of something organic and human into a thing*—and to this "thingification" calls special attention.

7. Karl Marx, *Capital* (New York: 1936), p. 83.

Manuscripts this criticism appears largely as a hostile examination of the concept of money. "Money," says Marx,[8] "abases all the gods of mankind and changes them into commodities. Money is the universal and self-sufficient value of all things. It has, therefore, deprived the whole world, both the human world and nature, of their own proper value. Money is the alienated essence of man's work and existence; this essence dominates him and he worships it." It is not only the socially significant point that under the commercial impulse the human individual becomes a mere commodity; it is also the more philosophic consideration that the rule of money signifies the complete domination of living men by dead matter—a triumph of mechanism over vitalism. "The devaluation of the human world," says Marx,[9] "increases in direct relation with the increase in value of the world of things. . . . The performance of work appears in the sphere of political economy as a vitiation of the worker, thingification as a loss and as *servitude to the object,* and appropriation as alienation." It is no wonder therefore that the worker is related to the product of his labor as to an alien object and that the more he labors the more powerful becomes the inhumane world of objects he produces and the poorer his inner life of self-determination. The very presuppositions of the Marxian humanism are what permits it to operate as a telling critique of modern industrial society—to find monstrous the devaluation of the human world through man's servitude to objects and his literal conversion into an object, and through this perception to add another dimension to the concept of alienation.

Hegel's *Phenomenology* appeared in 1807. Marx's *Economic and Philosophic Manuscripts* were written in 1844. Ferdinand Tönnies' great work *Gemeinschaft und Gesellschaft*[10] appeared in 1887 and marks, I think, the third moment in which the meaning of alienation has been fixed for the modern world. Perhaps

8. *Early Writings,* p. 37.   9. *Ibid.,* pp. 121f.
10. Ferdinand Tönnies, *Gemeinschaft und Gesellschaft: Grundbegriffe der reinen Soziologie* (Berlin: 1926). All references will be to this edition. The work has been translated into English by Charles P. Loomis in the American Sociology Series as *Fundamental Concepts of Sociology* (New York: 1940).

the term "alienation" is not as central to Tönnies' analysis as it is to the work of Hegel and Marx, but the underlying idea of *Gemeinschaft und Gesellschaft* expresses a sense of the state at which Western society has arrived, a kind of sociological "fall from grace" which gives the term "alienation" much of the pathos and persuasiveness that it bears in the body of contemporary existential thought.

These three thinkers—Hegel, Marx, Tönnies—form a seamless web of modern criticism. As Marx draws upon Hegel, so Tönnies draws upon Marx, and in fact in that curious preference for sensualism as against the dangers of abstraction, which strikes one so forcibly in the *Economic and Philosophic Manuscripts,* is already implicitly the salient point that the whole of *Gemeinschaft und Gesellschaft* sets out to prove. Hegel's perception is metaphysical and Marx's is more narrowly economic, but Tönnies manages to set forth the sociological explanation of the sense of fragmentation and thingification which the works of Marx and Hegel express. The son of a prosperous peasant family, he experienced in person the consequences of the new rationalism as the ancient rural culture of his native province of Schleswig-Holstein was forced to submit to the mechanization and commercialization of the industrial revolution.[11] The result was his famous distinction between community and society, the former an association of intimacy and closeness with ties of blood and

11. In his own intellectual "Lebenslauf" Tönnies attributed the genesis of his principal work to bookish and theoretical influences. See *Die Philosophie der Gegenwart in Selbstdarstellungen,* ed. Dr. Raymund Schmidt (Leipzig: 1922), p. 211: "Meine eigene Theorie wuchs in einem gewissen negativen Verhältnis zu Ihering. Die Kritik ist, wie gar manches andere, im Gewahrsam meines Pultes geblieben. Aber aus der Verbindung meiner Hobbes-Forschung mit dem Studium der Nationalökonomie und des Naturrechtes, der historischen Rechtsschule und der Rechtsgeschichte, der vergleichenden und ethnologischen Jurisprudenz, daher besonders auch aus Kenntnis der Bücher Maines und seiner Formel 'von Status zu Contract,' die ich bei Herbert Spencer wiederfand, sind einige Grundgedanken meiner Schrift 'Gemeinschaft und Gesellschaft' entsprungen." But his passionate feeling for the place of his birth also can be read between the lines of his account, and it is by no means impossible that precisely his early familial experiences gave to his intellectual sources their persuasiveness. This must particularly have been the case apropos of Sir Henry Maine.

immemorial tradition, the latter an association of limited purposes and loyalty, reasonable, cold, contractual in nature, and where only a segment of the self enters in.

It is true that Tönnies' presentation of *Gemeinschaft* and *Gesellschaft* are as of ideal types for sociological analysis, almost as *entia rationis,* but it cannot be denied that they were suggested by the course of Western social development since the Middle Ages and that quite without explicit intention they propose a dimension of alienation obvious to all who have experienced the contrast between the industrialized and the folk society. The life of *Gemeinschaft* develops in permanent relation to land and homestead. It can be explained only in terms of its own existence, and therefore its reality is in the nature of things. It is the "natural form" of organic human beings.[12] *Gesellschaft,* on the contrary, is the construction of an artificial aggregate of persons who although associated remain separate and aloof from one another in spite of certain uniting factors of calculated interest. Persons are distant from one another and isolated rather than close and emotionally united, and this provides its own feeling of remoteness and distantiation from the immediacies of life and existence. Tönnies provided an elaborate psychological grounding for this social dichotomy. *Gemeinschaft* is the product of man's "natural" or "integral" will (*Wesenwille*), and *Gesellschaft* is the product of his "rational" or " calculative" will (*Kürwille*). The first is a spontaneous expression of natural disposition; the second is the deliberative and prudential process of the rational mind. It is not necessary to assess the adequacy of this psychologizing, for what counts in Tönnies is the concept of the development from *Gemeinschaft* to *Gesellschaft* and the pervasive underlying sense of loss. In his final book, *Geist der Neuzeit* (1935), published almost fifty years after the first great work, Tönnies returns to his theme in even more explicit terms

---

12. *Gemeinschaft und Gesellschaft,* p. 24: "In dauernder Beziehung auf Acker und Haus entwickelt sich das gemeinschaftliche Leben. Es ist nur aus sich selber erklärbar, denn sein Keim und also, in irgendwelcher Stärke, seine Wirklichkeit ist die Natur der Dinge. Gemeinschaft überhaupt ist zwischen allen organischen Wesen, menschliche vernünftige Gemeinschaft zwischen Menschen."

to contrast medieval unity with modern atomization, the sympathetic relationship between relatives and friends with a daily contact with aliens and strangers, a world of permanent rural homes with a world of changing, impersonal urban dwellings, the intimacy of folk art and handicraft with the impersonality and mathematical impenetrability of modern science. Through it all like a bright, tough thread runs the contrast between the satisfactions of the old-fashioned intimate life and the cold impersonality of the modern urban world.

I have presented these ideas of Hegel, Marx, and Tönnies not in order to weave the fabric of social criticism which dominates our epoch but to indicate the historical grounding of the components of the concept of alienation as it enters into existentialist speculations of today. For it is my belief that the intellectual core of the idea is fixed during that crucial eighty-year period of metaphysical construction and social criticism which begins with Hegel's *Phenomenology* and ends with Tönnies' *Gemeinschaft und Gesellschaft*. In Hegel the awareness of the destruction of the community of faith and a nostalgia for its return is the source of a metaphysics that reads the fall from unity as the alienated fate of reality itself. In Marx a perception of the monstrousness of capitalist exploitation and the consequent dehumanization of man reads all human degradation as a reduction to the status of the manipulable inanimate object. In Tönnies the pathos of the passing of the warm social microcosm of folk society and its transformation into a macrocosm where social relations have become cold and calculated transactions suggests that human value varies inversely with social distance and that immediacy is the cradle of all human good.

It is important, I think, that the multiple uses and the plural significations of the term "alienation" in contemporary discourse not blind us to the links between them and to the core meanings, fixed in the nineteenth century, in which they universally participate. When one speaks of alienation from God, from nature, from values, or from the self; when one details the feelings of loneliness, abandonment, estrangement, homelessness, and

anxiety; when one points to the dissociation of life and meaning
or to the aloofness and lack of participation of the alienated
man, to his fragmentary encounters with others, estrangement
from what is real, and internally divided self; beneath the
heterogeneity of situation and variations in emotional tone lie
concepts that at once define a value term, constitute the source
of a judgment, and serve as the foundation for a pervasive
critique of the self and of society.

Alienation is essentially a state of disvalue, the subject of a
negative judgment; and if we inquire what substantive values it
denies, we shall find them respectively to be (1) unity (as with
Hegel), (2) organicity (as with Marx), and (3) immediacy (as
with Tönnies). In every case the use of the term implies an
axiological dualism, a valuational contrariety, and the essential
pairs in this case are therefore, I think, three: (1) the unified or
integrated versus the divided or fragmented; (2) the organic, the
sensed, the human, versus the mechanical, the abstract, the thinglike; and (3) the immediate and the feelingful versus the impersonal and the distant. *Fragmentation, mechanization, distantiation,* are the three dimensions of alienation, and every usage,
however remote, will in some sense presuppose, or explicate, or
explore one or more of these crucial aspects.

Within these dimensions it is always possible to distinguish
further the locus of alienation—whether between the self and the
objective world, or within the self between aspects or functions
that have become separated or estranged, or within the social
structure where class divisions or the performance of overly seg-
mented roles may have led to an incongruity between personal
development and institutional expectations—but for existentialism
these sociological distinctions are perhaps less important than
that between the objective state of separation or estrangement
on the one hand and the subjective state of feeling of the
estranged personality on the other. Since the time when Nietzsche's and Kierkegaard's preoccupation with the emotions of resentment, nothingness, nausea, guilt, bad conscience, dread,
abandonment, and self-contempt was found susceptible of analysis

by Husserl's phenomenological method,[13] existentialism has exploited the fertile field of the so-called existentialist emotions as much in literature as in the formal philosophic treatise, and the nausea of Sartre's Roquentin (in *La Nausée*), the affectlessness of Camus' Meursault (in *L'Étranger*), and the grotesque furniture of Sartre's hell (in *Huis Clos*), with its assemblage of dead objects in a vast hotel of endless rooms and corridors, have passed for commentaries upon the human condition as well as fictive reconstitutions of imaginative experience. But the existentialist tropism for forms of feeling should not blind us to their objective source, and the emotional fog that has surrounded the term "alienation" should not distract our attention from the modes of fragmentation, mechanization, and distantiation to which its continual use implicitly points.

With respect to its treatment of human alienation, existentialism as a philosophy has one significant advantage over merely psychological or sociological analyses: it can provide the facts of twentieth-century alienation with a metaphysical grounding; it can treat alienation with that phenomenological respect that anchors it less in the relativity of the shifting social context than in the eternal condition of man. In this respect its general preference is for the strategy of Hegel rather than of Marx, and it sees alienation not in the light of historical contingency (and thus of revolutionary action), but rather as a permanent structure of human experience.[14] And for this same reason it is wise to separate within the writing of the existentialists those works of purely contemporary social criticism—like Jaspers' *Die Geistige*

13. For further elaboration of this point see Albert William Levi, *Philosophy and the Modern World* (Bloomington, Indiana: 1959), pp. 390–96.

14. But in this particular respect Sartre is the paradoxical case. His analysis of alienation in *L'Etre et le Néant* often suggests that this is situational, permanent, and ineradicable, while his political writings (somewhat journalistic in character and almost always published first in *Les Temps Modernes*) echo the orthodox Marxist line: that the proletariat is the heart of France, that the French Communist Party is its authentic voice, and that unity under its banner will bring the revolution and the end of alienation. One might say that the strife in Sartre's mentality between Hegel and Marx is reflected in his life in the dual roles of systematic philosopher and strident political journalist.

Situation der Gegenwart (*Man in the Modern Age*) and Marcel's
Les Masses contre l'humain (*Man Against Mass Society*), which
despite their trenchancy are profoundly unoriginal and derivative[15]—from the basic texts like Sartre's *L'Etre et le Néant*, Heidegger's *Sein und Zeit*, and Jasper's *Philosophie*, where within
the very texture of each philosopher's most systematic construction is to be found the equivalent of a treatment of situational
alienation, whether or not the term itself appears as an explicit
analytical tool. In the nature of the case, my future examples
must be merely illustrative rather than exhaustive, but I want
now briefly to show how, with respect to alienation, the heritage
of Hegel, Marx, and Tönnies appears in the decisive works of
Sartre, Heidegger, and Jaspers.

Of the two major themes of existentialism—the analysis of
being and the centrality of human choice—it is the second to
which Sartre is primarily committed, and since therefore his
energies are devoted more to human decision than to ontology,[16]
we should expect his treatment of alienation to occur as some
aspect of the pathology of choice. Indeed his most noteworthy
analysis views it as the protean forms of irresponsibility and self-

15. Marcel sees the degradation of modern man in the misplaced idea
of "function," in his bondage to the timetable and the schedule which sub-
ordinates the emotional necessities of lived time to the mechanical necessities of clock time. Jaspers' argument is similar. He is obsessed by the
tension between technical mass order and the requirements of genuine
human life, and to the humanistic criticism he learned from Dilthey and
Simmel he adds the fear of mechanical organization and bureaucracy which
he learned from Max Weber. We have heard all this before. Fragmentation
and mechanization are no new message. Only their integration into the
complex of existentialist theory is of philosophic interest.

16. I agree that this point is arguable. Sartre surely has learned much
from Hegel, and in fact the preliminary ontology of *L'Etre et le Néant* is
Hegelian through and through. It is almost for this reason profoundly unoriginal and serves, I think, largely as a kind of introduction to the brilliant phenomenology of human action which follows. Sartre's metaphysics,
as has been often noticed, does little more than explicate the fissured universe, the split between the for-itself and the in-itself, between the reflexive
and the prereflexive subject; but this is more introductory than substantive.
One might say that in Sartre a preliminary (and derivative) "ontology of
alienation" à la Hegel prepares for a later (and brilliant) "phenomenology
of alienation" à la Marx.

deception which are assumed as the self seeks to escape from the givenness of its freedom—as the plural possibilities of *la mauvaise foi*. It is of course first necessary to remember the curiously dogmatic and unpersuasive theory of human freedom which Sartre presents—that freedom is not an acquisition laboriously won or intermittently exercised, but the built-in quality of human consciousness, which is the kind of "nothingness" that is groundless, contentless, and eternally striving to encompass the objective Being that it is not. For the initial postulation of the qualities of consciousness contains the definition of its alienation: for subjectivity to substitute objectivity; for potentiality, determinateness; for responsibility, the force of circumstance.

Alienation in the philosophy of Sartre takes many forms, cognitive as well as functional, so that it may consist in a philosophic belief, an emotional attitude, in a disposition to act, or in the quality of an act itself, but all have in common the presupposition of habit and the denial of fluidity. Thus a canvassing of the rich phenomenology of *L'Etre et le Néant* will reveal among others the following specifications of alienation: "to be ashamed of one's subjectivity," "to deny that one is free," "to believe in the illusion of the permanent self," "to deny the radical contingency of the world," "to depend upon objective considerations," "to deny that the self is pure potentiality," "to seek determinateness instead of fluidity," "to make mechanically the typical gestures of my state," "to seek in one's attitudes the solidity of rock." It is true that when Sartre himself attempts to generalize a meaning for the multiple patterns of bad faith, his words are reminiscent of Hegel—he finds it to be "un certain art de former des concepts contradictoires, c'est-à-dire qui unissent en eux une idée et la négation de cette idée"[17]—but sustained attention to his argument will reveal, I think, that his concrete treatment of alienation is far closer to the insights of Marx. His intrinsic mode of perception is Marxist, not only in a similar indignation that finds in the expressions of bad faith various sorts of human depravity, but also in the curious equation of bad faith with the impera-

17. Jean-Paul Sartre, *L'Etre et le Néant* (Paris: 1955), p. 95.

tives of bourgeois conventionality. To free oneself of bad faith is frequently for Sartre to throw off the trappings of false privilege, and his contrast between the good faith that glories in the free act of genuine choice and the bad faith of a reliance upon a supernatural guarantee of values comes remarkably close to the words of Marx in "Bruno Bauer, Die Judenfrage." But even these are superficial resemblances. What is crucial is that underlying Sartre's extensive treatment of bad faith is the perception—which is also the essence of Marx's treatment of alienation—of the organic, the sensed, and the humanly free, versus the mechanical, the abstractly determined, and the thinglike. Sartre's critique is therefore at once a denunciation of abstract functionalism and of the thingification of personality. There are some men, says Sartre—like caretakers, overseers, gaolers—whose entire social identity is a negation, whose selves are defined by the objects to which they are related. A few pages later this insight into the automatic, functional, and repetitive character of the life style is typified in the waiter in the café—his movements too quick and precise, his manner too automatically patronizing, his acts and his voice seeming to be parts of a machine as he performs the mechanical dance that testifies to the rigidity of his condition. For the role of waiter is a set of abstract specifications, a form of existence in a "neutralized" mode where one "exists" "en faisant méchaniquement les gestes typiques de son état."[18] Here is the alienated personality par excellence, he who makes mechanically the gestures typical of his condition with its clear implication (suggested previously by the early Marx) that the origins of human alienation are implicit in the necessities for a social division of labor.

Society takes many precautions to imprison a man in the role that he must play, as if in perpetual fear that he might escape and suddenly as an expression of his freedom break away and elude his condition. But social habituation is reinforced by personal insecurity. In bad faith a new method of thinking and of self-consideration appears which patterns itself not upon the

18. *Ibid.,* p. 100.

infinite malleability of consciousness but upon the opacity and solidity of objects. A hateful security arises out of "thingification"—through the cowardly assumption of a permanent self. The confidence of the waiter depends upon seeing himself as a mechanical object. The safety of the frigid woman lies in viewing her frigidity as "physiological"—that is to say as inherent in the object that is her body. The anti-Semite by adhering to anti-Semitism makes himself into a tight bundle of unchangeable attitudes; he has chosen for himself "the permanence and the impenetrability of rock." Sartre's metaphors are revealing, and the continuous appeal to "hardness," "impenetrability," "recalcitrance," "solidity," and "obstruction" which stud his work show that the constant presence of *Verdinglichung* has permeated his consciousness even at the level of verbality and style.

There is one other place at which alienation or "thingification" enters Sartre's work, and it is the very point at which his theory of social relations is poisoned by his cynicism and make impossible that very fraternal rebellion against the strictures of bourgeois injustice which his practical Marxism inconsistently and paradoxically invokes[19]—I mean his treatment of "the look" and his concept of sociality as mutual aggression, appropriation, exploitation. It is impossible to discuss this in any detail, but the entire third part of *L'Etre et le Néant*, "Being-for-Others"—with its insistence that the function of another's gaze is to transform one into a thing, that social striving is the quest for domination, and that love itself is but the appropriation of the alien body of the other—presents with infinite refinement a Hobbesian state of nature in psychological guise. Alienation is here the rotten center of all social relations, and it cuts off Sartre's philosophy from the primary values of an optimistic sociology (the felicities of genuine communal feeling or the transports of a selfless love) more

19. The paradox is clear. Sartre's social psychology never really gets beyond the isolated and atomic self sunk in its own obsessive freedom. But his political theory postulates and actually finds comradeship and concerted action based on sympathy and shared goals in members of the proletariat. How bridge the gap? One might say that Sartre's theory of liberty makes his theory of fraternity impossible. Of that other great French value, equality, he has little explicitly to say.

drastically even than in the case of Hegel, Tönnies, or Marx. It is for this reason above all, I think, that Sartre's long-promised ethical system has never appeared and indeed, if I am not mistaken, can never appear. With such presuppositions one can produce a clinical psychology or a social pathology, but not a moral philosophy.

In Sartre a preliminary analysis of being has served as an instrument for the assertion of the centrality of human choice. In Heidegger it is just the opposite. He is an ontologist, almost in the classic tradition, and if he gives considerable attention to the phenomenology of the human condition, it is neither for psychological nor sociological reasons but as an adjunct to his explication of his central concept of *Dasein*—"being" or "being-there." He therefore presents a peculiar problem in the quest for alienation among the existentialists. Because of his inveterate habit of producing a metaphysics through the ontologizing of human emotional experience (which a positivist might describe as the pathetic fallacy raised to the dignity of an ontological method), it is never completely clear to what extent he is a critic of the conditions of human life and to what extent the neutral author of a merely descriptive metaphysics. He himself insists throughout upon the latter,[20] but it is necessary, I think, to read between the lines, and here, if I am not mistaken, there seems always to be an implicit reference to spoilage and to the deterioration of values. *Sein und Zeit* has two primary treatments of alienation:[21] the first is in the sections "Das In-der-Welt-sein

20. Concerning "Das alltägliche Sein des Da und das Verfallen des Daseins" Heidegger says: "Mit Bezug auf diese mag die Bemerkung nicht überflüssig sein, dass die Interpretation eine rein ontologische Absicht hat und von einer moralisierenden Kritik des alltäglichen Daseins und von 'Kulturphilosophischen' Aspirationen weit entfernt ist." *Sein und Zeit* (Tübingen: 1957), p. 167. Concerning the title "Das Verfallen und die Geworfenheit," he says, "Der Titel der keine negative Bewertung ausdrückt . . . ." *Ibid.*, p. 175. And finally: "Die existenzial-ontologische Interpretation macht daher auch keine ontische Aussage über die 'Verderbnis der menschlichen Natur,' nicht weil die nötigen Beweismittel fehlen, sondern weil ihre Problematik *vor* jeder Aussage über Verderbnis und Unverdorbenheit liegt. Das Verfallen ist ein ontologischer Bewegungsbegriff." *Ibid.*, pp. 179f.

21. *Ibid.*, pp. 113–130, 166–80.

als Mit-und Selbstsein. Das Man," and the sections "Das alltäg-liche Sein des Da und das Verfallen des Daseins." To each of these I should very briefly like to turn.

Heidegger's first treatment of the alienation of being is that which follows from its quality of being in the world—its every-dayness ("das Dasein in seiner Alltäglichkeit"). An existential analysis shows that Being is here constituted by its being with others and that just "the dominance of the other" (*der Botmäss-igkeit der Anderen*) is the source of its alienation.[22] For the other is no determinate other but the neutral mass of an anonymous "they" (*das Man*) and the essence of social living, now metaphysically interpreted, is that loss of autonomy which comes from the abandonment of the self to the indeterminate other. The self has thus lost the dignity of its private character—it is public in the worst possible sense, and its *Dasein* has fallen prey to "decay" (*der Abständigkeit*), "averageness" (die *Durch-schnittlichkeit*) and "leveling" (*die Einebnung*).[23] It is precisely this dependent publicity of the self which constitutes its degrada-tion and distinguishes it in its "inauthenticity" from the condition of "an authentic self-existence" (*das eigentliche Selbstsein*).

Heidegger's second treatment of alienation practically equates it with "the deterioration of being" (*das Verfallen des Daseins*), which he proceeds to spell out as the vices of idle talk (*das Gerede*), pointless curiosity (*die Neugier*), and essential am-biguity (*die Zweideutigkeit*).[24] This deterioration is an existen-tial consequence of the situation of *Dasein* in the world—a struc-tural feature of the universe rather than an accidental and his-toric occurrence. It represents, therefore, the kind of alienation which is never overcome.[25] I use the term "alienation" here with

22. *Ibid.*, p. 126.
23. *Ibid.*, p. 128: "In den herausgestellten Seinscharakteren des alltäg-lichen Untereinanderseins, Abständigkeit, Durchschnittlichkeit, Einebnung, Offentlichkeit, Seinsentlastung und Entgegenkommen liegt die nächste Ständigkeit des Daseins."
24. *Ibid.*, p. 175.
25. *Ibid.*, p. 176: "Die ontologisch-existenziale Struktur des Verfallens wäre auch missverstanden, wollte man ihr den Sinn einer schlechten und beklagenswerten ontischen Eigenschaft beilegen, die vielleicht in fortge-schrittenen Stadien der Menschheitskultur beseitigt werden könnte."

some confidence, for unlike Sartre, who never explicitly related "aliénation" and "mauvaise foi," Heidegger specifically equates *Entfremdung* with *das Verfallen des Daseins* and with the *Uneigentlichkeit* that is its essence.[26] It is precisely this alienation in which being is cast down and sinks in the bottomless nothinglessness of an inauthentic everyday existence. ("Das Dasein stürzt aus ihm selbst in es selbst in die Bodenlosigkeit und Nichtigkeit der uneigentlichen Alltäglichkeit.")

It is characteristic of Heidegger as a metaphysician that he should view the deterioration of being as essential to the structure of *Dasein* itself and equate its falling away with a compromised and inauthentic existence. But in relating this deterioration to the preoccupations of the here and now and the triviality of daily existence, there is an unmistakable reference to social milieu, and a perspicuous reader will see in his two treatments of alienation a critique alike of *Gesellschaft* and *Gemeinschaft*. The first implicitly attacks the impersonality, abstractness, and conformity of the stratified industrial society, but the second could have been directed against an overromanticized version of the more primitive *Gemeinschaft*. Idle gossip, curiosity, and ambiguity are precisely the everyday vices of the folk society (as Flaubert in *Madame Bovary*, as Dostoievsky has so brilliantly shown in *The Possessed*), and one who resists the abstract activity of ontologizing will perhaps find in the reflections of this proud and solitary figure traces of resentment against the unwelcome inquisitiveness of Freiburg and other more primitive villages of the Black Forest region.

I should like to add a few brief comments about Jaspers. Jaspers' thinking is in some respects much more diffuse than that of either Heidegger or Sartre, and it is therefore difficult to find in it a single term that stands for alienation and plays the same role as, for example, *Uneigentlichkeit* or *Verfallenheit* for the former or "mauvaise foi" for the latter. But that alienation plays its part in Jasper's philosophy there can be no doubt. Its presence and its character are nowhere better illustrated than in his

26. *Ibid.*, p. 178.

intellectual autobiography, "Über Meine Philosophie," written in 1941.[27] At one point he says, "We are so exposed that we constantly find ourselves facing nothingness. Our wounds are so deep that in our weak moments we wonder if we are not, in fact, dying from them." And a moment later the social foundation of alienation is laid bare: "The community of masses of human beings has produced an order of life in regulated channels which connects individuals in a technically functioning organization, but not inwardly from the historicity of their souls. The emptiness caused by dissatisfaction with mere achievement and the helplessness that results when the channels of relation break down have brought forth a loneliness of soul such as never existed before, a loneliness that hides itself, that seeks relief in vain in the erotic or the irrational until it leads eventually to a deep comprehension of the importance of establishing *communication* between man and man."[28] Here is that same sense of distantiation which is classically set forth in Tönnies, and the cure is seen to lie in that immediacy of communication which is to be found only in a true *Gemeinschaft*.

Jaspers' philosophy is haunted by the sense of loneliness and isolation (even in his later "Mein Weg zur Philosophie" he says of his youth: "Die Einsamkeit war nun das Problem."), and it finds expression at two chief points in his systematic thinking: in his treatment of the confrontation of the self with transcendence and in his constant insistence upon the necessity for communication.[29] Man only becomes authentic, only achieves the reality of being as he devotes himself to *the other*, and the other may be either the community of other men or the limiting horizon of higher values which may be called transcendence. "The thesis of my philosophizing," says Jaspers, "is this: The individual cannot become human by himself. Self-being is only real in communica-

27. Karl Jaspers, *Rechenschaft und Ausblick: Reden und Aufsätze* (München: 1958), pp. 392–450. The quotation immediately following is from p. 400.

28. *Ibid.*, pp. 403–4.

29. See his *Philosophie II* (Berlin: 1956), Chapter 3, "Kommunikation," and Chapter 6, "Freiheit."

tion with another self-being. Alone, I sink into gloomy isolation—only in community with others can I be revealed in the act of mutual discovery."[30]

Alienation for Jaspers thus has both a cosmic and a social dimension—as it arises in isolation from one's fellow men or from narrowness in the face of ultimate values. As an essential "limitedness" or "unrelatedness" with mankind it is a failure of communication and before the totality of the universe a failure to come to grips with transcendence. Here, too, as in Heidegger, a sense of the isolation of man, already prefigured in Tönnies, once more makes itself felt. In Heidegger the cure for alienation lies in man's return to the sense of his own being through which the pathos of "rootlessness" and "homelessness" is overcome. In Jaspers the cure lies in the establishment of real community and in a broadening of cosmic horizon.

Thus far I have tried to show that however weary we may be of the ubiquitous and frequently imprecise use of the term alienation in contemporary discourse, we must recognize it as the essential evaluative concept for personal orientation and social criticism in the modern world. Following a procedure usual in the history of ideas, I have attempted to chart the stages through which its intellectual content has been fixed—in Hegel's metaphysical critique of fragmentation, Marx's strictures against the thingification implict in the system of capitalist production, and Tönnies' contrast of the impersonality of the modern social system with the feelingful immediacy of the folk society. Finding, therefore, that fragmentation, mechanization, and distantiation constitute the core meanings of the term, I have tried very briefly to sketch out how these appear in the systematizations of existentialist philosophy.

Unlike other philosophies of the recent past, like logical empiricism or linguistic philosophy, existentialism has arisen as a direct consequence of, and perhaps as a specific effort to redirect, the fate of man in the modern world. It was therefore inevitable that a concept of basic personal and social import should

30. *Rechenschaft und Ausblick,* p. 415.

find its reflection in existentialist systems. How as an existentialist will you utilize the idea of alienation? If, like Sartre, your major theme is decision, choice, and therefore freedom, you will find it to consist in the self-denial of freedom, in becoming solid and thinglike in a moral immobility, and in bad faith. If, like Heidegger, your basic theme is being and especially the *Dasein* of man's being, then you will be concerned with every instance in which being is compromised into inauthenticity, with impersonality *(das Man)*, and with the various deteriorations of being in gossip, prying, and ambiguity. If, like Jaspers, you are concerned with both of these themes, but particularly with a kind of phenomenology of the feelings of isolation and unworthiness, then you will stress silence, anxiety, and the felt diminution that comes from failure in communication and the narrowing of cosmic horizon. Bad faith, inauthenticity, failure in communication, are the concepts through which existentialism effects a translation from the moods of personal insecurity and social disorientation to the intellectual world of systemization and understanding—concepts through whose formalization perhaps may lie catharsis and relief.